In a culture where materialism has driven the global village of mankind to the brink of inhumanity, this work is a breath of fresh air and relief to the collective psyche of our generation. Sunday hits a home run again, and in light of the demise of the global economic system built on unbridled greed, this subject is timely and necessary.

—DR. MYLES MUNROE
BFM INTERNATIONAL, NASSAU, BAHAMAS

Pastor Sunday is a humble, prayerful, and powerful apostle who is mightily impacting the world through raising up and releasing spiritual sons and daughters to plant explosive churches that move in the spirit of faith to touch heaven and change Earth.

—PAUL DAVIS
WORLDWIDE MINISTER AND AUTHOR OF GOD VS. RELIGION

Pastor Sunday Adelaja gives us so much to think about in his new book. It will force you to think in a new way and then take action.

—PAT WILLIAMS
SENIOR VICE PRESIDENT, ORLANDO MAGIC

In his latest book, *Money Won't Make You Rich*, Pastor Sunday Adelaja skillfully lays a solid foundation addressing the morality of earning, sharing, saving, and spending money like a wise master builder. All the while he places top priority on the advancement of God's kingdom as the proper place to lay up treasure. Each chapter builds toward a rewarding crescendo, teaching its readers how to systematically reach financial freedom by hard work and wise investing as they use the index of character and spiritual wisdom as the pillars to build on. Pastor Sunday has done a marvelous job of teaching the readers how to realize freedom from serving money or from allowing it to control our lives. The book reaches its climax as it outlines the keys necessary for us to become millionaires in order to serve kingdom purposes and to be a blessing to our families and those less fortunate.

—MARCUS D. LAMB
PRESIDENT/FOUNDER, DAYSTAR TELEVISION NETWORK

Money Won't Make You Rich provides an incredibly stable foundation upon which to build your financial life. There is more wisdom on any one of these pages than in many books I have read on the topic of finance and wealth. It should be mandatory reading in high schools and colleges and should be taught by every church or organization that desires to lift people out of poverty.

—**MICHAEL Q. PINK**
AUTHOR OF *SELLING AMONG WOLVES* AND *RAINFOREST STRATEGY*

I have been to Pastor Sunday's church and witnessed the passion of his persona. This book shows that passion with some excellent principles on economics as it relates to the church, the individual, and the world at large. You cannot help but be impacted, and I highly recommend it.

—**DR. PETER J. DANIELS**
AUSTRALIA

I am quite impressed by the curriculum and rich content of the book. I suspect it is going to be the next handbook or alternative MBA manual for kingdom businessmen as well as young Christians aspiring to make a success of their lives and ministries. I can hardly wait to get copies for my wife, siblings, and friends. I have been blessed to read this manuscript.

—**AYODELE ADEBOYE**
BUSINESS CONSULTANT, NIGERIA

The principles God has given Pastor Sunday will work anywhere in the world, from his native Nigeria to the economically challenged former USSR, where he now pastors. Whether the national economy is in boom or bust, the Word of God has power. Imagine immigrating to a nation as a despised minority and then being elevated to leading the nation's largest church and scores of self-made millionaires. This is the testimony and the proof of Pastor Sunday's ministry.

Money Won't Make You Rich is a timely word for every Christian. In this book, Pastor Adelaja explores the causes and dynamics of poverty for an individual's life, a community, or a nation. Sunday explicitly parts the sea between the truth and deception of how Christians can receive wealth. His doctrine shows us how we can operate within an imbalanced world economy. These are revolutionary words for revolutionary times, which require a new generation of Christian leaders. Pastor Adelaja asserts that we can become channels to pour out God's resources. Even you can become a millionaire. Are you ready to rumble?

—BISHOP HARRY R. JACKSON JR.
SENIOR PASTOR, HOPE CHRISTIAN CHURCH
IN THE WASHINGTON DC AREA
FOUNDER AND PRESIDENT, HIGH IMPACT LEADERSHIP COALITION

Many people operate under the delusion that smarts or connections are primary tools for success. Sunday pricks these incomplete beliefs and lays out foundational truths—that sound principles, destiny, dedication, and excellence will set every person free from poverty and the slavery of money and facilitate their entry into their personal destiny. May many be consecrated unto God's purposes through this book.

—DAVID TAY
KINGDOM RESTORERS, SINGAPORE

Wealth creation, the kingdom way, requires an individual's commitment to be engaged in the Lord with all his heart, his mind, and his soul. Pastor Sunday warned of the fault lines in our world, while appropriately guiding the reader through the principles into kingdom wealth creation processes, recognizing that money is nothing more than just a tool used for the purpose of discovering one's value and attitude in life toward the fulfillment of the gospel of the kingdom, and his response to that value in the gospel of salvation.

—DR. PHILIP TAN
MANAGEMENT SCIENTIST, ALLIANCE DYNAMICS GROUP

Throughout Bible history, while God constantly uses messengers to bring a message to His people or the nations, once in a while God chooses to make the messenger the message. Hosea was one of them. In our day and time, God has picked yet another man named Sunday Adelaja and has made the man the message. God has prospered this man from very humble beginnings in Nigeria, Africa. God has His reasons for prospering this man, and my sense is that God is about to give birth to a movement that will result in many of God's people becoming millionaires so that our millions can be used to solve the many problems out there.

—APOSTLE GEORGE ANNADORAI
GOLDEN GATE CLUB 1000 / SHALOM SINGAPORE

Finally, a book about the reason wealth creation is biblical. Pastor Sunday has given us an excellent contribution to understanding money and wealth from a biblical perspective that is refreshing. This is not a "get rich" prosperity book, but a balanced treatment of a biblical view of wealth creation and its role in building the kingdom of God. Well done! I recommend it highly.

—OS HILLMAN
PRESIDENT, MARKETPLACE LEADERS;
AUTHOR, *TGIF* AND *THE 9 TO 5 WINDOW*

Sunday Adelaja is a leading figure not only in Ukraine but also in the world. He has a spirit of faith driven by his compassion for people. The word he speaks is one of authority!

—BILLY JOE DAUGHERTY
VICTORY CHRISTIAN CENTER, TULSA, OK

Some are called to churches. Some called to cities. Sunday Adelaja has a fresh word for the nations! His experience with the Lord, his compassion for people, and his commitment to the kingdom make Sunday Adelaja a world-class leader with a world-class vision to build a world-class army to change the world for Christ. If you desire to have maximum impact in your life, this world-class book is a must for you today. Read and reap benefits for a lifetime.

—KENNETH C. ULMER, DMIN, PHD
PRESIDING BISHOP, MACEDONIA INTERNATIONAL BIBLE FELLOWSHIP

Sunday Adelaja is an indisputable success in his family, in his church, and in his nation. This book will help you grow personally and spiritually. Read it and *succeed*!

—PETER LOWE
FOUNDER AND CEO, GET MOTIVATED SEMINARS

I have heard and read a great deal about Pastor Sunday and about the work he is doing. All those who do great things go through attacks such as Pastor Sunday has endured.

—U.S. PRESIDENT BILL CLINTON

The most successful in contemporary European churches is the Ukraine-based ministry of Sunday Adelaja.

—PHILIP JENKINS
DISTINGUISHED PROFESSOR OF HISTORY AND RELIGIOUS STUDIES,
PENNSYLVANIA STATE UNIVERSITY

Thank you for your contribution to our common victory. Your conscious work is a considerable factor in that victory. It was you who protected democracy in Ukraine, standing for its high ideals and not considering your own interests. I am convinced that as long as there are people in Ukraine who have the same civil position, dignity, and spirit as you have, everything will be all right in this country.

—VICTOR YUSHCHENKO
PRESIDENT OF UKRAINE

Through Pastor Sunday's endeavors, we have become bold and fearless people who are able to stand for truth, liberty, and God.

—LEONID CHERNOVETSKIY
MAYOR OF KYIV

In today's fatherless world, where men abdicate their roles and shun responsibility, God must raise up fathers who will accept responsibility for families, communities, and nations. Sunday Adelaja, a fatherless child, has become a father to a nation. This book reveals the Father's heart and inspires us to act on what is right.

—J. DOUG STRINGER
FOUNDER AND PRESIDENT, SOMEBODY CARES

Sunday Adelaja is one of those new breed of men who are influencing a nation and modeling a new style of missions. While there are some men who see success in another church or nation and follow their example,

Pastor Sunday is that example that men from around the world hear about and follow. He is a cross-cultural missionary who has made a new mold of what missions can do to touch a nation. I consider Pastor Sunday a modern-day hero of the faith.

—**PASTOR ROBERT BARRIGER**
CAMINO DE VIDA, LIMA, PERU

The Embassy of God is the biggest church in Ukraine and well organized with different areas and ministries. Pastor Sunday is a unique man. It makes no difference that he is black or that he is Nigerian or that he is not from Ukraine. This is a big church that keeps growing every day.

—**VASILIY ONOPENKO**
CHAIRMAN OF THE SUPREME COURT OF UKRAINE

God has raised up Sunday Adelaja to lead men and women to a deeper understanding of their spiritual destinies. Read this book, and let the journey begin.

—**BARRY BLACK**
CHAPLAIN, U.S. SENATE

Nothing like the Embassy of God has ever been seen before in Ukraine.
—**BRITISH BROADCASTING NETWORK (BBC)**

The Embassy of the Blessed Kingdom of God for All Nations church has ballooned from a ministry for society's troubled into this ex-Soviet republic's first true megachurch.

—**ASSOCIATED PRESS (AP)**

Pastor Sunday is a man with a mission.

—*WALL STREET JOURNAL*

MONEY
won't make
you
Rich

SUNDAY ADELAJA

Charisma
HOUSE
A STRANG COMPANY

Most STRANG COMMUNICATIONS/CHARISMA HOUSE/CHRISTIAN LIFE/ EXCEL BOOKS/ FRONTLINE/REALMS/SILOAM products are available at special quantity discounts for bulk purchase for sales promotions, premiums, fund-raising, and educational needs. For details, write Strang Communications Book Group, 600 Rinehart Road, Lake Mary, Florida 32746, or telephone (407) 333-0600.

MONEY WON'T MAKE YOU RICH by Sunday Adelaja
Published by Charisma House
A Strang Company
600 Rinehart Road
Lake Mary, Florida 32746
www.strangdirect.com

Unless otherwise noted, Scripture quotations are from the New King James Version of the Bible. Copyright © 1979, 1980, 1982 by Thomas Nelson, Inc., publishers. Used by permission.

Scripture quotations marked KJV are from the King James Version of the Bible.

Scripture quotations marked NIV are from the Holy Bible, New International Version. Copyright © 1973, 1978, 1984, International Bible Society. Used by permission.

Design Director: Bill Johnson
Cover design by Bill Johnson

Library of Congress Cataloging-in-Publication Data:

Adelaja, Sunday.
 Money won't make you rich / Sunday Adelaja.
    p. cm.
 Includes bibliographical references.
 ISBN 978-1-59979-458-7
 1. Wealth--Religious aspects--Christianity. 2. Money--Religious aspects--Christianity. 3. Poverty--Religious aspects--Christianity. I. Title.
 BR115.W4A34 2009
 241'.68--dc22

                                    2008039087

First Edition

09 10 11 12 13 — 9 8 7 6 5 4 3 2 1
Printed in the United States of America

Dedication

I wholeheartedly dedicate this book to all the poor people of our world, and to GS Micro-Finance Bank, which is poised to elevate forty million people from poverty in the next twenty years! Ride on, GS MicroFinance Bank, to set this generation free from abject poverty and lack!

Contents

Preface

─────────── ⤢ ───────────

A WORD FROM
THE AUTHOR

CONGRATULATIONS, DEAR FRIEND, FOR EVEN PICKING UP THIS book. Get ready, because your life is about to be drastically transformed!

This book might become one of the major adventures of your life. *Money Won't Make You Rich* is one man's journey of poverty, struggles, studies, money, wealth, and wealth creation principles. This book will surely not leave you where it found you.

You're about to be mightily enriched and empowered!

I came from true abject poverty in Africa. I didn't even have a pair of shoes to wear until I was twelve years of age. Our family might have lived on less than a dollar a day, and I never even had or saw a toy of any kind as a child!

Instead, my body still carries the scars of injuries and wounds that I acquired while trying to make a living in the jungles of Africa.

Miraculously, less than forty years later, not only did I make my first million in United States dollars, but also I was amazingly able to do this without being involved in any active business. Because I am a full-time pastor and itinerary speaker, I opted for passive earning, which came by adhering to certain laws and principles of wealth creation.

More incredible is the fact that I was able to make my first million dollars in a short span of only nine months!

In two years I was able to prove the efficiency of these wealth creation principles and reproduced more than two hundred people who now have a capital base of more than a million U.S. dollars each—even though they basically had nothing when I met them. Most of them were those generally referred to as "down-and-outers"—including former drug addicts, petty traders, bandits, and worse.

In the process of taking this journey of wealth creation, both for others and myself, I have come to some critical conclusions I wish to share with you in this book:

1. Becoming a millionaire is not a big deal; it is easy!

2. Everyone who sincerely wants to can become a millionaire.

3. Money won't make you rich!

4. Our world can overcome world poverty—if we have the heart to do so.

5. Money is only worth making if it is going to be used as an instrument to set others free.

6. God created money for the same reason as all other things—to serve His purposes.

7. Ignorance is the biggest challenge of our age; it is our biggest killer!

WHAT DOES IT MEAN TO BE RICH?

It is my hope and prayer that this book will spark a movement that will end the gruesome statistics of poverty and lack in our world today.

- Can you believe that 80 percent of people in the world today live on less than ten dollars a day?

- Three billion people live on two dollars a day, while one billion live on less than a dollar a day!

- Fifty thousand people die daily because of poverty-related causes!

Money won't make you rich, because it is not meant to do so.

To be rich is to understand the meaning of money and wealth and to know the difference between the two. Money is not necessarily wealth, so most people who desire to be rich are not necessarily looking for money. What they are actually looking for is wealth.

Money only comes to people who are already rich or wealthy in spirit and soul, so it's actually not money that makes you rich—you are rich before money even comes your way. Money only responds when these elements are in place, and until such a time, money won't move in your direction.

Money won't make you rich, because a man who is poor in spirit is poor altogether, even when he has a lot of money in his pocket. Money without the wealth of the soul is equaled to a compilation of sorrows and regrets. Only God enriches without adding sorrow to it.

Money doesn't come to *good people*—because there are millions of good people who aren't rich.

Money doesn't come to *educated people*—because there are so many educated people living middle-class lives in our world today.

Money doesn't even come to *churchgoers* or *Christians*. If that were the case, then our churches would be filled with millionaires!

As a matter of fact, money doesn't necessarily come to *businesspeople*, as so many are struggling even to make ends meet.

Money only comes to those who are already rich in the knowledge of the laws of money. If you are not already rich in your mind, then money won't come to you. Until you are rich in your mind, you're not rich at all.

So what is wealth?

Wealth is the subtotal value of assets owned by a person. The original meaning of *wealth* was: "to possess great qualities, values and virtues." In essence, a person wishing to be rich is actually thinking in terms of all the things he wants and needs.

What, then, is money?

Money is what economists call "legal tender," and it is something that is generally accepted as a means of payment, exchange, and pricing. Money is what we use to measure wealth, because it is the easiest way to move and handle wealth.

The information in *Money Won't Make You Rich* begins to have more meaning when you look at it from the prism of the above-mentioned definition. You can have wealth without necessarily having money, because money won't make you rich. On the other hand, you can have money without being rich, because you need to first be wealthy, both in assets and virtues, before you can be truly rich.

Money is only a strip of processed wood or metal, so it's not worth exchanging your life for. Instead, you should seek first to build the wealth of both material and inner values, and then money will begin chasing after you. You must be rich before money comes to you.

Money has two effects on people: either it rules and controls, or it is mastered and controlled by its owner. The effect it has on you is determined by whether you are first wealthy in assets and virtues.

In this book I have endeavored to share truths with you that will surely enable you to become financially free—if you will only abide by the laws of money that are revealed. More importantly to me, I want to not only set you free from poverty and lack, but I also want to set you on fire to become an instrument of financial freedom to all men wherever they are.

BECOME SET FREE FROM
THE POWER OF MONEY

When people of God are empowered financially, they can easily pursue their God-given ambitions, goals, and purposes. Many people have dreams and aspirations that are not fulfilled because of a lack of money.

Many of God's projects suffer for the lack of money. I believe this book will help end this dilemma in the lives of many. *Money Won't Make You Rich* is not just a book about money, purpose, and poverty, however. This book's larger emphasis is setting people free from the power of money.

Money has a way of possessing people, and only the wise can overcome its influence over the soul. Remember: either you master money or you serve it. Money is a good slave but a bad master. This book will teach you how to become a master over money. You can be truly rich by mastering and walking in the tested laws and principles of wealth creation.

Read on, my friend, and join the army of those who are empowered financially to go and destroy the evil of poverty and mediocrity in our world.

Come, and let's make history together!

Much grease to your elbow!

YOURS IN HIM,
PASTOR SUNDAY ADELAJA
KYIV, UKRAINE

CHAPTER ONE

THE REALITY OF
POVERTY IN OUR WORLD

CONSIDER TWO DIFFERENT SNAPSHOTS. THE FIRST IS OF A stereotypical suburban family from Kansas City, Missouri, surrounded by all their material belongings. The family of four (two requisite children) stands in front of a luxury home, compared to world standards. Outside the home are two expensive cars and a brand-new minivan. Scattered around the family home are rooms full of furniture, including an eighty-six-inch-long sofa, king-sized bed, oriental carpets, various wardrobes, several television sets, radios, telephones, computers, CDs, DVDs, iPods, several bathrooms, modern kitchen equipment, and a library of books. All together, the family owns hundreds of items of every conceivable nature. This depicts the life of a typical family in the United States.

The second snapshot shows a statistically average poor family from a village similar to the Nigerian village of Idomila Ijebu-Ode, Ogun State, where I was born and raised. All of the family's few earthly possessions are scattered in front of their thatched-roof hut, where the family of ten lives with a goat, a pig, and some chickens. There are few cooking and washing implements. The only food is cassava, a type of yam. There are sticks used for digging and a bundle of wood for firewood, but no electric utensils because there is no electricity in the

1

village. The family owns almost no clothes besides what each family member is wearing. Their toilet is a hole in the ground outside the hut. All that they own, put together, amounts to maybe a dozen items. This depicts a family with no possessions and little opportunity. It depicts the picture of an earlier century.

On a global scale, most people more closely resemble the Nigerian family than the American family. The stark reality is that unlike the typical American family, more than half the people in the world have very little to call their own.

The World Bank defines extreme poverty as living on less than the equivalent of one U.S. dollar per day. Moderate poverty is defined as living on less than two dollars a day. By that definition, a man earning three U.S. dollars per day or ninety U.S. dollars per month is not poor. This may seem ludicrous to those living in Western countries. Nevertheless, more than a billion people live on less than a dollar a day, and nearly three billion live on less than two dollars per day. In other words, about half the world lives each day on less money than the price of a cup of Starbucks coffee.[1]

As alarming as these facts may be, what's more alarming is that such things could be happening in this twenty-first century. How can a generation that lays claim to such technological breakthrough and innovation allow such disparity to continue unchecked? Unfortunately, most Americans and people in the Western world as a whole are generally oblivious to the abject poverty and utterly detestable conditions in which the rest of the world lives.

DRIVEN BY NEED OR GREED?

When westerners are confronted with the blunt facts of global poverty, it becomes immediately apparent that most of the material things they pray for are more driven by *greed* than by *need*. Greed makes us want more than we can handle. It makes us heap up things until we have to acquire more living space just to keep it all. Greed is the spirit that drives corporate America. It's why corporate downsizing has become so popular while top-level executives earn ridiculously exorbitant bonuses.

Greed is pervasive within the Western culture (as well as most of the leadership of the developing world, especially in Africa), and the church is not immune to its vices. We seem to have forgotten that God only promised to meet our needs, not to satiate our greed. The sad reality is that greed is vigorously promoted from the pulpit and by those who are supposed to be the pillar of truth and justice in society.

My intention here is to sound the alarm and awaken the conscience of people in order to see injustice come to an end. It is not an attempt to judge anyone; rather, it is an attempt to incite awareness in the hopes that we would work to reform our unequal world.

If we have problems using this absolute definition of poverty, we can also look at poverty as a relative idea. That is, we can see poverty as something socially defined, or something that depends on a particular social context. Such a relative measurement would ask us to compare, for example, the total wealth of a segment of the poorest people in the world with the total wealth of a segment of the richest people in the world. If we do that, these comparisons will be even more bleak and unsettling.

A recent study published by a senior World Bank economist showed that the richest fifty million people in Europe and North America have roughly the same income as almost three billion poor people collected from around the world.[2] This 1 percent of the world's population takes as large a piece of the pie as the small slice handed to the world's poorest 57 percent of people. Using another illustration, if we use the poverty line as defined by the countries of North America and Western Europe, then the poorest 10 percent of Americans are better off than a full two-thirds of the world's entire population. The World Bank recently reported that twenty-four developing countries with a population of three billion people are beginning to integrate into the global economy, with a per-capita growth of only 1 percent in the 1960s up to 5 percent in the 1990s.[3] Even so, the state of world economics and the ratios of poverty between the Western world and the developing world are very dramatic. It is no secret that there is inequality among nations.

Certain countries of the world have most of the money while others have very little. There is also inequality within nations, for it is a fact that within poor countries there are rich groups of people whose incomes compare to the incomes of wealthy groups in the more developed nations. Our sense of goodness and fairness suggests a more equitable distribution of the income of the world. Our sense of fairness and rightness says that within a country, some should not be living in mansions while others scrounge around for food in garbage dumps. It is hard to understand why distribution of wealth is so unequal. Our sense of what is just and appropriate cries out and asks why.

REASONS FOR INEQUALITIES

Why do some countries have so much and others so little? One explanation is that this situation is a result of the market economy. Rich countries are rich because they supply things that are scarce but in high demand. Poor nations are poor because they supply too many things for which there is relatively little demand. This explanation, however, seems somewhat simplistic and does not answer the question of poverty in poor nations such as South Africa, which supplies the world with diamonds,[4] and Nigeria, which is the world's ninth largest producer and supplier of oil,[5] both commodities that are very much in demand.

Whatever the answer might be, it is clear that inequalities in the world cry out for some form of remedy. As President George W. Bush said at a meeting of the Inter-American Development Bank, "A world where some live in comfort and plenty, while half of the human race lives on less than two dollars a day, is neither just nor stable."[6]

One way the world attempts to come to grips with poverty on an international scale is through the concept of foreign aid. This is where poor nations receive money to encourage their growth and economic development. Reasonably rich nations donate money to alleviate the conditions of poverty in poorer nations. This is especially true when richer countries tout their moral responsibility by pointing to the size of their foreign aid budget. Despite the fact that there seems to be no objective evidence to prove foreign aid stimulates economic development in poor countries, the rich nations continue pledging more money in aid to the world's less-developed nations.

The reality of poverty is that one-third of deaths, some eighteen million people each year (fifty thousand per day), are due to poverty-related causes.[7] That is three hundred million people since 1990, the majority women and children, roughly equal to the population of the United States. Every year nearly eleven million children die before their fifth birthday.[8] These are horrible, sobering facts. Can the Christian church do anything to solve the problem of worldwide poverty and the inequality of wealth distribution? Aside from foreign aid and the economic theories of supply and demand, is there a spiritual dimension to poverty? The following chapters do not discount economics, but they go beyond the economic sphere to blend the laws of economics and spirituality and to address the individual hearts of men and woman as they submit to God in their quest to overcome poverty.

This book is not a study of world poverty or economics, but it does seek to answer the question, Is the Christian and the Christian church relevant to the eradication of poverty in the world today? I wish to address Christians, who have access to biblical solutions to this problem, and I want to tell you my thesis right up front: *Christians around the world must become kingdom minded in order for us to help resolve the problem of poverty in our world today.* The purpose of the church is not to have people come in and sit down. Rather, it is to go out and change cultures by establishing God's value system. Moreover, this includes God's value system regarding money and wealth. Poverty is not God's will for anyone, and it is outside kingdom purposes for Christians to be struggling in the area of finances, whether personal or societal.

Being kingdom minded is what the apostle Paul calls being "transformed by the renewing of your mind" (Rom. 12:2). I have written in other books about applying the principles of the kingdom to the church, and now I want to apply those same principles to individual Christians on questions of money, wealth, and personal finances. Remember, God's kingdom principles apply to money as much as they do to anything else. World poverty is agonizingly real. It will never improve until individual Christians affect the culture of life, change the culture of nations, and improve their own financial situations. Thus, the economic growth of the world must be the priority of individuals in obedience to the teaching of Scripture and the principles of the kingdom of God.

Hence, the reason why a Christian desires financial freedom is not just to meet his or her needs but also to become an answer to the challenges of our world.

The Great Commission of Matthew 28:19–20 is not only about rescuing souls and planting churches. It is about much more. The Great Commission tells us to make disciples of all *nations*. Nations are cultures, and cultures are to be transformed and redeemed by Christ's church taking dominion over God's entire creation here on Earth. The purpose of the Great Commission is to change cultures, and this means the church needs a new model or style of missions. God is not satisfied with our church-minded approach. He created everything, and He wants His principles to rule everywhere. That is our assignment in the Great Commission—to permeate the world with the nature and principles of God and to be the Lord's representative in our spheres of influence. If we are in a place, then God is there!

Only the redeemed can improve our world. That is why God is calling Christians all over the world to take up the challenge of conquering the mountain of finances to subdue the earth for God.

THE GOSPEL OF PROSPERITY

This book is not about the American dream or the well-being of any individual. It is not about getting money for personal gain, and, as will be evident, it is not about the so-called prosperity gospel. There are many wolves in sheep's clothing when it comes to teaching financial prosperity. Of course God prospers people, and I believe this as strongly as anyone does. Nevertheless, there is a good deal of error in most American prosperity preaching, as in most countries where the prosperity gospel is preached. It is important to address this matter now so that there will be no mistaking this book for the teachings of the so-called prosperity gospel.

THE MAIN ERRORS OF THE
PROSPERITY MOVEMENT

The prosperity gospel teaches that one prospers only when giving. Giving is the main emphasis. This is false. True prosperity comes not just when we give but also when we know the laws of money and discipline ourselves to abide by them. This is the difference between being rich or poor. Although there is an important place for the law of giving, it is only one of many laws. By itself, it will fail to make anyone sustainably wealthy.

There is a very sympathetic story of a young couple who was sent out with their little child as missionaries by their denomination to a different part of Ukraine. Their situation was so bad that they didn't even have money for a bed or a mattress, and so they ended up *sleeping on the floor*! In Africa and other third-world countries, this could be something quite common, but for it to happen in the center of Europe is out of the ordinary!

They had been commissioned to go out and save people; meanwhile they didn't even have the bare minimum for basic living. This young couple was so desperate that they were about to leave the ministry when they came across my teachings on financial freedom.

Subsequently, they started listening to these teachings and applying the principles to their lives. As a result, three years later, even though they are still full-time pastors, they have been able to make their first million U.S. dollars. As a matter of fact, things were so bad for them that they didn't have any starting capital. The young pastor had to borrow one hundred fifty dollars from his father's pension for their first investment.

What is most painful about this story is that the couple had been serving in their charismatic denomination for fifteen years prior. They had been taught that all that is needed for financial prosperity is to be a good Christian, be active in ministry, faithful in giving tithes and offerings, and other additional giving to various church projects.

They did this for fifteen years faithfully, even dedicating their lives to be missionaries—yet the money never came! As they continued to abide by the teachings of the church, they likewise continued to become more and more impoverished. This is because they were not following the whole truth of kingdom prosperity—only half the truth. Half truth however cannot get the job done. Half truth is equally as dangerous as a lack of truth. One aspect of the truth will not make you financially independent. Giving only is not enough to bring you to substantial wealth.

This man is now traveling all over Ukraine and Europe, teaching about these real principles and how ignorance caused him to live a miserable life in poverty, and conversely, how the truth has set him free for financial abundance to minister freely!

In most cases, when Christians teach that the only way to be prosperous is by giving to the church or ministry, the only person who becomes wealthy is the one on the receiving end or those who have control of the collection. Usually, this is the pastor, televangelist, or radio preacher and his or her inner circle. This leads to a situation where many pastors, especially those of most megachurches, live in the lap of luxury and excess while large portions of their flock can barely afford three square meals a day. It is important that you understand I am addressing the issue of *imbalance*. The truth is, many megachurch pastors are quite talented and hardworking. Many have been able to create their own wealth from their book sales and other private enterprises. There is nothing fundamentally wrong with being prosperous and living well from one's own exploits. However, there is something fundamentally wrong with exploiting the weak and the innocent for personal gain. There is something wholly unsettling about a Christian leader whose taste for the good life exceeds his sense of justice. This imbalance is not in harmony with the teachings of Jesus Christ.

My focus in this book is to help my readers attain financial freedom. The focus is on *your* well-being, not just that of some preachers. For that, I want to introduce what I believe to be a more biblical model for prosperity. Unlike the corporate model used by most churches where wealth is only accessible to a few at the top of the pyramid, this model is a kingdom model, which empowers all. This model has produced more than two hundred millionaires in just two years in the church that I currently lead. The majority of these people started with nothing.

Many were in debt when they started their journey to wealth. All glory belongs to God for giving us the wisdom and insight and for vindicating His Word.

For the preachers of prosperity, financial prosperity is much more than a blessing—it is the right of every believer who claims it. In fact, God wills wealth and riches to all His children. The prosperity movement presents an erroneous view on the gospel of prosperity by limiting wealth creation to the power of confession. You often hear them teach that what you say is what you get, or "confessing it means possessing it." Start speaking about it and it will come into being as God creates what you are speaking. This is the *Wheel of Fortune* approach to faith, and it amounts to extortion because it purports to teach people how to make God work at their behest. Most teachers of prosperity teach an incomplete aspect of financial empowerment. They emphasize faith and belief and never teach about the production of goods and services, and often because they are not comfortable with having to release their controlling grip on the congregation. They never tell their people that true prosperity comes by getting involved in the process of production because they themselves do not understand it. They emphasize faith, belief, and sowing a financial seed, and never teach about the production of goods and services.

THERE IS SOMETHING WHOLLY UNSETTLING ABOUT A CHRISTIAN LEADER WHOSE TASTE FOR THE GOOD LIFE EXCEEDS HIS SENSE OF JUSTICE.

Amazingly, the Donald Trumps of this world profess no faith at all, and yet they sit on top of the pile in the world of finances. It is high time we begin learning the importance of producing goods and rendering services as a prerequisite to being wealthy. It is not enough just to bring money to the church or pastor; if we do not produce goods and services, we are deceiving ourselves if we expect to gain or sustain wealth. Because of this kind of teaching, even in rich Western societies

like the United States, you often find most people living in the clutch
of persistent need instead of living in the abundance they profess. This
always shocks me when I travel through the United States.

There is another problem with the prosperity movement: it tends
to put the emphasis on the needs of the person. Unfortunately, this
has produced more self-centered Christians and "what's-in-it-for-me?"
Christians. It talks about paying bills and meeting the needs and
desires of life (such as cars and houses). I believe, however, that the
main purpose of money is not to meet needs, but first to accomplish
God's purposes on the earth. Of course, the Lord meets personal
needs, but that is not the main reason to desire wealth. God wants us
to be rich so we can carry out His purposes. He is more interested in
making us channels of blessing to others rather than islands of blessing
to ourselves. This theme will recur throughout this book.

POPULAR SCRIPTURES BUT
FALSE INTERPRETATIONS

"The wealth of the wicked is laid up for the righteous" is a major doctrine
in prosperity-preaching circles. The emphasis is on the fact that God
wants to take wealth from the sinner and give it to believers. Proverbs
13:22 does say, "A good man leaves an inheritance to his children's children, but the wealth of the sinner is stored up for the righteous." This
is true, and the Bible does not lie. Nevertheless, when preached this
way, there is contradiction in the very principles of God's nature. The
principles of the justice of God would not allow collecting the wealth
of the wicked to give to the Christian, because the Bible teaches in
Proverbs 10:4 that the diligent worker will prosper, no matter whether
that worker is a believer or not. God makes people rich because of diligence and hard work, not because they are followers of one or the other
prosperity teacher. There is yet a more tragic consequence of this direction of thinking; which is that it warps the underlying sense of love,
kindness, and fairness of its subscribers. Whereas the Bible teaches us
to love our enemies, this kind of teaching ends up causing us to hope

and pray for the downfall or misfortune of the unbelieving wealthy, so we can dispossess them of that wealth we have been eyeing.

The way to look at the meaning of Proverbs 13:22 is that we reach wealth when the righteous produce a better product than anyone else on the market. This is because the righteous will produce goods and services not only to impress people but also to please God. The transfer of wealth that prosperity teachers should emphasize is not God taking from the wicked to give to the believer, but rather people buying from the righteous in exchange for the best quality of goods on the market. Remember, there is no transfer of wealth without Luke 16:10–12: "Whoever can be trusted with very little can also be trusted with much, and whoever is dishonest with very little will also be dishonest with much. So if you have not been trustworthy in handling worldly wealth, who will trust you with true riches? And if you have not been trustworthy with someone else's property, who will give you property of your own?" (NIV). The point here is that the wealth of the world comes only to the believer who produces better goods or services than others in the market. Because most people buy from him, he exchanges his goods for the wealth of the world and the wicked.

"The wicked desire the plunder of evil men, but the root of the righteous flourishes" (Prov. 12:12, NIV). In this scripture, the Bible tells us that only the wicked desires the plunder of other men, even if the man with the plunder is an evil man. It is still wickedness to desire what you did not work for. It is even more alarming that this kind of teaching is coming from a pulpit of a church, because the church is supposed to be a pillar and foundation of truth.

On the other hand, the second half of this verse says: "But the root of the righteous flourishes," which goes a long to tell us that if we are really righteous we will be productive and do things better than other men. That is what the word *flourish* indicates. We are supposed to not just be productive but also exemplify excellence and perfection in our work. When something flourishes, everybody is attracted to it. When we flourish in what we do, in the goods we produce, in the services we offer, all other people who wish to flourish will come to us. That is what I mean when I say that the wealth of the wicked will only come to the righteous when the righteous do things better than the rest of the world—so much so that everybody is attracted to them to buy their products and deploy their services.

Some prosperity preachers use another passage of the Bible to push their wares: when the children of Israel left Egypt and God told the Egyptians to give their gold and silver to the Israelites. (See Exodus 12.) They use this as an example of God giving the wealth of the world to the believers, and it sounds nice—except that the children of Israel had worked very hard for a very long time in slavery and forced, unrewarded labor for that gold and silver. For several years, Pharaoh did not pay the Jews for their labor. They were working without compensation, so in this case, God was proving He is a God of justice. He would not allow the Israelites to leave Egypt without being compensated for their years of hard labor. Technically, this was a transfer of wealth on a very large scale, but as you can see, God did not violate His own principles of justice in order to make His children rich and happy. Israel's newfound wealth was amassed over the course of several centuries under Pharaoh's hand. They had built his temples and his cities and received nothing for their toil. The gold and silver were simply God's way of compensating the children of Israel for their services.

The basic premise of this book is that prosperity must have as its top priority the advancement of God's kingdom and His righteousness (Matt. 6:33). Christians can build this kingdom by understanding the concept of wealth and touching the whole fabric of society through the creation of wealth. When properly allocated, wealth can become the solution to many of society's problems. Not only can Christians experience financial freedom, but that freedom also affords them the ability to be committed to radical kingdom service.

HOW THE SYSTEM WORKS

There is a popular belief that all people are equal and that everyone has an equal opportunity to make money. This is a cover-up. Even though God makes us equal, manufactured systems work to the advantage of some and to the disadvantage of others. Only a select group of about

5 percent of the world's population has solid and correct information on how to get rich. In addition, you can be sure they have the system constructed in such a way that all things work together for their good and that no one breaks the order.

Outside this cadre of wealthy leaders active in promoting their own self-interests, the rest of the whole world suffers because people do not know the truth about the spiritual dimension of money and riches. The truth is there is more than enough money in the world, and anyone can have a share of this wealth. Because of a lack of knowledge, however, the vast majority of us do not have access to it. I consider this an unfortunate situation, and the time has come to apply the remedy of knowledge and information. Unbalanced prosperity teaching has failed to deliver on its many promises. Within the church it has created a structure similar to that of the world where only those at the top attain wealth. That is why I so strongly resent it. Rather than reducing the scourge of poverty, it has only made it worse by failing to apply the whole counsel of God to the problem.

PRACTICAL WISDOM
FOR ASPIRING MILLIONAIRES

1. Successful people know that success is not a gamble or a matter of chance.

2. Successful people know that all success comes by hard work.

3. Real success is a lifetime of learning.

4. Successful people have conditioned themselves to learn from others and from their failures and successes.

5. Successful people learn by practicing what they know on a daily basis.

6. Successful people know that true education is what you get for yourself and by yourself. It is not what someone gives or tells you.

7. Successful people know that true success in life does not come by luck. A lucky man is not a successful man.

8. True winners know that they must develop skills and acquire knowledge before becoming truly successful.

9. A successful man is one who has the knowledge, skills, and expertise that brought him to success.

10. Work your way to success, and don't expect it to come by accident.

KINGDOM PRINCIPLES FROM CHAPTER 1

1. Over a billion people live on less than a dollar a day, and nearly three billion live on less than two dollars per day.[9]

2. The richest fifty million people in Europe and North America have roughly the same income as almost the three billion poor people collected from around the world.[10]

3. The poorest 10 percent of Americans are better off than a full two-thirds of the world's entire population.

4. The reality of poverty is that one-third of deaths, some eighteen million people each year (fifty thousand per day), are due to poverty-related causes.[11]

5. Christians around the world must change cultures by establishing God's value system.

6. World poverty is agonizingly real. It will never improve until individual Christians affect the culture of life, change the culture of nations, and improve their own financial situations.

7. The reason why a Christian desires financial freedom is not just to meet his or her needs, but also to answer the challenges of our world.

8. God is calling Christians all over the world to take up the challenge of conquering the mountain of finances to subdue the earth for God.

9. When Christians teach that the only way to be prosperous is by giving to the church or ministry, the only person who becomes wealthy is certainly not the giver but rather the person or group at the helm of the ministry.

10. The main purpose of money is not to meet needs but first to accomplish God's purposes on the earth.

Chapter Two

WHY EVERY CHRISTIAN CAN BE A MILLIONAIRE

ANY YEARS OF EXPERIENCE HAVE CONVINCED ME THAT IF money does not serve the kingdom, then it perverts, spoils, and destroys its owners. Therefore, our motives must be right when it comes to interest in gaining money and riches. If we realize we have gone off track spiritually, we need to humble ourselves before God and renew our covenant with Him. One woman in our church made a covenant to give God all her earnings and leave only 5 percent for herself. God blessed her abundantly with many business deals and wealth because she put herself in a position of total reliance on God. This woman still keeps 5 percent and gives God 95 percent. These boundaries protect her from any kind of trap. She gives to God's work by using her money to minister to the needs of others and her society, not just to the church or other Christian ministries, which, by the way, she also does with joy.

If our trust is only in the material things we possess—things like our houses, our cars, our summer cottages, or our insurance plans—then how pathetic and vain is our faith! This makes us the most laughable of people, and there is no reason why anyone outside the faith would want to commit to Jesus Christ! Of course, we can justify our need for many of these things in life, but the point here is that these are just things that make our life easier. Life is much more than the things we own.

If we measure our lives by the things we own, we have no more hope than any other unbeliever.

The Bible teaches a vital life creed—*everyone who has something should behave as if he or she has nothing*: "As having nothing, and yet possessing all things" (2 Cor. 6:10). Having material things, we need to see ourselves in the right perspective without them. If we notice ourselves thinking and daydreaming about money all the time, then we have allowed the idol called mammon into our hearts. For this we need to repent and break free from its control. The beauty of the spirit life is a real freedom: a soulish detachment from the idolatry of material things. Our overoccupation with and overwhelming pursuit of these things, to the very detriment of the kingdom, is proof enough that we are enslaved by the love of money, which is the source of all evil. We have to search our hearts and imagine ourselves without cars, without nice clothes, without beautiful homes. Would we feel miserable? Then we have failed the test. If a person depends on outward, visible things, that person is not free but enslaved. That person has the love of money, which is the source of evil.

That is why Jesus told the young rich man to sell all his possessions before he could inherit the kingdom. (See Matthew 19:21.) The wealthy man failed the test because he loved his riches. He could not imagine himself without them. You are not free until you can imagine yourself being happy without all these material blessings. If you cannot, then you do not really own those things; they own you.

We often think that people who have money are the ones with the love of money, and since we do not have much of that valuable commodity, we are free. What a deception! It is usually the other way around. Predominantly, the rich are free from the love of money, and that is why they have it. They usually do not suffer from the disease of loving money. It is those who constantly think, dream, and worry about money who are 100 percent addicted to it.

Now, the rich are certainly not free of their own problems. The main problem the rich really have is that they often trust in their riches, making it their fortress instead of God. Hence, the rich man or woman has a harder time giving out to the poor. We are not to be servants of money, for that is not our destiny. God calls us to be masters of money. If money is *our* master, our lives will show its fruits: pride, self-centeredness, dishonesty, greed, envy, and phoniness. No, we are to master money, not the other way around. Money is merely a tool, a means by which we meet our needs and accomplish the purposes of God. We must learn to rule over money, because if money means more to us than just a piece of paper, we are depending on it too much one way or the other. What is money, anyway? It is just processed wood or metal, just a piece of paper. Perhaps that is why the Founding Fathers decided to put the words "In God we trust" on the front of the U.S. dollar, meaning, "We don't trust in this piece of paper, but in God." Yet people risk their lives for this treated paper. They serve it instead of serving the Creator.

We used to have a currency in Ukraine called *karbovanez*, which was replaced by the current *grivna*. Why did the *karbovanez* cease having value? It no longer has value because the government changed the currency. Germany used to have a currency called the *mark*, but now a "mark" is a blurry spot or streak on a piece of paper. As Christians, we must learn to see our present-day currencies the way we see past currencies—as pieces of paper that no longer have value. I am speaking of value *to our souls*. Our inner minds must not rely on the money we have; we only allow it to serve us and meet our outward needs and resolve issues of life with no soul attachment whatsoever.

Some people think they have freedom because they have capital. However, is capitalism or any other "ism" the way out, or is it all an illusion? We should not be living by the laws of capitalism but according to the laws of freedom, the laws of the kingdom, putting the values of God above all earthly things. When our earthly lives are over, we will live in eternity by the laws of the kingdom, but the condition is that we start living by these laws now.

THE HAZARD OF THE LOVE OF MONEY

What causes people to deceive others and do repulsive things? The answer so often is the love of money! If we are believers, then we need to realize that nothing holds us here on Earth. Life is in Christ Jesus, not money. Then why does a believer need to learn about finances? We need to learn this so we can be free from the power of the love of money over us. Only the truth makes us free. When we understand God's principles about finances, we can then sow money to please God and do His will here on Earth. We want to be free of the love of money so completely that we can control any amount of it without it perverting us with its influence. We want to use it for God's purposes. There are only two options with money: either it serves you or you serve it.

Knowing the truth about money and money principles frees people from bondage. This is especially important for capitalist, free-market countries, because the system of those countries makes people work hard at jobs, sometimes keeping them on a leash of ignorance. As a result, we do not know some basic things about money except how to spend it. We become slaves to our jobs in the desire to make a good living and end up serving money. The kingdom of God, however, works differently. It is the only successful alternative to the system of this world. We must master money to make it work for us while remaining free from the world system; we must work for God in order to dominate the world with the principles of the kingdom of God.

> IF MONEY IS *OUR* MASTER, OUR LIVES WILL SHOW ITS FRUITS: PRIDE, SELF-CENTEREDNESS, DISHONESTY, GREED, ENVY, AND PHONINESS.

Consider an interesting testimony from a woman I will call Nicole:

One businessman, who was my husband's pastor, wrote a very effective syllabus consisting of forty principles taken from King Solomon's Proverbs. King Solomon was wise, wealthy, and had a very clear head about him. As Christians, we also want to have clear heads, and we remind God about it while forgetting to use our heads. I used to be like that, but after going through this program dealing with work ethics, money, character, business, worldview, and everything having to do with everyday life, I realized I did not have the right knowledge of money and needed to study, change, and develop.

When God called me to be a missionary, it never crossed my mind I would ever need to know anything about finances. I was so wrong. Ninety percent of the people who came to me for help had financial problems, and I did not have answers for them. I could only pray for them, and I realized that as a Christian I also had a responsibility to know about finances. I needed to know more than others did, because as a missionary, I will answer before God about what I taught people.

I wanted to share the knowledge I had learned in this curriculum when I first began working in Colombia ten years ago, and now this course is taken by one hundred and eighteen thousand members of police departments all across the country, along with sixteen thousand prison guards. Even prisoners showed an interest in this program. The government covers all expenses! Recently we came back from Kenya, where the mayor of a large city asked for seventy copies of this course for all his advisors. In Guatemala, thirty-six thousand students go through this program every year.[1]

From Nicole's testimony, we can see that for a Christian, there are real advantages for knowing the laws of money. In Nicole's experience, she is set free to go as a missionary while her investments work for her and supply her needs. She does not need to worry about health or life insurance; neither does she need to go around begging for support. Mastery over money allows her to serve God while her money works for her. Thousands of people all over the world, from government leaders to average people in the market, need to learn financial principles. Even one empowered person can make such a huge difference and help to alleviate poverty and ignorance in our world.

SHUN FEAR

Do not let failure be an option. Do not be afraid of anything, including fear of failure itself. It is not failure itself but fear of failure that is the biggest obstacle on the path to success in a Christian's life. Failure makes us stronger, more flexible, and more decisive, but fear of failure paralyzes one's thoughts and actions and hinders us from doing the things required to make it on the way to success. One young reporter asked Thomas Watson, the founder of IBM, how he became successful. Mr. Watson answered, "Would you like me to give you a formula for . . . success? It's quite simple, really. Double your rate of failure."[2] Success is on the other side of failure, so have courage to move forward.

Millionaires who made their money by plain hard work do not have a gambling addiction, but they are always ready and willing to take a well-thought-out risk that leads straight to their set goals and the achievement of a greater reward. Psychological preparation is the key because it is the biggest indicator of our readiness to become prosperous.

Every time you face a risky situation, you should ask, "What is the worst that can happen if I move forward?" Then, just like J. Paul Getty, the oil billionaire who made his money the hard way, make it your assignment to be sure the worst will never happen. The fact that everyone is afraid of failure is understandable and legitimate. We are all afraid of poverty and bankruptcy. We are all afraid of making a big mistake and falling behind. Very wealthy people who make their own money are usually those who intentionally and consciously resist this fear and take steps accordingly to move forward.

Ralph Waldo Emerson offered powerful advice when he wrote:

> Make it your habit to do things you are afraid of. If you do what you are afraid of, then your fear dies. When you are brave, this invisible power rises up inside of you and your every act of courage leads to the increase of your courage, which makes you stronger and braver when you confront fear in the future. Every time you do not have a guarantee of success, take a step and move forward, and your fear will decrease as your courage and

confidence increases. Finally, you will reach a stage in your life when you are not afraid of anything.

I think the best moment from the movie *Apollo 13* is when everyone thought they would lose the spaceship and Gene Krantz, the head of flight control for NASA, declared in a loud voice, "Failure is not an option!"[3] Our task is to become millionaires who make our own money to serve kingdom purposes. Our task is to devote ourselves to this one goal and work at it every day. When difficulties and fears arise, remember, failure is not an option. We need to get hold of this mentality, for more than anything else it will be the guarantee of our financial success.

WHY EVERY CHRISTIAN CAN AND SHOULD BE A MILLIONAIRE

When I first became a pastor, I was living in comfort—but never in abundance. Then one day I came in touch with the parable of the talents in Matthew chapter 25, and God opened my eyes. For a period of one year, I meditated on this Scripture passage, and this led me to discover the need to do more study on the subject of wealth. Finally, I realized that everyone could become a millionaire. Before I could preach on this new revelation, however, and if anyone was going to believe me, I had to prove these principles by first becoming a millionaire myself. Moreover, I had to do this without stealing or misappropriating money from the church that I oversee!

I felt for sure that the rich were rich because they understood the laws of money, something about which I had to acquire more knowledge. Therefore, I gave myself two years to convert theory into actual possession of a million dollars. Using the principles of wealth creation and following the laws of money I am teaching in this book, I was able to make my first million U.S. dollars in nine short months. Today this sort of thing is a common phenomenon in our church, as over the last two years I have been able to raise more than two hundred millionaires in the Embassy of God. Prior to that, every one of those people had an income of less than one thousand U.S. dollars per month!

Every Christian can be a millionaire, and, actually, it is easy to become one. It is just a matter of knowing the principles involved. Becoming a millionaire is not only for some special people who are born with golden spoons in their mouths. It is for people who know the true nature of the laws of money and the biblical secret of success. They have learned to maximize this knowledge in their lives.

TEN REASONS WHY EVERY CHRISTIAN CAN BE A MILLIONAIRE

1. God said we should be the head and not the tail, which means we should be first and not last. (See Deuteronomy 28:13.)

2. All gold and silver belong to God. As heirs of God, we have a legal right to it, but it must be used for His glory. (See Haggai 2:7–9.)

3. We are God's highest creation, and we are commanded to possess and dominate the earth. Wealth plays an important role in fulfilling the command to dominate the earth. (See Genesis 1:26–28.)

4. Our eyes make the difference. (See Proverbs 20:12–13.) Both the rich and the poor have this in common: "The LORD is the maker of them all" (Prov. 22:2). God is rich unto all His children, but He does not determine your financial status; your knowledge of wealth creation principles does.

5. Money is necessary to live in a material world. What oxygen is to the physical body, money is to the material world. (See Ecclesiastes 10:19.)

6.   We were commanded to be fruitful. Without money, our ability to bear kingdom fruit is minimal. (See Luke 13:6–9; John 15:1–7.)

7.   A Christian is a giver and abides in wealth. The blessing of the righteous exalts a city. (See Proverbs 11:24–26; Luke 6:38.)

8.   Christians are in a covenant with God, and this opens heaven to us. We have unlimited access to heaven's resources because of our relationship with Jesus Christ. (See Malachi 3:8–12.)

9.   Christians have the power to gain wealth. We have access to God's wisdom, favor, empowerment, and ability to create wealth. (See Deuteronomy 8:18.)

10.   God takes pleasure in the prosperity of His people. This gives us heaven's backing to be prosperous for His glory. (See Psalm 35:27.)

EIGHT REASONS WHY EVERY CHRISTIAN SHOULD BE A MILLIONAIRE

1.   We must carry out the Great Commission. (See Matthew 28:18–20.) Our instruction, then, is to bring Christ to the people of the world, train them, and release them to change the world they come from.

2.   We are commanded to clothe, feed, and house the needy and the poor. We need to be wealthy to do these things! (See Matthew 25:31–46.)

3.   Our job is to manage the earth for God. (See Jeremiah 49:2–3.)

4. It is good stewardship. Our ability to faithfully manage wealth produces in us godly qualities. (See Matthew 25:14–34.)

5. It is shrewd to use the wealth of the world for eternal purposes. (See Luke 16:8.)

6. Christians should accumulate wealth to demonstrate how not to trust in riches, because trusting in riches will always disappoint. A man setting his mind and his heart on money will be equally disappointed whether he gets it or not. (See Proverbs 11:28; Mark 10:23–25.)

7. We cultivate our land and keep it. The creation of wealth enables us to build the great qualities of managing and protecting wealth.

8. As one of the righteous, a Christian leaves an inheritance to his children's children. (See Proverbs 13:22.) It empowers us to fulfill this scriptural legacy and prepares the future generation for upward success.

PAY GOD FIRST AND YOURSELF SECOND

For anyone to become wealthy, the first thing to learn is to pay yourself second! Each time we receive our salary, we first pay for our rent, car, fuel, gas and electricity, and other bills. This means we are actually paying other people first from our salary. Because of our money, others are keeping themselves above water. That is the logic behind commercial advertisement—it is aimed at your pocket, not at meeting your real needs. It is only when we pay our creditors or buy from them that they achieve their goal. Meanwhile, we part with our money only to keep on going back to work and expecting another paycheck.

Then the same thing happens repeatedly. We receive our salaries only to give the money to others, including the grocery store owner, the gas station owner, the hairdresser, or the property owner. This is not bad if we actually pay ourselves also, but unfortunately, the vicious cycle of paying others first never ends. This repetitive system is a deterrent to us. Therefore, it makes all the sense in the world for the person making the money to pay himself or herself first after paying God. Whenever we put aside an amount of money for our future or for our children and prosperity, we are actually paying ourselves. Any amount we retain from our salary is the only amount we actually get, and we give everything else away.

Common sense says we must all learn the discipline of saving a certain amount of money for ourselves before we begin our spending spree. We must consciously plan to put aside a certain percentage of our income for our future. Depending on one's commitment to saving, that amount could range from 10 percent to 50 percent of one's income. We like to spend, but saving is another thing entirely. The average savings rate in the United States is negative .5 percent,[4] compared to 20 percent in Europe.[5] In Japan, it is even higher.[6] In America, wealth is evaluated not on what one has saved in the bank but rather on what is in the yard, in the garage, or in the house.

I have noticed that people who have not disciplined themselves to give tithes and offerings will also find it difficult to discipline themselves to pay themselves. I believe this is because they have not learned to first pay their essential obligation to God. So pay God first and yourself second before you begin meeting your needs.

SEVEN STEPS TO SAVING

Here are seven steps to keep in mind when laying aside money for your future and the future of your family.

1. Begin by paying your tithes and offerings as an automatic practice.

2. It is better if you can inform your bank to automatically transfer funds to your church account.

3.   Instruct your bank to transfer automatically a designated amount from your paycheck to your "Pay Myself Second" bank account.

4.   Try paying yourself no less than 10–30 percent of your normal income, and 80–90 percent of your extra income.

5.   Whatever percentage you decide to put aside (not less than what is recommended above), put it aside consistently.

6.   Putting money aside in savings must become so automatic that it functions as an automated system for you.

7.   Put money saved in a fixed deposit with a guaranteed interest rate, such as a bonds deposit, or use a savings account.

SAVINGS THROUGH
ECONOMIZING YOUR SPENDING

Most people tend to find reasons why they cannot afford to save. Maybe you are one of them! They often complain of a small income or expensive bills and other responsibilities that will not permit them to pay themselves. The truth is, you should not try saving a large amount immediately, but instead discover that it is actually *time* that multiplies money. The problem is not in how much or how little you *earn*, but how much or how little you *spend*. If you receive a million dollars monthly and spend as much, then you will never be truly wealthy. What determines wealth is not how much you receive, but rather how much you can save. To the extent you are able to reduce your expenses, you will be able to receive God's wealth.

The paradox of money is that people tend to spend more than they earn. The Bible says that when wealth increases, those who spend it also increase (Eccles. 5:11), but that should not be true of believers. That is why we must learn by practicing saving, even while we are earning small amounts of money. If we master this now, we will be able to save more when we make more. This is a consumption-oriented society. Yet the Bible teaches us to prepare for the future with confidence, and to do that we need a realistic savings plan. Part of trusting God includes saving for the future.

NONESSENTIAL EXPENDITURES

If we determine to save from the amount we would have spent on nonessential and unnecessary items, we would discover we could actually become wealthy. Some of us spend excess money on expensive boutiques, expensive restaurants, mobile phones, flashy clothes, first-class transportation, and so on. There is a long list of unessential expenditures we all waste money on daily. Think of your own list.

We can all save five to ten dollars daily simply by refraining from noncompulsory daily expenditures. A daily cup of coffee could cost three dollars or more, and a muffin to go with that coffee another two dollars. Candy or chewing gum or other cash-register items might add another couple of dollars, and then soda could be another two to three dollars. If we spend money on unnecessary things every day, it could total up to as much as one hundred fifty dollars per month, *or two thousand dollars each year.* What would happen if we put that same money into an account yielding a 10 percent annual return? In forty years, we could earn close to a million dollars. Savings can add up that dramatically. Let's examine some calculations below.

SAVINGS ADD UP

If you begin saving $5 each day that you would normally spend on nonessentials, in one week you would save $35, and in one month, $150. In one year this would amount to around $1,825. If you include 10 percent compounded interest monthly, you could anticipate the following accumulated wealth:

- Two years—$3,967

- Five years—$11,616
- Ten years—$30,727
- Fifteen years—$62,171

With 10 percent interest compounded monthly and a monthly investment of $300 ($10 a day for thirty days), after one year, the total would be $3,770. The totals continue to rise with each year:

- Two years—$7,934
- Five years—$23,231
- Ten years—$61,453
- Fifteen years—$124,341
- Thirty years—$678,146
- Forty years—$1,897,224

Does it seem impossible to invest $300 to $400 each month for your future? Then begin with $100 per month, an amount almost anyone can afford to set aside. Investing just $100 per month will reap huge benefits for you at retirement age, a time when you will no longer have the strength to labor. If you save $100 cash per month for forty years, you have only saved $48,000 at retirement. However, if you invest $100 per month at 6 percent interest compounded monthly (just leaving the money there to compound), the earnings would be $199,150, four times more than you could save in cash. Remember, this return reflects using only a fixed-deposit banking account. The money earned is apart from one's salary, business, stock investments, and so forth.

THE CULTURE OF SAVINGS AND INVESTMENTS

1. Keep some part of your earnings for your future. This is the "pay yourself second" principle.

2. Ten to 50 percent of your salary should go to work for you. Money in the purse is only gratifying to the soul; so put more of your money into your savings plan and less in your purse for immediate and easy spending.

3. Learn to live according to your purse (i.e., what you eventually have left after servicing your savings plan), and learn to live on less than your salary.

4. Don't be in a hurry to invest. Take great caution so that you do not lose your money. Remember, quick gain is deceptive. Many have said that if you want to make a million dollars, you have to endure a million dollars' worth of pain. Gain usually takes time. The first principle of investment is securing the principles of righteousness and honesty.

5. Analyze your priorities. Discipline yourself to save and invest, and thereby later attain increasing wealth. Money cannot quench desires; only discipline can tame desire.

6. Develop a budget, and live by it. A budget defends your priorities from casual wishes, and it helps to differentiate between the two.

7. Save for uncertain times such as old age or unexpected circumstances. (See 1 Timothy 5:8; 6:10.)

8. Accumulate wealth first in small amounts, then larger amounts as you learn and become more capable. Your goals should be simple and definite.

9. Be focused, and concentrate your efforts to acquire more information, new networks, strategies for better service, and cheaper and better products.

10. Beware of lending out money. You are not a bank, so do not bring others' burdens on yourself.

PRINCIPLES OF WEALTH CREATION

Money is not necessarily what you should desire. The crucial thing is wealth. Keep in mind that money is not the same thing as wealth. *Wealth* pertains to all the things we want and need, things like food, clothes, cars, houses, and so on. *Money* is a recent invention, but wealth has been here for many thousands of years. You can have wealth without necessarily having money. For example, if you could have all the things wealth brings, you certainly would not need money. In many ways, it really does not matter how much money you have, especially if you are in a place where you cannot spend it. Then why does the subject of money always arise when talking about prosperity, wealth, and riches? Money is the way we move wealth, and money is necessary in a modern world where you have to buy most things from someone else. The one who understands the laws of money—multiplication, retention, diligence—is on the way toward wealth.

Here are some principles of wealth creation:

1. Know your passion, know your love, and know what really gets you excited.

2. Study hard and obtain the best knowledge possible in your area of calling.

3. Look for opportunities to build great relationships.

4. Make sure you are seeking to resolve problems and give good service. Think of whom your knowledge can benefit, and render your services to them. Make sure you can offer something to the people you know. Focus on helping each person to resolve at least one problem.

5. Find out how much money and how many properties you have, and turn everything into investments or assets.

6. Make sure to keep some part of your earnings for the future.

7.   Make sure that you invest 10 to 30 percent of all your earnings (50 percent if possible).

8.   Cut down on your expenses and invest the rest.

9.   Make sure you have a mentor. Find competent people who can lead you in the process of wealth creation.

10.   Reach for success by developing your passions, desires, and drive to make money.

11.   Get to know the laws of money and follow them. Money comes to those who understand it.

12.   Know that self-discipline is the greatest asset and the number one rule of wealth creation. To create lasting wealth, you must be able to master and discipline yourself so that you can adequately follow the laws of money and wealth creation.

Now that you have read most of this second chapter, where I've endeavored to prove to you that becoming a millionaire is not a big deal, I would like to challenge you to stop here and repeat all the truths and principles you have been given above. Sit down and analyze your financial situation, and task yourself on the new things you have learned so far.

For example, make up your mind on how much you want to put aside weekly or monthly from your income. Moreover, take another step further by investigating the best financial institutions that could likewise give you the best returns on your money.

In short, try to put into immediate practice what you have learned so far before you are engulfed by other truths in this book. Remember: knowledge is nothing until it is established by action.

PRACTICAL WISDOM
FOR ASPIRING MILLIONAIRES

1. Successful financial life begins with a successful saving mentality.

2. Save to invest in your future.

3. One of the keys to saving is never to spend on what you can do without.

4. You either waste money, spend money, or invest money.

5. Fools waste money.

6. The mediocre spend money.

7. The wise invest money.

8. Investments become your future and assets.

9. Fight against pride in your life.

10. Always recognize the fact that we are only the managers and trustees of God's property.

KINGDOM PRINCIPLES
FROM CHAPTER 2

1. If money does not serve the kingdom, then it perverts, spoils, and destroys its owners.

2. The main problem the rich really have is that they often trust in their riches, making them their fortress instead of God.

3. You must master money to work for you while you are free from the world system and to work for God to dominate the world with the principles of the kingdom of God.

4. Every Christian can be a millionaire, and, actually, it is easy to become one.

5. Your job is to manage the earth for God.

6. It is shrewd to use the wealth of the world for eternal purposes.

7. For anyone to ever become wealthy, the first thing to learn is to pay God first and yourself second!

8. The problem is not in how much or how little you earn, but how much or how little you spend. What determines wealth is not how much you receive, but rather how much you can save. To the extent you are able to reduce your expenses, you will be able to receive God's wealth.

9. Beware of lending out money. You are not a bank, so do not take others' burdens on yourself.

10. To create lasting wealth, you must be able to master and discipline yourself so that you can adequately follow the laws of money and wealth creation.

Chapter Three

MONEY DOES NOT MAKE YOU RICH

D O NOT LOVE MONEY! LOVE GOD; LOVE YOUR FAMILY; LOVE friends and neighbors! Love people, but never love money! When you fall in love with money, it possesses you. By itself, money does not truly make you rich. It is neutral. That is why we need to acquire moral wealth before acquiring large amounts of money. Most people do the opposite. They put all their energy into amassing monetary wealth while ignoring the development of their character. The end result is that instead of them controlling their money, the money begins to control them.

Money also enslaves. If we are not prepared to manage wealth and riches, they will eat us alive. This may be difficult for some to believe, but it is nonetheless true: money will not make you happy. We use money to solve certain problems, which may produce a temporary sense of fulfillment or happiness, but it is never a true source of a joyful life—Christ is. If anyone thinks people are unhappy because of a lack of money, they are gravely mistaken. The reason many are unhappy is because either they have not understood the basic truths of life, or they simply refuse to live by them. For those convinced money is required for happiness, they need to know that mammon itself is responsible for this deceit.

If the concept of money is to work for you and not against you, you must grasp these three crucial facts: money does not make you rich, money enslaves, and money will not make you happy. A fourth and similar principle says that God entrusts money to the pure in heart. "Now godliness with contentment is great gain" (1 Tim. 6:6). In the world at large, even evil and unscrupulous people make money, but it possesses and controls them. Therefore, everyone who wishes to attain lasting financial prosperity has to work on developing a righteous and pure heart.

Righteousness is true wealth, for it is the possession of God's character. Whoever possesses this character trait is content, no matter how much money they have or do not have. Righteous men and women fear the Lord and follow His commandments, and when they do, evil cannot touch them. The entire world's wealth could never corrupt a righteous person, because the righteous rule over wealth and not the other way around. Money neither controls nor dominates them. They are free to use and channel it as God's Spirit directs them without the fear of loss.

I want to tell you a sad story. There was a young woman who loved to shop. She could not pass by any department store or boutique in the mall without going in and buying something. Neither her first nor her second husband could satisfy her desire for shopping. Her third husband, however, was a millionaire who did not bother her about her expenses. Excited about her unending stream of resources, she went on a spending spree. She bought anything and everything she wanted. She even went shopping in London, Paris, and Zurich. Even though she bought everything she coveted, in the end she was still not satisfied. You see, it was not the money or the things it could buy for her—there was an empty space inside that only God could fill. In the search for a beautiful life, this woman became a drug addict.

This story repeats itself every day across America. How many times have we seen relatively poor people become rich overnight after winning the lottery, only to lose it all in a few short years? Not only do many of these lottery winners lose all their money, but also some even end up having their properties confiscated and become debtors. Unable to overcome the despair of having to return to their former lives without money, some have even taken their lives.

The verse says, "Godliness *with contentment...*" By contentment, we mean a deep gratitude and appreciation to God for where we currently are and with what we currently have. The ability to be content is a quality that should be valued more than gold. Whoever has this trait is already a wealthy person. That rich young woman in the story above lacked contentment with the way things were. She could not be content, for in the end nothing satisfied her.

If God sees that we are not content with what we have, He will definitely not entrust us with more. If we are not content with one hundred thousand dollars, then fifty million will not do the job either. Not even a billion dollars will bring about satisfaction. That is the logic behind the love of money—the more you have, the more you want. We need to train ourselves to be righteous and become prosperous in our souls before seeking financial prosperity.

> WEALTH IS NOT A MIRACLE; IT MUST BE EITHER EARNED OR CREATED.

Many people pride themselves as righteous when they have nothing. However, I have seen repeatedly that riches can bring out the true color of people. If we already have certain assets, then we should search our hearts and see how content we are with what we have. Inner discontentment and frustration are reasons enough to stop expecting further financial blessings, at least for now. Of course, one can go out into the world and start making money by worldly means, but in the end, this is not the solution. Money will destroy us if that is all we are seeking. Money should bless and not kill its possessor.

Before God trusts us with money, we need to learn to see it as any other useful tool, like a simple piece of paper. Consider yourself successful if large sums of money do not excite you or cause you to become greedy. There are people who cannot control themselves when they see money in front of them. Try to give an unprepared man a million dollars, and he will most likely destroy himself.

AM I FREE OR NOT?

The mere fact of not having much money does not mean we have overcome greed. How do we identify our true feelings? Just consider the prospect of having millions of dollars, and imagine how you would feel. How do you feel when you think about coming into large sums of money overnight? Do you usually envy lottery winners or people who just suddenly got lucky with money? When you look at stacks of large bills, how does it make you feel?

If you feel indifferent, then you have victory over money. If you failed the test, maybe you should think twice about asking God for big money. Thankfully, He loves us too much to entrust us with large amounts of it before we are ready. God does not want us to suffer, and therefore He does not bring money our way unless and until we are ready for it. If God is to trust us with wealth, we must get rid of all the passion and excitement we hide in our hearts for money. That is the source of true financial victory, not the money itself.

As for me, I learned to live my life in a way that money does not rule over me. That is why in the time of need, money always comes to me. My thoughts are not about money, and I am constantly aware that I have authority over it. Some people will not even leave their house without money. This seems to be a bigger problem among men than women. Some men do not even tell their wives how much money they make because they do not want it taken away from them. In most families, the biggest conflicts are over money because it has great meaning and a disproportionate place in their lives. Often, people lose control when they start making "big" money. Wives cannot recognize their husbands anymore because these husbands were not set free from the love of money before it became theirs.

No millionaire I know carries money around. Why should they? Money for them is just an exercise in numbers. They are worth millions but often do not even carry a wallet. This is because these people are free from the power of money. On the other hand, people who have nothing often try to show off by carrying big, fat wallets around, counting their money in full public glare, because mammon has enslaved them.

We have to learn to have the right attitude before God entrusts us with money. For this, we need to realize that money is just a means, not an end. It is a tool and resource in the same way a hammer, nail, or screwdriver is a tool required for a specific task. Just as we use a car as a means of transportation, so too money is used as a means of solving certain problems. If it means more to us than that, it will become our master.

We are not supposed to treat money like a miracle that comes by itself. We earn it, but it is disruptive in the wrong hands. The fact that there are lotteries all over America with million-dollar jackpots does not negate the principle that money was meant to be earned. Many examples can be found of people who win large sums of money, only to return to their old, often penniless lifestyles within a short number of years. Some who were homeless returned to homelessness, just as homemakers became homemakers again. This is because they came into money when they were not ready for it, and they never learned that money must be under human control, not the other way around.

It is a question of who the master is. Learn to master the laws and nature of money rather than expect it to come to you as a miracle. Wealth is not a miracle; it must be either earned or created. Many Christians, especially in developing countries, are sitting in churches expecting God to bless them with money, instead of learning the principles of wealth creation. That is a great pity. These Christians are no better than someone playing the lottery, because neither is attempting to create or earn their wealth—they just want to win it.

We need to work to make money and be ready for it when it comes. Most people are capable of making a lot of money, but not everyone has the skills to retain it. It is not how much you *make* but rather how much you *keep*. This is a secret to financial success. Money that comes easily is like snow that falls on our heads and melts just as quickly. People who are expecting money through a miracle, and those who play the lottery, fall into this category.

BE FINANCIALLY FREE

We read in Ecclesiastes 10:19, "A feast is made for laughter, and wine makes life merry, but money is the answer for everything" (NIV). I learned one extremely important truth when I learned that people who are not free regarding money are not free at all. There are two kinds of financial freedom—one may decide either to live without money altogether, which seems almost impossible in our modern world, or to possess and control so much money they are free to spend any amount needed or desired. Most people will never experience this kind of freedom. Ninety-five percent of the world, which means the vast majority of Earth's inhabitants, is utterly dependent on money. It controls and directs their lives. The lack of it limits their desires and visions. It dictates their lifestyle and controls their actions. It tells them what they can eat, what they can wear, where they live, and where they go. Largely, money or lack of it is the proprietor of their lives.

It is tragic when a person does not have a place to live, when people go hungry, or when a church does not have a building to gather in for worship. It should not be that way! Money should not stop us, nor should it limit us or become an obstacle to us in any way. Money should not determine what we can and cannot afford. We must rule money and not allow it to rule us, because God predetermined we would have authority over all things, including money.

I hope I've been able to convince you in this chapter that money is not what makes you rich or happy. Like I've said earlier, what is worth spending your lives on attaining is righteousness and contentment, which is true wealth.

Get this right: If you will do more work on yourself, your character, and on your inner man, then you will get to a place where you are absolutely content and satisfied with God's blessings in your life. If you will pursue righteousness, contentment, and integrity—dedicating yourself to attaining these virtues—you will discover it will be easier for you to rule over money. More so, God finds it easier to trust you with wealth and money because your heart is right.

PROCESS OF PRODUCTION

Even though God blesses, it works to our disadvantage without our involvement in the process of production. Like I had said earlier, we can become no better than gamblers and lottery players. We cannot just sit in church and pray to God to make us millionaires, rich and wealthy, without actually getting involved in the production of goods and services. It is no different from the ills of a welfare culture that creates a people with a welfare mentality. It ultimately destroys the fabric of a society by weakening the value system of hard work and responsibility. Genesis 2:15 tells us that God required even Adam to go through the process of production by telling him to till the ground and keep it. God is trying to tell us that the most important thing in wealth creation is not really the money involved but the process by which it is created.

God could have just commanded the earth to be cultivated by itself through a miracle, or command the angels to come and do the upkeep of the garden—that is even a better miracle. But God did not do that, because He designed man to do it.

In that process of cultivating and tilling the ground, not only is production made possible, but man develops himself as well. As he works and goes through the process of production, he discovers more of his abilities, and his hidden potentials are released. He becomes a cocreator with God, and he enriches his knowledge by discovering more of nature and of the product he is trying to create. So, "the process" is important for both the man and the product. When preachers tell people to only give, and then expect a miracle, they have not helped the man. They have to go beyond that and encourage their people to learn the process of production of either goods or services.

Going through processes helps both the man and the product. It is easier for a man that is content and righteous to be involved in the process of production because he is already satisfied and derives more joy in just being a blessing and a benefit to the earth and to others. He is no longer pursuing gain and greed, but when a man is only interested in gain and profit, most often, greed is behind it! We should be more interested in the blessing that the process brings rather than the profit we are going to get in the end.

Money, therefore, is a by-product of the process of production of goods and services. That is to say that money is a reward for goods and services. It is a compensation for going through the process of production. So when people play the lottery or pray for financial miracles without the process of production, it is more a manifestation of greed than blessing. That is why the Bible says that God blesses a diligent worker rather than an idle person who is just hoping for blessings to rain down from heaven on him. You need to learn to be happy and rich in virtues before physical and material wealth will follow.

PRACTICAL WISDOM
FOR ASPIRING MILLIONAIRES

1. They understand the true nature of money as a force to be dominated, subdued, and directed for good. They know money is a good servant but a bad master, and they never allow it to rule or guide their lives.

2. Money is only the tool; it is never the goal. Or, we may say it is a means to an end and not the end in itself.

3. Stability, peace of mind, and joy in the family are far more important than money.

4. True millionaires live below their means. Everything they own they can easily afford. (See the example of Paul in Philippians 4:10–19.)

5. True millionaires are cash-flow conscious. (See Deuteronomy 28:8.)

6. They let common sense, patience, and self-control dictate their wants and needs, rather than the attractiveness of something. They would rather live without things than buy them on credit.

7. They are resourceful problem solvers, using what they have—not what their neighbors have—to meet their needs.

8. They know how to maximize their time, talent, and resources.

9. True millionaires know how to explore the time, talent, and resources of others to the maximum.

10. They understand the value of a dollar and the decency of work.

KINGDOM PRINCIPLES FROM CHAPTER 3

1. Do not love money! Love God, love your family, and love friends and neighbors.

2. Money does not make you rich.

3. Use money to solve specific problems, not to make yourself happy.

4. The ability to be content is a quality that should be valued more than gold.

5. Money should not determine what you can and cannot afford.

6. Money is a good servant but a bad master.

7. Stability, peace of mind, and joy in the family are far more important than money.

8. The process of production is more beneficial than the profit we receive at the end.

9. Pursue righteousness, contentment, and integrity. Dedicate yourself to attaining these virtues and God will find it easier to trust you with wealth and money because your heart is right.

10. True millionaires know how to explore the time, talent, and resources of others to the maximum.

Chapter Four

MAXIMIZING OPPORTUNITIES FOR FINANCIAL PROSPERITY

HERE ARE SOME TIPS ABOUT USING OPPORTUNITIES TO THE fullest in order to achieve success in your chosen sphere. The first tip is this: never stop learning. Continuous education is the minimum requirement for achieving success. There are endless resources to learn from before becoming proficient in any given area. In reality each one of us has more intellect and skills than we will ever be able to use if we practice self-development and constant learning.

COMMIT TO CONTINUOUS EDUCATION

I want you to know you are smarter than you think. If you apply your mind, there is no obstacle you cannot overcome, no problem you cannot solve, and no goal you cannot achieve. Your brain is like your muscles in that it strengthens with practice. In sports, the more we train for a certain kind of sport, the better we become at it. It is the same thing with the brain. The more we learn, the more we build the capacity to learn. The volume of your studying determines your learning.

Continuous education is the key to opportunity and success in the twenty-first century. It will have a substantial impact on personal gains.

Make a decision today to become a student for life in order to grow and become better at what you do. In order to live a life of continuous education, follow the following three rules of practical advice.

RULE 1: Spend from thirty to sixty minutes every day reading materials pertaining to your area of specialty or interest.

By reading every day for an hour, you will be able to finish almost any book in a week. That equals fifty books per year, and five hundred in ten years. According to the Library of Congress, 59 percent of people polled had read fewer than ten books in the previous year.[1] Fewer and fewer people are doing any reading at all, so think of the advantage you will have in your field. Reading for an hour each day will make you more knowledgeable, more competent, and better as a specialist.

RULE 2: Use your time wisely, listening to teaching CDs while driving your car from place to place.

On average, Americans spend one hundred hours each year commuting to work.[2] That is as much as twelve to twenty-five forty-hour workweeks, or three to six months of actual working time. It would be the equivalent of one or two semesters in a university. That is a lot of time, particularly wasted time. Why don't we make our cars mobile education centers? Many people became millionaires through headphone self-study from these kinds of CDs. That is why self-education is the biggest radical accomplishment in the sphere of education since the invention of the typing machine.

RULE 3: Attend every possible seminar and course that can help you become more qualified in your trade or profession.

The combination of reading, listening to teaching CDs, and attending professional workshops and seminars will lead to a life of continuous education that will have a great impact on your career.

Ongoing education also comes in packages that are more formal—adult courses in high school, college, or the university. According to the Office of Continuing Education, in one Midwestern university alone (Purdue) there were more than twenty-eight thousand people active in noncredit continuing education courses for the 2003–2004 school year.[3]

In credit programs, almost two thousand were taking undergraduate courses that same year, and two and a half thousand were in graduate programs covering all the academic departments, as well as fields such as teacher education, technology, consumer and family sciences, and many other areas. Of the grand total, 66.7 percent were women. And these continuing education figures represent just one institution. This is an indication how important nonstop learning is. It bears repeating: nonstop education is the key to opportunity and success in the twenty-first century.

Proverbs 23:5 says: "Cast but a glance at riches, and they are gone, for they will surely sprout wings and fly off to the sky like an eagle" (NIV). Choose a subject that will help you become more effective and qualified in your sphere. Make it your project, and study it to the end. Attend courses and read books on this subject. Ask God for the spirit of understanding to be teachable.

ANALYZING REASONS FOR FINANCIAL FAILURE

The reason for poverty in some people's lives is not because God likes them less or gave them less to work with. There are various tangible reasons for poverty in different countries of the world, depending on the region. Some of these are natural disasters, such as earthquakes, hurricanes, tornados, floods, droughts, and other natural disasters that do not allow people to rise up and be successful. Another tangible reason for poverty is dictatorship in a country, which is the situation in forty-three developing countries, according to the U.S. Department of State.[4] The corruption of the government suppresses freedom of speech and religion, the right to fair trials, and does not allow wealth to get to ordinary people. Many dictators commit torture, murder their political rivals, and starve their own people.

In democratic, free-market nations, however, there is absolutely no reason for people to live in poverty. In these countries, the reasons for poverty are not always attributable to bad government. Even in cases where there is corruption in government, people still manage to make money. Neither is it attributable to the fact that one lives in a poor country, for even in the poorest countries there is wealth, just as in the richest countries there is poverty. No, I believe the main reason for poverty anywhere is that people fundamentally lack understanding of the laws and functions of money. As I pointed out earlier, money comes to those who know how it works.

UNDERSTANDING THE LAWS
THAT GOVERN MONEY

Understanding the difference between assets and liabilities

The difference between assets and liabilities is extremely important to grasp. The poor acquire liabilities while the rich acquire assets. An *asset* is a possession that brings income to your pocket, income that also appreciates. A *liability* is something you own that requires expenses on your part to maintain. A liability is also something that depreciates. The cars we drive and the houses we live in are liabilities because of expenses required for upkeep.

The vast majority of people think that money is only for meeting certain needs, such as eating, dressing, or driving a car. Yes, money plays such roles, but my message in this book is that if you only use money for meeting certain needs, you will never be rich. You will always lack real wealth and will become a slave who works for money only to spend and spend. Remember the parable of the talents where we learn that the first law of money is not to spend it.

It is a rare thing to get money accidentally, such as winning a lottery, or inheriting it, or marrying into a rich family. That kind of money comes and goes, but its not enduring wealth.

Understanding that money, just like a seed, is meant to be multiplied

Money functions as a seed. What do we do with seeds? We can eat them, but that would be unwise. If we consume the seeds, next year will come and we will not have anything to eat, because we have not sown a thing. "Whoever does not sow does not reap" is a universal law. Therefore, we must turn the money that comes to us into planted seeds. Even small amounts can multiply. In the next chapter we will look closely at the parable of the talents to learn more about the laws of money. That parable illustrates this fact: God will not swing into action on our behalf, and He will not give us something big if He does not see our faithfulness in small things.

We are smart and can overcome any obstacle. Even so, Jesus said that some people in the world are smarter than we are, and no wonder. They have learned the main purpose of money. One of the lessons of the parable of the talents is that money cannot be stored, but rather needs to be put to work. We think sometimes, "I am a believer. I pray to God, and I serve Him. God will bless me." This is not smart. Not if it means you are just going to sit around and wait for the blessing. No matter how much you pray, God will not give you much, because He knows you will consume everything anyway. God does not sit in heaven with a money-printing machine, waiting for us to ask for riches so He can drop a few bundles into our laps. God gives us power, authority, intellect, wisdom, and ideas—in other words, the abilities—to make money ourselves (Deut. 8:18).

> IF YOU APPLY YOUR MIND, THERE IS NO OBSTACLE YOU CANNOT OVERCOME, NO PROBLEM YOU CANNOT SOLVE, AND NO GOAL YOU CANNOT ACHIEVE.

Some Christians have said to me, "Why do I need to work if God provides for me?" Of course, we bless each other in the body of Christ, but if we are continually asking God or the brethren for money all our lives, like the wicked servant, God will dismiss us from His presence into the outer darkness. Jesus said to the evil servant, "Go out of my sight. Your place is in the outer darkness." (See Matthew 25:28–30.) In Deuteronomy 8:18, we learn that God gives power to obtain wealth. It says, "Remember the LORD your God, for it is he who gives you the ability to produce wealth" (NIV). Notice something: God does not give wealth, but rather He gives the power and ability to gain wealth. The first talent or the first money that comes to us is not for spending. Sow it into good soil, which is the beginning of producing fruit, or profit. This is the difference between the rich and the poor: the rich make profit from their money and the poor consume their money quickly, afraid someone will take it from them.

Understanding the difference between an investment mentality and a consumer mentality

A savings culture is the first step to wealth. The second is investment. As soon as you complete the first condition and start receiving returns on your money, the next question arises—how to keep it. Keeping money does not mean burying it somewhere. We have all heard about investors who put money into different projects. We also know people put money in banks in order to keep or save it. These are the smart things to do. Too many people do the opposite when they get some money in their hands. They count how far the money will go and then go out and spend the money on new clothes or new shoes, expensive cars, extravagant travel, and so on, until the money runs out. This is because most people lack the knowledge and understanding of the laws of money. That is why the poor get even poorer. If all of a sudden you came into one hundred fifty thousand dollars, would you go out right away to buy an expensive car without thinking about how those expenses would only bring more expenses?

Understanding the difference between financial discipline and instant gratification

It is no surprise that businesspeople invest billions of dollars into advertisement. Why do they do that? Because millions upon millions of people watch commercials and then run to the stores to give their money away on the things they have seen advertised. Money goes from hand to hand; the rich get richer and the poor get poorer. That is why I have been stressing that the most important step to wealth is to retain money through savings. Everyone must start his or her financial journey with a philosophy of savings, because in time the small becomes big. True investment begins with a culture of saving. After savings, then we will begin to have something to invest and multiply.

We must discipline ourselves to control the lust and desire to spend money. The man or woman who puts aside his or her desires and does not rush out to exhaust his or her money has power and control over it. One hundred or fifty dollars could turn into a million in five years through the law of money and really take care of children and grandchildren.

Do not eat your firstfruit. If you are in need, wait a little bit, and from your returns, you will be able to buy whatever you need. A twenty-six-year-old man who used to be addicted to drugs came to our church and received Jesus into his heart. He was flat-out delivered. This young man did not finish high school, did not go to college, and had absolutely no work experience. What he decided to do might sound crazy. With ten cents, he bought two plastic bags, went on the commuter trains, sold the bags, and made some money. Then he went and bought more bags with the money he made from the previous sales call. In a year, he started little stalls in different stores, had four people working for him, and was making two hundred fifty thousand dollars a year selling plastic bags! This is the power of money in circulation.

That man came to understand the very nature of money. If he did not have the right understanding, he probably would have sold a few hundred bags and then used up the earnings without realizing it. He would still be walking from train to train with his plastic bags today. This is how many people unknowingly spend large amounts of money. No one can ever become rich by focusing only on spending instead of saving, no matter how little or how much.

This is what the wise person knows, and so he disciplines himself and invests the money to get more returns, rather than spending it immediately. Let the money multiply itself many times over—and then enjoy it more. The person with power over money will never be poor. Those without that power tend to pursue a flamboyant lifestyle, thinking that their extravagant lifestyle and careless spending is what wealthy people do. That is not so. The rich are very accountable for their money.

Most people look at the 5 percent of the population that owns 95 percent of the world's riches, and dream of being like them. This is a dangerous illusion. That kind of desire will only lead to becoming servants of the rich instead of their equals. The rich do not spend their first earnings or profits on flamboyant lifestyles. Only the poor and the proud do that in their attempts to appear rich and affluent. They drive cars they cannot afford and live in houses they cannot pay for. Moreover, when it comes to fashion, they wear all their wealth on their backs. They derive some sick satisfaction from the mere appearance of being wealthy, when in reality it is all an illusion. In their efforts to keep up the illusion, they must spend even more of what they own so little of. Hence, they progressively become the slaves of those who already have more than enough.

MAXIMIZING OPPORTUNITIES

As we can see from this chapter, a whole lot of people are poor, not because God is not good to them and not because life does not give them a whole lot of opportunities, but, unfortunately, many never seem to see the opportunities they have! Successful people have learned to take advantage of opportunities. However, before you can take advantage of opportunities, you have to be able to see these opportunities first.

Our ability to see opportunities is very crucial for wealth creation. For example, at the beginning of this chapter, I spoke about taking advantage of the time you spend in your car and other chances for study, thereby maximizing your time for productivity.

People who do this will succeed in life. On the other hand, people who don't maximize their time live in lack and poverty because they did not see their time as an opportunity that can be converted to wealth.

This is very closely linked to the passage we see in Proverbs 13:23, where the Bible says that there is a lot of food in the field of the poor, yet the man is called "poor"! So why is he poor? Because he has refused to maximize the provision that God has given him. Also, because he has failed to manage and structure the resources in his hand.

These and other reasons stated above are responsible for failure in life.

SACRIFICE BEFORE PLEASURE

If the man that is given one hundred dollars per month will invest the money in a profitable project on a regular basis, then as we witnessed in the previous chapter, even a one hundred dollars could make you a millionaire—if the principles of money are followed.

Everyone should take advantage of time and compound interest. Unfortunately, the poor people around us are actually becoming poorer, not just because of the system we live in, but also because of their mind-sets of comparing themselves with the wealthy and the flamboyant lifestyle they see around them. When the poor do not know the true lifestyle of the wealthy, and the principles that the wealthy had observed before achieving this lifestyle, the poor will be deceived into pursuing only the end results without observing the preliminary laws of money that the wealthy had already observed.

It is important for the poor and the rich to know that before they spend any amount of money on pleasure, they have actually made ten times the equivalent of this money that would be spent on pleasure.

If these laws are followed, we will succeed in reducing the amount of poverty that we have in our culture and society today.

There is an inspiring story of one of the Armenian pastors in our church. Roughly two years ago, he, his wife, and two small children were suffering desperate circumstances. They were cooped up in a small, one-bedroom apartment, earning only three hundred U.S. dollars monthly. They could hardly afford to eat or use the public transport system.

Due to this situation, he managed to keep money aside and bought about three hundred cassettes of these financial lessons. He tried listening to them several times, and initially he didn't quite understand what I was saying because he actually couldn't read or write! He had never finished elementary school as a result of being expelled from four schools while growing up.

Even though he was absolutely desperate to come out of poverty, he just couldn't because his mind was not used to learning. Nonetheless, with absolute determination, he took hold of those cassettes and started listening to them every day. It took him about a year to listen to all three hundred tapes four to seven times! All of a sudden his eyes of understanding opened and he began to comprehend the principles of money that are stated in this book.

As he started applying these principles over the subsequent year, he accumulated an asset worth of over two million U.S dollars! He is now training 500 people to become millionaires too! Out of those

500 candidates, on the last count, he already had 255 people who were making between ten thousand and fifty thousand U.S. dollars per year.

This is why I want to challenge every Christian reading this book not only to practice these principles in your own life, but also to go forth and teach them to others also so that you could contribute to reducing the ache of poverty in our world.

RULES OF FINANCIAL EQUILIBRIUM

The next thing to know about money is how to balance expenses and income. No matter how much money we have, even if it is a billion dollars, it will eventually run out. The main problem for many people is that they run out of money before their next paycheck. As I stated earlier, Proverbs 13:23 says, "A poor man's field may produce abundant food, but injustice sweeps it away" (NIV). This Scripture says there is plenty of food in the fields of the poor. If that is true, then why are some people poor? They are poor because their "food" is decreasing due to lack of order, management, and knowledge. They do not understand how money functions, and they do not know the laws of money. It is easy to learn these things, but the more information we have about money, the better we can control it.

Another testimony we have is that of a young and beautiful girl. She came to our church as a student, twenty years old and a sorry sight! I can distinctly remember her because the day she first stepped into the church, she was wearing tattered and torn clothes. She had come to Kyiv from the countryside from another region of Ukraine.

Even though her circumstances were horrible—she was surviving on less than two dollars per day—she went ahead and bought all the cassettes of these financial teachings. She put her mind to studying them for six consecutive months and then began applying these principles of financial equilibrium to maximize her two dollars. By this time she was almost twenty-one, she began spending the next year implementing these principles and teachings so that by twenty-two she had already made her first one million dollars—still being a full-time student!

Today she is heading up the young businessmen's club in our church whose aim is to help young people between the ages fourteen and twenty-five to earn an income of ten thousand dollars per month.

At the moment, the club boasts over three hundred members, which all goes to show that nothing is impossible when we follow the truths in this book.

EIGHT RULES OF FINANCIAL EQUILIBRIUM

1. When we use or put our seeds to work, it multiplies. By disuse, it depreciates and loses value. For example, when we refuse to use our muscles, we lose our strength. The same applies to finance. Use it—that is, plant it—or lose it. If we take piano lessons and then refuse to practice, we lose the obtained skills. The same is true with capital.

2. Storing money away without putting it to work will lose its original value over time.

3. Money will always leave the hand of those who don't put it to use, and come to the hands those who will multiply it. For example, the man with one talent—which he didn't use—lost it to the man with ten talents.

4. The key to increase is always investment. A good steward keeps what he or she receives, then uses and increases it through investments.

5. Those who invest their "talent" are entrusted with more.

6. The reward for being trustworthy is more trust.

7. The steward who buries his sum loses what he has, and he will see it given to another.

8. Life is based on laws, and understanding the laws of money will bring greatness.

PRACTICAL WISDOM
FOR ASPIRING MILLIONAIRES

1. The foundation of life is laws and principles, not superstitions and mystery.

2. Successful people know that life is time and time is money. They do not waste it but maximize it.

3. Great people reign by what they know; hence, they are always seeking knowledge.

4. Successful people love work.

5. Curiosity is the lifetime hobby of successful people, and opportunities do not pass them by.

6. Great people are reliable, stable, and truthful.

7. Quality and excellence are the watchwords for people who achieve success, and they desire to be the best in every area of their lives.

8. Strong achievers are always confident about their abilities.

9. People at the top are ready to go the extra mile and make the necessary sacrifice to reach their goals.

10. The successful man or woman considers details, facts, and fragments.

KINGDOM PRINCIPLES FROM CHAPTER 4

1. In reality, you have more intellect and skills than you will ever be able to use if you practice self-development and constant learning.

2. Self-education is the biggest radical accomplishment in the area of education since the invention of the typing machine.

3. The key to saving is to never spend money on what you can do without.

4. You may waste money, spend money, or invest money.

5. An asset is a possession that brings income to your pocket—income that also appreciates. A liability is something you own that requires expenses on your part to maintain. A liability is also something that depreciates.

6. God does not give wealth; He gives the power and ability to gain wealth.

7. True investment begins with a culture of saving.

8. The sin of *indolence* is doing nothing; the sin of *insolence* is passing the blame to others.

9. Life is based on laws, and understanding the laws of money will bring greatness.

10. Successful people are successful because they have learned to take advantage of opportunities.

Chapter Five

FINANCIAL FREEDOM
AND THE
BASIC LAWS OF MONEY

As God's children, our goal should always be to be financially free and to depend on our Maker alone. Accordingly, nothing should control our lives but Him. To live like this, however, requires that we first conquer the love of money and rise above its controlling power. "A feast is made for laughter, and wine makes life merry, but money is the answer for everything" (Eccles. 10:19, NIV). Yes, feasts are for fun, but money is required for them. No money; no party. The simple and indisputable fact is that we need money. We need it to make a feast for God, for our families, and for our generation. The Lord tells us in Psalm 23 that He will prepare a table for us in full sight of our enemies. Notice that even God wants to prepare a table for us. He needs something to work with from our end, which is why we must apply ourselves to work.

Money is responsible for fun. As I said earlier, there are two ways to be financially free—either we have no financial responsibilities, making us independent of the influence of money; or we have a surplus supply of money, making us free from the worry of responsibilities. The first scenario would only apply to a small segment of society, such as children or homeless people. Therefore, the only reasonable way to be finally free would be to have money in abundance. The fact is, we derive satisfaction from things other than parties, nice clothes, comfortable shoes, good cars, and so on. These things are as much a source of satisfaction as they are the source of monetary responsibilities. Still, if you were to try living without them for a year, I seriously doubt whether you would have much fun. Without funds, there is nothing to eat, no gas for our cars, and no clothes to wear.

What did Solomon mean when he said, "Money is the answer for everything"? This means it brings answers or solutions to all questions of life. Everywhere I go, I hear people complain about the lack of money. There is not enough money in Germany, England, Africa, the United States, or Ukraine. Remember, 95 percent of the money in the world is concentrated in the hands of only 5 percent of the world's population. The other 95 percent (almost six billion) struggle to grab a part of the remaining 5 percent. Those in possession of the money are the ones who know the principles of wealth creation.

Here we have two major contrasts in financial profiles. As many as 95 percent of the world's people have a shortage of money, and the other 5 percent have abundance. The first group consists of people trying to solve the problem of not having enough money. They work from morning until night to make money. Therefore, they end up being slaves to it. The latter group of 5 percent has their needs and the needs of their children covered. Thus, their only challenges are how to steward their money so that it keeps on turning over interest for them daily and how to avoid paying taxes. This is another perk the wealthy 5 percent enjoy—they do not pay taxes. What a contrast! Those who can least afford it shoulder the nation's burden of paying taxes, while those who could easily afford it get off scot-free! It is little wonder the rich get richer while the poor are forever getting poorer.

THE LOVE OF MONEY

It is not money itself but rather the love of money that is the root of all evil. When people love money, they are not free from it. People whose thirst for money drives them to that extreme commit a vast majority of the crimes committed in society. As strange as this is, it is not the people with credible wealth but people who do not have money who are usually the ones most affected by the spirit of mammon. As I mentioned earlier, having an excess of wealth creates its own problems, and it has ruined many people. However, a lack of money and the desire to have it is responsible for most crimes and violence.

Just a cursory glance at history will reveal the extent to which this is true in America. Crime flourished during the Great Depression at an alarming rate, even by today's standards. From the street gangs to the more sophisticated crime rings, there were myriads of activities among them, all aimed at making money. At the writing of this book, because of the recession, bank robberies have increased in America over the past year.[1]

However, the love of money is seen not only in the multiplicity of crimes being committed by the poor, but also in legal activities at the institutional level. Since *Roe v. Wade*, circa 1973, over fifty million babies have been legally aborted in America. Some see no wrong in this, while others consider it morally reprehensible. Whichever end of the spectrum you stand on, abortion is a multibillion-dollar federally funded business that continues to flourish under government protection. Antiabortionists in America have fought long and hard to have the laws overturned for the protection of the unborn, but to no avail. Why the killing of the innocent unborn is allowed to continue can only be explained by the love of money.

The same can be said of the pornography industry, which enjoys protection under the First Amendment. It does not take a genius to see the negative impact of these things upon society. If time permitted, we could talk about the greed of Wall Street speculators and the effect they have on the price of oil and, consequently, the global economy. The love of money affects people from every segment of society. It impacts the rich, the poor, and even our institutions.

You are either the master over money, or you are its slave. Either you make money serve you, or you will end up serving it. Most people believe they are free from the love of money. You can test yourself by asking, "What am I working for?" If it turns out you are working for money alone, then you might be its slave. Christians should not work just for money. Instead, every Christian should go to work with one goal and one purpose in mind—to bring the kingdom of God into the sphere where he or she works. We are His ambassadors in the marketplace. If we are working at a job only because we must survive, then the potential exists for money to control our actions and rule over us.

Survival makes us resort to all manner of desperate acts. Kingdom dwellers must never be motivated by survival but by purpose. Jesus went to the cross because He was not concerned about His longevity. He had a single purpose in mind and would not be deterred by threats or criticism. For Jesus, survival was never an issue. He lived and died for the will of the Father. That was His purpose. Therefore, the first purpose of employment should be to bring God's kingdom to rule in our workplace. God gives us plans for making His name known and getting His will done. Paychecks and promotions are just God's way of rewarding our faithfulness in seeking His kingdom first.

For me, work is service to God, a way of establishing the kingdom of heaven on Earth. Of course, I want to have a decent salary, but a decent salary is not my primary goal. Instead, I want to be an example to my co-workers that God will provide everything necessary in life. If you are motivated by something different than that, you need to change. All work should be service to God; money is only a by-product of such services.

WHO IS YOUR GOD?

The tragedy of the twenty-first century is that people—especially in the West—serve money instead of making money serve them. It is sad to see how so many have become slaves to money. It is true the Lord wants us to prosper, but there is a purpose for prosperity. It is ultimately for the prosperity of God's kingdom in this world. While acquiring riches, avoid stepping away from the boundaries of that goal. If you devote yourself to this purpose, uprooting all selfish ambitions and egoism from the heart through repentance, then the Lord, who looks at the heart, will sanctify you and make you a channel for His glory.

When you devote yourself to the promotion of God's kingdom, you can prepare for blessings. God does not give money so much as He *entrusts it* to those who are pure in heart. He can only trust those who are dedicated to working tirelessly to establish His rule.

These are the principles that move us toward wealth before we actually receive financial blessings. They must be deeply entrenched in our hearts. Would you like God to entrust you with millions? If your answer is yes, what will you do if someone actually gives you five million dollars? During one of the numerous seminars I conduct in our church, I asked these two questions, and I want to share some of the responses I received from people who thought they were ready to be millionaires.

1. *I would fast, pray, and ask God what He would want me to do with the money.* Yet this is no answer at all, because if we do not already know what we need money for, then we really do not need it. Money comes only in response to vision, because when there is vision, money moves in its direction. Vision leads to provision.

2. *I have a few ideas. I would buy a piece of property and build a rehab center. I would buy buildings for other ministries and help them financially.* This sounds worthwhile and spiritual, but spending money that way only leads to spending *all* the money reserved, and soon that person is penniless again. Before spending money on charities, multiply it first.

3. *I would invest the money in arts and media for the Word of God to be preached on television and in theaters.* This answer is similar to the previous one in that this mindset only devours the finances instead of generating a source by which it would constantly generate more and more funds for future use.

4. *I would build houses for homeless people. I would also give money to students who can't pay for their education.* A wrong understanding of money makes people assume that their first duty to money is to spend it. On the contrary, the first law of money says do not spend it; invest it instead.

5. *I would invest the money and make a profit. Then, I would buy a building for the church.* This answer is much better. The responses I received in my own congregation show that only one out of five Christians understand what to do with money. Wise people know they only spend the proceeds from one's capital, but never the basic capital.

These answers point to the fact that most of us are not prepared enough for God to entrust us with money. He also knows how each one of us would really use the money. One thing is certain—God will never entrust wealth to someone not ready to handle it. He is our Creator, and He knows us better than anyone else does. He also knows whether we would have enough wisdom to make the right choices. For most of us, a single day would probably be enough to dispose of the money and be left with nothing. This is the problem of not knowing and abiding by the laws of money.

THE PARABLE OF THE TALENTS

In the twenty-fifth chapter of the Gospel of Matthew, Jesus told the parable about the talents and thereby explained the laws of money. The servant hoarding the talent and not investing it was punished and rebuked for his wickedness. The other two servants received three and five talents of money each, which they invested and multiplied, and their rewards were handsome. If we are going to invest money, we need to know how to do it and what to invest in. Many people go bankrupt because they sow good seed into bad soil, and that is the surest way to lose one's hard-earned money.

It is obvious that the first servant did not have an appreciation of the value of the talent committed to his trust and had not learned enough to know how to invest properly in moneymaking ventures. Preparation for riches implies rich saturation on the inside with God and His kingdom principles. Usually, riches do not come suddenly. The reason is that God uses a systematic approach to entrust us with money and wealth.

At first, He may give us one thousand or five thousand dollars just to test our wisdom in its use. However, maybe He has a million dollars in mind for us. What we do with the one thousand or five thousand dollars will determine whether we will get the rest of the money God is keeping for us. So, even though God intends for all His children to live in abundance, only a few will, because most do not possess the knowledge necessary to bring the millions to them.

Churches receive tithes and offerings every week, but most of them run their budgets to the limit way before the month is over. This problem reflects ignorance of what the Bible teaches us to do. In the parable of the talents, the servants that were given three and five talents multiplied them for their master. On the other hand, the servant given only one talent chose not to invest it and earned himself a stiff rebuke and stern punishment. Why are we surprised that there are few millionaires in our churches? There will never be many people with significant money to benefit the church as long as we do not understand the concept of money. Stewardship is demanded from each one of us, including nations, nongovernmental organizations (NGOs), and even churches. If a church is not a good steward of the tithes and offerings of the people, God cannot trust that church with more money. God expects us to multiply some of the money and keep it for the future to carry out His will on the earth.

THE BASIC LAWS OF MONEY

The first law of money is *multiplication*. The two faithful servants did not *spend* the money given them, but rather *multiplied* it. Even the third servant did not spend his money, as we often do, but he stored it up and hid it away. Yet this man was condemned. I have advised the pastors of our daughter churches to take 30 percent from the monthly tithes and offerings and put it aside for savings and investments. I tell them to turn this money into a harvest, in other words, put it aside for multiplication and not spend everything right away on rent for the building and the other needs of the church. If 30 percent is too much, I tell them to start with 10 percent. The important thing is to begin with something. If a church would be a faithful steward of God's resources this way, then that church could teach individual congregants to do the same with their individual incomes. This is the first law that the parable teaches.

The second law of money, which the third servant failed, is *retention*. The servant failed in this because he did not even retain the money entrusted to him. After hiding the money for some time, the initial amount given to him had depreciated through inflation. Even though he gave it back to his master upon his return, it was not intact as he had so smugly thought; hence, the master's disappointment. Therefore, the second law of money is to retain it. We are often tempted to spend the money coming our way on pressing and legitimate needs, but wise people keep it in their possession before investing. Every time God gives us talents, He expects us to multiply them. It is irresponsible to spend money before it multiplies. Churches and individuals tend to find excuses why they cannot invest, especially giving excuses of the IRS and tax-exempt situations. Remember, excuses are the comfort of mediocre people.

If God trusts you with five talents, multiply them by ten or even thirty before spending them. Moreover, remember that you can only spend the profit from your multiplication of the original talents, not the seed itself, because the seed belongs to God. Spending all of one's salary every month before any of it multiplies is contradictory to the laws of God and human logic. The Lord often does not trust us with money, because we do not understand His ways. We think Jesus was just sharing a nice, quaint parable about money when, actually, He is teaching us how to live. No matter how small your income, keep a part of it for multiplication. Jesus rewards those who multiply what they have, as Matthew 25:21 records, "Well done, good and faithful servant!

You have been faithful with a few things; I will put you in charge of many things. Come and share your master's happiness" (NIV). The same applies to local churches. If we keep on giving excuses, then we are only encouraging our members to do the same thing—first, to be irresponsible with little, and then to start begging God for a financial breakthrough. What a paradox!

We see the third law of money exemplified in the two faithful servants who were diligent. Diligence means making a meticulous, conscientious, thoughtful, and careful effort in rendering service. It is not just doing something right, but also doing something thoroughly and effectively. Diligence delivers excellence, quality, creativity, and the highest standards possible. (See Proverbs 12:24; 22:29.) Money comes to those who are diligent and who know what to do with it. The servants were faithful because they multiplied their seeds while retaining the original seed and then simultaneously multiplying the seeds again. This third stage is the stage of *investment.*

A revelation from God is a reliable starting capital. Every day the Lord brings drug addicts, prostitutes, and alcoholics to our church in Kyiv for whom we need to care. Who will take care of them, and who will pay for it all? The funds will come from the tithes and offering from the church. How can we multiply these when most people in Ukraine are poor and struggling financially? We do it by diligent savings and investments. Many of my fellow citizens have apartments costing in the neighborhood of $150,000 to $200,000, and yet they do not have money for food. Why not sell the apartment or take a loan on it and buy another one outside the city at a cost two or three times cheaper? Why not invest the rest of the money in real estate and resell it later? Using this principle, a man in our church now owns five apartments instead of one and reports that in three years he will be a millionaire.

Money comes to people who know what to do with it; their knowledge is like a magnet that attracts more riches. We need to stop poverty, and, if we are to stop poverty, it must begin in our minds. I want to relate to you the testimony of another one of our church members, who I will call Kate.

I serve God in the worship team. One day I heard the Lord telling me to take responsibility for the building of the church. Confused, I thought to myself, "How am I going to do this?" But God simply repeated His request: "Take responsibility and be in accordance with My will. I will send money through you. This is your task, to receive it and apply it according to My purpose." I agreed to be this channel for God. I had been working in real estate for the last nine years, and the whole time I have been practicing the principles of God regarding money.

I both invest and give. God is faithful and blessed me abundantly. Whenever I had some decent amount of money, I would pray vigorously to find out where the money was supposed to go. By God's grace, I was able to rent an apartment for a minister. Then I found out that a church had a problem keeping up with payments for the rent of their building. I felt the Lord telling me to start paying the rent for them. Since this was such a big responsibility, I asked God for a confirmation. I really wanted to know that the Lord was going to do this thing through me. I had been trying to sell an apartment that was on the real estate market for three years. Therefore, I asked the Lord to help me sell the apartment as a confirmation that whatever I heard was from Him. The next day there were several people vying for the apartment! God told me He is giving billions of dollars to churches and that there will be companies working directly and exclusively for the kingdom and its needs. I believe the time will come that the Lord will bless me so much that I will be able to live on 5 percent from the profit and give the rest.

Notice that Kate gives not just to meet her needs. She first invests to multiply her capital (seed) numerous times over, and only after that, she gives from her overflowing profits to meet the needs around her.

Indeed, the Lord is ready to give large amounts of money to Christians dedicated to the kingdom of God. We need to be ready to give as much as God says to give and not just tithes and offerings. We must remember, however, that there are conditions. One condition is integrity. We need to have God's character, purity, and honesty. We need to be ready to suffer rather than to bring reproach to God's name. If you do not bring God's holiness into your field of work, then you are not ready for true blessings. As I have already stated, God *entrusts* finances and does not *give* them. Can He trust you with wealth, or are you an untrustworthy servant? To be trustworthy, you must be faithful in living by the laws of money first before you could expect to be God's channel of financial blessings.

MY WAKE-UP CALL

I will share my story of how God gave me a wake-up call about how much I had been an unfaithful servant in the area of personal shameful stewardship, as well as in the churches finances. At this time, we were running well over fifteen thousand in membership, yet we never had as much as a million U.S. dollars in our savings account. Our financial life was a constant pocket-to-mouth experience. Whatever we got was what we spent. The paradox here was that when we were only a one-thousand-member congregation, we had exactly the same challenge as we have now.

When we had only one thousand members, we were collecting twenty thousand U.S. dollars in offerings monthly, and at the end of the month, we were always out of money until the following service. In spite of the fact that we now had over fifteen thousand members and were receiving ten times more in offerings, we still had the same problem. As our income grew, so did our expenses. It was a puzzle I could not solve. We prayed, fasted, and expected wealthy converts to bail us out, all to no avail.

Needless to say, that same cycle was repeating itself in my personal life as the pastor and in the lives of most of our members. This situation continued until a fateful day when God challenged and rebuked me from the Book of Matthew, chapter 25. After I finished preaching to my staff on the lazy and wicked servant who hid his talent, God began to open my eyes to the knowledge that I was worse than that servant. I could not believe it because I prided myself on pastoring the biggest church in the nation. Yet, God was telling me I was worse than that "wicked, lazy servant" (v. 26).

After long sessions of meditation, I realized that this parable was actually a lesson on what our attitudes should be toward money—not just talents, as in gifts or callings only. It was a lesson about money management. God made me realize that if the first law of money was to multiply it and not spend it, then I failed a test as an individual and as a pastor. I also failed in the second law of money, which is retention. I did not retain what I got. I failed worst of all in the third law, which is investment of God's resources. I learned that you should never desire to make money as a minister—if you do, you are greedy and worldly. It does not matter if you are going to use it for God's purposes or not. The scriptures in the Book of Acts, where the disciples decided to concentrate on the Word of God and fasting while the others served the table, remained very strong in my memory. I dared not think about it.

> IT IS NOT MONEY ITSELF BUT RATHER THE LOVE OF MONEY THAT IS THE ROOT OF ALL EVIL.

However, from Matthew 25, God showed me I was not a good steward of His resources. Moreover, Paul and other apostles actually worked apart from preaching, praying, and fasting. They gave a good account of themselves, both as ministers and as merchants in the marketplace.

What totally shattered my charismatic dogma was when God pointed out to me that the wicked and lazy servant was better than I was because he at least obeyed one of the laws of money. I, on the other hand, had failed all three of them. The wicked servant in the parable at least understood that money was not to be spent. That may explain why he did not spend his one talent. However, I was failing miserably in this first law. I began to imagine where I would be financially if I had at least kept what God had entrusted into my hands, both on a personal basis and for the church finances. Then I broke down in repentance.

On one hand, I was repenting, but on the other hand, I was justifying my actions. I kept telling myself that if I had not spent the money, I could never have covered all the church's expenses and mine. We needed to pay not only our rent and utilities, but also numerous other bills, including bills for our many outreaches. The spirit of self-justification was all over me until I finally understood that God was telling me to start with a minimum of 10 percent. That 10 percent would later be invested for multiplication. A ten-time multiplication gives me the total amount collected originally. If I do this every month and invest at least 10 to 20 percent annually, the compound monthly and yearly interest would be enormous.

That is exactly what I started doing. By the end of that year, we already had over a million U.S. dollars in our church's account. I realized that as soon as you begin to apply these financial laws into your business, God begins to open supernatural contacts, relationships, and other doors of unlimited opportunities to you. Again, that was exactly what happened to our church and to me. As soon as we started applying the principles, our income began to grow tremendously, and this happened even without the church membership knowing. When the members began hearing of the changes, however, another miracle took place. Some of the most faithful businesspeople in the congregation saw the sense and wisdom in this approach to church money. They began offering incredible business and investment opportunities to the church, leading us to gain in returns the minimum of 30 percent annual interest on all our investments. Some of them offered to multiply our resources at the expenses of their own time, energy, and gifting.

When I saw how this principle worked for the church, I then decided to be a good steward of my personal finances and income as well. As I applied these principles in my life, God opened up doors, enabling me to make my first million dollars in nine months. It was after this that I decided to study the topic more thoroughly and then begin teaching the church all I had discovered. I taught these principles of economic and financial empowerment for the next two years on a weekly basis. As a result, we produced over two hundred millionaires in a span of two years, as I said earlier. Today I have started a millionaires club called Club 1000, aimed at raising up one thousand Christian God-fearing and kingdom-minded millionaires, warriors against poverty and financial ignorance.

I would again like to give you an illustration from the life of the young twenty-year-old girl who came to our church with nothing, and in less than two years earned her first million dollars. Today she is helping to raise up other young people financially who have a heart for the kingdom of God.

Well, she is one of the people who, after listening to all of these teachings and then applying them to her life, made up her mind to live below her income status. That is to say that even though she was earning ten thousand dollars per month, she refused to buy a car, house, apartment, or any other lavish expenditure. She continued to rent an apartment and use public transportation.

She contributed fifty percent of her income to various kingdom projects, and the rest she continued to invest and multiply, leaving a mere 1 percent to live on—and, in her own words, "To live as a queen."

My reason for telling you this story is because it is so unlike many others who try to live *above* their financial status. Many will even go so far as to take out a loan so that they can live extravagantly, when, in reality, they can't afford it at all!

She understood that she should not be concerned with public opinion and social expectations. She decided to abide by the laws of money—even after she had earned substantially—and continue to multiply her money before expenditure.

This is actually the pattern of all truly wealthy people, to live below their true financial standard and instead continue with investments and multiplication. Hence, the saying remains true: *the rich get richer as the poor get poorer!*

THE TWENTY BASIC LAWS OF MONEY THAT I TAUGHT TO MY CONGREGATION

1. God made us to live by laws, not by miracles or mysteries. Money comes to those who know and abide by its principles.

2.   Knowledge of the law of money is the key demand for wealth. To obtain this knowledge, find mentors, coaches, teachers, and partners for wealth.

3.   The first thing to do with money is save.

4.   Income does not determine wealth; knowledge does.

5.   Minimize expenses.

6.   Don't steal. Pay your tithes and taxes. For a secure future, pay all your debts.

7.   Wealth comes by investment. Save in order to multiply the savings, retain by minimizing costs, and multiply by investment and production.

8.   Don't listen to the dictates of money—it is a good tool but a bad master.

9.   Wealth does not come by working harder, longer, or even wiser. It comes by applying principles, time, energy, your mind, and your money. (See Luke 19:24–26.)

10. It is easier to obtain wealth in poor surroundings than in rich or developed surroundings with already-maximized potential, so never complain about your circumstances.

11. Ignore social expectations demanding a certain standard of social behaviors.

12. Money does not come because someone is good, spiritual, or lucky. It comes to those who know and apply the principles of money. (See Proverbs 6:6–11.)

13. There are no limits in life except those of the mind.

14.   Don't keep liabilities. Keep only assets.

15.   The reason for failure in life is ignorance and laziness.

16.   Do not despise the day of small beginnings. Start with small savings.

17.   The windows of heaven are open to send blessings, not money. God sends ideas and designs, but He does not send money. (See Deuteronomy 8:18.)

18.   Let God become your partner.

19.   Money comes by cultivating your land and producing goods and services. Genesis 2:15 says: "The LORD God took the man and put him in the Garden of Eden to work it and take care of it" (NIV).

20.   God's blessing is important for enduring wealth without sorrow. God's blessing is the guard against evil. In Proverbs 10:22, we are told, "The blessing of the LORD makes one rich, and He adds no sorrow with it." Never love money. Instead, love God, and you will be able to subdue money.

As you can see, I am trying to give you as many laws and principles in this book—in a summarized version, compared with what I taught my members in the church. Each one of these laws took me a month to communicate to my members because the bottom line is not just to give them the information and the laws, but what is even more important is to change their mind-sets. When it comes to money and wealth creation, belief system is the key. As you can see from the stories I've told above, it took me a lot of breaking and humiliation before God before I could change my own religious concepts to line up with the new revelations that God was giving me. It is possible that you, my dear reader, are now in the same position that I used to be in with my religious stereotypes and belief system that didn't allow God to answer my prayer for financial breakthrough.

Therefore, I would like to challenge every reader at this junction to examine yourself, as to your own concept of ministry and finances that you have come to believe because of one dogma or another. I would therefore like to encourage you not to just read through these laws and principles, but to actually dig deep into yourself in honesty, examining these new points of view that have been brought to you in this book. Pray about it and sit down to write down on paper the areas where you need to change and make amendment in your personal finances and ministry finances.

In the beginning of this chapter, I gave you the example of the responses that members of my church gave as to how they would spend five million dollars if they were given it. We saw that most people who were dreaming of becoming millionaires one day actually had the wrong attitude toward money altogether. Their attitudes were more sentimental than financially logical.

Because of this, they might be working and struggling through life, dreaming of becoming wealthy one day, but yet fail because their zeal is not according to knowledge. I can assume that most people might be in that category, and you can decide for yourself which of the five respondents you are. The lesson this is giving us is that we must strive to gain adequate knowledge of money first before striving to gain wealth. Make sure you don't just strive to learn these but that you also understand them very well. Don't just read them, but study them diligently before you step out to apply what you have learned. The more you know about the principles of money, the better for you in application.

PRACTICAL WISDOM
FOR ASPIRING MILLIONAIRES

1. Steadfast millionaires find their joy and contentment in life by pursuing their God-given dreams, not in pursuing material acquisition.

2.   They study and work hard to learn more, and then they convert that knowledge into profits.

3.   True millionaires invest not just their money, but also their time in getting more knowledge and wisdom. Even their hobbies help them to grow financially and personally.

> Then I realized that it is good and proper for a man to eat and drink, and to find satisfaction in his toilsome labor under the sun during the few days of life God has given him—for this is his lot. Moreover, when God gives any man wealth and possessions, and enables him to enjoy them, to accept his lot and be happy in his work—this is a gift of God. He seldom reflects on the days of his life, because God keeps him occupied with gladness of heart.
> —ECCLESIASTES 5:18–20, NIV

4.   True millionaires shun opportunities to get rich quickly and get-rich schemes. They prefer building their wealth in widespread ventures.

5.   True millionaires like to understand what they are doing. They focus on building and controlling each step of the way.

6.   Legitimate millionaires live below their means and do not concentrate on living big.

7.   Faithful millionaires are givers but not wasters of money, both in the family and in the church.

> If anyone has material possessions and sees his brother in need but has no pity on him, how can the love of God be in him? Dear children, let us not love with words or tongue but with actions and in truth.
> —1 JOHN 3:17–18, NIV

8. True millionaires understand that they are blessed to bless others.

    I will make you into a great nation
        and I will bless you;
    I will make your name great,
        and you will be a blessing.
    I will bless those who bless you,
        and whoever curses you I will curse;
    and all peoples on earth
        will be blessed through you.
                    —GENESIS 12:2–3, NIV

9. They build a future for their children and grandchildren, and they support their churches and other Christian ministries.

10. Genuine millionaires are frugal in that they control their expenses and do not waste anything.

K I N G D O M
P R I N C I P L E S
FROM CHAPTER 5

1. The only way to be finally free is to have money in abundance.

2. Ninety-five percent of people have a shortage of money, while the other 5 percent have abundance.

3. It is not money itself but rather the love of money that is the root of all evil.

4. Christians should not work for money, but instead, every Christian should go to work with one goal and

one purpose in mind: to bring the kingdom of God into the sphere where he or she works.

5. Work is service to God, a way of establishing the kingdom of heaven on Earth.

6. All work should be service to God, and money is only a by-product of such services.

7. Money comes only in response to vision, because when there is vision, money moves in its direction. Vision leads to provision.

8. It is irresponsible to spend money before it multiplies.

9. Money comes to people who know what to do with it; their knowledge is like a magnet that attracts more riches.

10. God made us to live by principles, not by miracles or mysteries.

Chapter Six

AVOIDING THE DECEPTIONS OF MONEY

ONE OF TWO CRUCIAL TRUTHS WE MUST RECOGNIZE IS THAT money alone does not make a person wealthy. The second truth is that only the morally wealthy can manage money the right way. When people love money and focus their prosperity on money, then money rules them. They probably will not come to church on Sunday, because money tells them to go to work. A person might have billions, but until that person is "free" from those billions in his or her mind, and understands that monetary wealth is not the source of prosperity, it will devastate and destroy that person. Let us not be so foolish as to let some paper with printed numbers on it own us. In this chapter, I will talk about avoiding the deception of riches. As I have said earlier, riches are very deceptive indeed and can manipulate us into doing all kinds of evil things.

Success is not an accident; it is subject to laws and principles. If someone really wants to attain it, it is possible to do so. More often than not, one accomplishes success after very hard work. It is a combination of many other factors too. For believers, success is fulfilling what God calls them to do. Everyone can attain success, because God has given everyone a brain and abilities. Of course, if you think you are nobody, or if you think you are a failure, it just means that you have yet to attain the knowledge successful people have. Something is in them you still have to discover.

The brain is more capable and powerful than you think. We all have so many untapped resources that we could explore for greater success, if we could only agree to work harder and go the extra mile. We need to stretch ourselves to the limit and train our brains to use our abilities and build the muscles of our intellect.

You need to study and learn the things that can make you into somebody, meaning a personality in God. There is no easy road to success in life. It takes hard work to build character, and character building requires much discipline and wisdom. Hard work usually comes before success. God is under no obligation to bless people who do not work hard. In fact, the Scriptures say: "He who tills his land will be satisfied with bread" (Prov. 12:11).

A person needs to have inner decisiveness and an honest desire to be fulfilled. This makes success goal driven, and to get there, we must set goals and accomplish them. Yet sometimes even a workaholic cannot reach success, because success also has definite elements of spirituality: "Unless the LORD builds the house, its builders labor in vain" (Ps. 127:1, NIV). The Lord will not put His hand, His mercy, or His blessings on us if we do not trust Him.

IS HAPPINESS FOR SALE?

As paradoxical as it may sound, it is possible to have a lot of money and not actually be successful. It is difficult to believe that having a lot of money does not make a person happy. After stockpiling all the money they wanted, many of Hollywood's richest people come to realize that happiness and success are not found in riches. The world may be trying to imitate Hollywood stars, yet they have some of the highest suicide and divorce rates in the United States, despite their so-called success or wealth.

One of the most tragic Hollywood figures is the famous Howard Hughes. He was young, good looking, and wealthy. Some say he was one of the wealthiest men in America, even by today's standards. By the 1960s, he was already a billionaire. Yet Howard Hughes spent the final years of his life wasting away in seclusion and misery, addicted to drugs and barely able to help himself. When he died in 1976, there was hardly anything left of him but skin and bones and several hypodermic needles, which were found broken inside his body. Howard Hughes left an untold fortune behind and many unanswered questions. What happened to this bright young aviator who once had the world in the palms of his hands? Why couldn't his wealth preserve him from such a wretched end? The saga of Howard Hughes serves as a grim reminder that true happiness and success are not found in money.

Some think success lies in a career. There is some truth in this, because a person who wants to reach success dedicates himself or herself fully to a calling. If someone does not become devoted—even fanatically devoted—he or she probably will not be successful. If a person is not a diligent worker, there is not much chance of any real success. As I said before, God is not obligated to bless people who do not work hard.

Eventually, successful people realize two things: there must be hard work to be successful, and monetary success by itself is not happiness. Many are disappointed to find nothing but emptiness at the top. "Have I worked all my life for this, to end up empty and alone?" "Is that all there is?" These are the sad conclusions of those who rely on their career as their source of inspiration in life.

This is why we need principles and guidelines from the gospel. They become the foundation for our success as Christians. It is indeed very boring and lonely at the top, but being at the top should not be our goal. Our goal should be fulfilling God's agenda and answering His call. If that takes us to the top, then so be it. It is a much better and wiser alternative to merely being "successful." Accomplishments and success in the worldly sense are only the means to gaining a greater platform from which to exercise the kingdom's influence. All things are to serve and advance His cause on the earth. Unless we always keep this truth before us, success will pollute and defile even the best of us.

Every time we try to get ahead, we need to be sure to build a very solid foundation in the family. The biblical principle says that family comes first, and then after family comes ministry or career. Many people are careerists who abandon their families for their career. That is not God's way. We need life partners to share the memorable moments of our difficulties and struggles on the road to success. The wife (or husband) of your youth can share your successes, failures, humble beginnings, and exalted heights.

Remember that God is your first companion in life. He is your senior partner in business and the Creator who gave you life. He is always by your side and the one with whom you will spend eternity. If you live by His principles, you will not be alone on your mountaintop. Your divine friend will always be with you and will be there for you amid difficulties as well as celebrations. God and the spouse of one's youth are the two basic pillars required to maintain life successes and accomplishments.

The Word of God says, "If you abide in My word, you are My disciples indeed. And you shall know the truth, and the truth shall make you free" (John 8:31–32). You can amass great wealth, but if you have no truth, it will enslave you. I know very rich people, and I can testify to hearing many sad stories about great wealth and the deception of riches. Believe me, you would not wish an enemy such a life. Some of them have put every effort into their careers while sacrificing their families. They are so consumed with loneliness when they go home that they resort to disreputable things at night just to fill their void.

There are people, many of them young people, who accumulated quick riches through one shady deal or another, and they spend their lives in casinos and social clubs. They are looking for joy and contentment. Perhaps they get into drugs, all in an attempt to be happy. But who can be happy without God? I have never met anyone who can prove there is happiness without God! No one and nothing can replace the Creator who fashioned us and knows our every desire. Without God, the more money a person accumulates, the more the feeling of emptiness settles inside. Life with an abundance of money and wild success is just harder and rougher than life without it. Only God enriches life without adding sorrow to it. All other successes outside of Him and His protection are full of sorrows and disillusionment.

NO ACCIDENTAL SUCCESS

Some believers think they are not lucky because they do not live like the rich. We have a man in our congregation who used to be a multimillionaire before joining the church. One day he said, "Everyone here has compassion for the homeless, the drug addicts, the poor, but what about people like me? Does anyone care for me? Being a millionaire, I had a lifestyle that afforded me anything I wanted. Yet, I was often envious of the poor, drug addicts, and the drunks. I did not drink, did not smoke, did not do drugs, but all the prostitutes in town knew me. I was possessed with adultery and perversion. I could not control myself, and I could not live with my wife. Do not ever try to accomplish success without the Creator. The more you try, the more you will regret your actions."

How do we attain solid success? "In the beginning was the Word, and the Word was with God, and the Word was God" (John 1:1). God should be before anything else. He is our covering, our foundation, the beginning, and the end. The truly rich are people who are first rich in God. To them, money is just a means for serving the Father.

Is there a formula for success and fulfillment? Yes, there is:

> I returned and saw under the sun that—
> The race is not to the swift,
> Nor the battle to the strong,
> Nor bread to the wise,
> Nor riches to men of understanding,
> Nor favor to men of skill;
> But time and chance happen to them all.
> —Ecclesiastes 9:11

This teaches that the combination of preparation and opportunity equals success. It is a biblical formula, and it is as easy as it seems. When preparation and opportunity meet, we are ready for success and elevation.

My testimony of how I came to Ukraine is a confirmation of this truth. In April of 1993, the first commercial TV station was established in Ukraine. An American came and invested money in it. Since it was an international project, they had to have an international department, so they needed someone fluent in both English and Russian. They started looking for someone suitable for the position, and when a friend called me in Belarus and invited me to Kyiv, I was the one who matched their requirements. They hired me, and immediately I had a two-bedroom apartment, a car, and a good paycheck. On the one hand, I was prepared as a professional, and on the other hand, an opportunity presented itself. Thus, I was fulfilled.

There was an opportunity to start an international department at the television news station, and my boss asked me to fill the position of an assistant director. Life and God are fair to all, and there is no partiality in God. God is faithful to His life principles. With hard work and deep preparation, one will always get an opportunity. No matter how tough life is, God is fair to everybody and gives everyone an equal opportunity. There are factors keeping us from using or even seeing opportunities, however.

OVERCOMING FEAR OF FAILURE

J. D. Parker once said, "There is no failure in the world; there are only people who don't know how to succeed." In order to be able to use opportunities that arise, we first need to overcome our fear of the unknown. People are afraid of moving, leaving their comfort zone, without knowing what is waiting for them on the other side. For example, I lived in Belarus for seven years and knew what to expect, but in Kyiv? God forbid something goes wrong in the new place. Eighty percent of people lose their opportunity because of fear of the unknown. Then they usually blame God, people, bad luck, or the enemy for their failure to grasp opportunity. Nevertheless, it is fear that makes them blind.

The second thing preventing people from seeing and using God-given opportunities is the lack of desire to change their lifestyle. When the Soviet Union collapsed and we had a period in history widely known as *perestroika*, most of the Russian population had to find different jobs or even train for different professions because in the new system business was done differently. Plants closed, and many skilled jobs were no longer required. Many people got involved in commerce, teaching, engineering, science, and so on, but in order to earn money, we had to accept the new way and change our attitudes. Many did not want to accept any new ways, and many of these lost their livelihoods due to inflation and economic depression. Those who overcame the challenges and adapted to the new system began living happy, productive lives. However, the lack of desire to change shattered others emotionally and physically, and this brought them into poverty.

PROSPERITY WILL COME WITH INNER CHANGES

Why do so many people perish in poverty? I suggest it is because of ignorance. They say, "This is how our ancestors lived, and this is how we will live, keeping our traditions." They forget that not so long ago their ancestors were in poverty. Our problem is not in our ancestors but in our refusal to change. We cannot keep doing what we have always done and expect great results—everything will just stay the same. In order to see new results we have to start doing new things. The art and ability to change is in the mystery of constant self-perfection and goal reaching. New information must be introduced to our cranium if new behaviors are to manifest. This is what change is all about. If we do not change, we will not be ready for the opportunities God gives us.

SUCCESS ISN'T ACHIEVED BY WELL-WISHING

Right now, many colleges and universities offer a variety of programs for new professions. These programs are for people in their thirties, forties, and fifties who are insecure or afraid of going back to school, not knowing that may be exactly what they should do in order to have opportunities to make them successful. Opportunities for success arise more than once. They appear numerous times during the course of our lives. We miss them either because of our ignorance or because of apathy. Sometimes a person has success, but because he relaxes and decides to stop growing, he misses the new opportunities God gives him. Opportunity and destiny go hand in hand.

Imagine you are invited somewhere, and you refuse to go, but your destiny happens to be waiting there. It could be a new acquaintance or a business proposition, a future spouse, or anything else. For instance, if I had refused the proposition to come to Kyiv when I did not even have money for transportation, I would not have become who I am today. We need to be serious, sober minded, and alert to be ready for new opportunities. It is disappointing when an opportunity comes and we are not prepared. I am sure each one of us can remember the time we made a wrong step. "If only I was more decisive...if only I agreed to that job proposition...if only I was smarter, or had a degree, or agreed to relocate."

Successful people are who they are because they make more effort than others do. A majority of people live without considering the possibility of a better life. Others never make any effort at hard work. They will say, "I have done my best." As a result, both types of people never make it. Successful people always go an extra mile. This effort is the preparation we need when opportunities arise. I do not consider myself the best preacher in Ukraine or Europe. Why then do I have such a big church? What attracts people? I think the secret is that I am always making an effort and trying to do more than enough. I always finish what I begin. After I accepted Jesus in my heart, I attended church for only six months before leaving for Belarus. Then, in the former Soviet Union, there were no churches, and I did not have a pastor. What I had was opportunity after opportunity to hear street preachers and attend seminars, conferences, and workshops, and these opportunities arose even though I lived in the midst of a nation of people who believed there was no God.

During those years, I was working on myself, working on my character, and studying the Word of God. I learned to make enthusiastic evangelistic efforts. At the age of thirty-three, I became the youngest pastor of the biggest evangelical church in Europe, and the only black person to lead an organization of 99 percent white people. I was also the only pastor to gather so many followers from a different race. After coming to the Christian faith, I was astounded at the realization that God forgave me. I could not fathom God forgiving someone like me. Then I decided I would faithfully serve Him to prove my gratitude.

When I heard that some believers pray for about one hour a day, I decided to pray three hours a day. When I heard that believers were praying three hours a day, I decided to pray six hours a day. In being faithful to Christ and His church, God has blessed me in ways I could never have imagined.

BE PREPARED FOR A FINANCIAL BREAKTHROUGH

We must value our time and the process of preparation, for to be truly successful, we must be people who go all out in whatever we do. The person who does the bare minimum, while expecting to accomplish the maximum, is setting himself up for failure. That person has an attitude of doing nothing to get something, hoping to be lucky in the end.

That attitude is the root of failure. Just trying to "get by" will cause us to miss out on happiness and success. Excellence, on the other hand, demands that we go the extra mile and double our efforts. Many people cannot accept blessings because they are not prepared. However, good preparation is the best antidote for fear. When we are ready, we can take risks, but when we are not sufficiently prepared, we are afraid.

It is clear that wisdom, understanding, and competence are results of thorough preparation, not qualities we are born with. Ecclesiastes tells us these qualities alone are not enough reason for success. We must match time and opportunity to these qualities. Opportunity is a result of perseverance. We may be prepared, but opportunity does not knock on our door every day. Remember, there is a time for everything. As soon as an opportunity presents itself, however, we will be able to take advantage of it only if we are well prepared.

Success is the result of preparation and opportunity intersecting at a specific time. All successful people, whoever they are, will tell us there was an opportunity they took advantage of at just the right time. They grabbed it and worked hard at it. A painter or a writer cannot predetermine when inspiration will come. It could come anywhere or anytime, even at the stroke of midnight. Inspiration comes when it comes, and it comes from above unexpectedly. God gives opportunity in His time, and it is up to us whether we see it and take it. If we know our calling, we must be ready for God's timing. "Hear, my son, and receive my sayings, and the years of your life will be many" (Prov. 4:10). Diligence is essential to wealth creation, while laziness is one reason for poverty. If we are to escape poverty, then we must live to do our work with diligence, whether we are Christians or not. Unfortunately, I see so many Christians who think that all that is necessary for a financial breakthrough is zeal in God's work, prayer, and being a good Christian. To some extent, this is true. These are wonderful principles to live by. However, when it comes to making money, God demands that we incorporate the principles of diligence as well. Praying, fasting, serving in the church, and spiritual zealousness certainly have their own important place, but make sure you are diligent and meticulous in your work as well. Then you can entertain a more realistic hope for major financial breakthrough.

Let us contrast the example of a Buddhist who is very diligent in his business with a zealous Spirit-filled Christian. If the Christian is zealous only about spiritual activities and yet very laid back when it comes to his business, then Proverbs 10:4 will not work for him, because he is not diligent. God is not obliged to make him rich. Whereas the diligent Buddhist will enjoy material prosperity because he has fulfilled God's condition for material blessing. God does not promise that only a diligent *believer* would come to wealth, but rather that *anyone* who will pay the price to be diligent would come to wealth. God loves the Christian brother; yes, he is going to heaven because he is saved, and he will be blessed in other areas. Yet, if he remains too laid back, he will be in financial lack because he did not fulfill God's requirement. Even though the Buddhist might not know Christ and might not enjoy other gifts of God's blessings, yet God is obliged to reward his diligence with wealth because He must keep His word.

How do we prepare? I could make many suggestions, but here are just a few. Base your life on biblical truths. We cannot adequately prepare for

> SUCCESS IS THE RESULT OF PREPARATION AND OPPORTUNITY INTERSECTING AT A SPECIFIC TIME.

life without a good knowledge of the Scriptures. Jesus knew Scriptures, and He used them all the time. Read books in your field of interest. Gather information on the Internet, in libraries, anywhere you can on the subject of your calling and interest. Prayer and fasting are extremely important ways to prepare for our calling. Every now and then, traveling and even magazine subscriptions will help in preparation for one's calling. It may be wise to keep an eye on the friends who surround us, and change friends when this is necessary.

If we want to realize our potential and strike blows for the kingdom, we need to learn how to change. For example, when I came to God, I still had friends who brought dirt into my life. I realized I had to stop those relationships because if I did not, they would have pulled me back into the world. When we come to Christ and live for God, we need to change our lifestyles in order to move forward. No one can effectively move forward while still looking back. Too much looking back will lead to failure.

If 95 percent of people in the world know little or nothing about finances, as I said earlier, then this means virtually everyone we meet every single day is living their myth about money. In order to reach a high financial level, we need to start building relationships with acquaintances who know the reality of money and wealth. This way we can learn from them about the principles they followed in order to attain their height. Get acquainted with those who are more knowledgeable than you are and who have a developed mind in this area. I have found that when I am talking to someone on any topic and feel like I am back in the first grade, it is probably because they are challenging me to learn and develop more. If I feel like a hero in my own circle of friends, then it stops my development and makes me satisfied. There is no growth and development in that.

Maybe in your circle of friends you do not have people who are able to challenge and teach you, but do not be discouraged. Authors of books can become your best friends. There has been an explosion of books on business and leadership. Good authors can offer readers much valuable advice. By studying their books and biographies, you can become friends with Bill Gates, Robert Kiyosaki, Bill Bartmann, Scot

Anderson, and Napoleon Hill. Soon you will realize you are finding your own niche by reading them and thinking like them. You can rub minds with great men and women through their books and teachings. You do not really have to meet them personally to receive valuable knowledge from them. If you think big and great, it is more likely you will become great. Never forget that God created you for greatness.

We are not ready to receive a financial breakthrough unless we work on our character and change where necessary so that when the Lord entrusts us with money, we will have the knowledge to multiply and maintain it.

Another reason to have acquaintances among the rich and successful is that often they have important information and can give advice to help make a decision. For example, you may have saved up a certain amount of money and are ready to invest it somewhere. It would be a tremendous asset to know someone who could help you make the first step.

LAYING THE FOUNDATION OF PROSPERITY

In laying the foundation of prosperity, often we must begin by working for someone else. This is just the first step—an in-between period to help in the accumulation of knowledge. During this period, even if you have only a small paycheck, there is still every reason to begin putting aside a set amount. Do not be discouraged; continue to put it aside faithfully. Making bank deposits of a hundred dollars every month, with accrued interest of 10 percent, will slowly increase your money. This is especially true over time. Time can multiply money if invested, or time can eat the money away if it is not invested with interest.

Most people are sure they do not have extra money to put aside because they have planned out their expenses a year in advance. It is clear these people need more knowledge at this point than they do money. In fact, it is my belief that the amount of money people make today is a direct result of how much knowledge they have. If your salary is about one to two thousand U.S. dollars monthly, it means that small amount matches your little knowledge. Why is it you cannot make ten thousand U.S. dollars a month? It is because you have not reached that level in your knowledge yet! How would you account for all that money right now? God knows that if He gives you that amount now, you would probably spend it all.

Where does the money of financially ignorant people go? You guessed it—into the pockets of the financially knowledgeable. Every second of the day the financially naïve are intelligently robbed by the financially knowledgeable through the enterprises of vision and advertising. It is a known fact that money will always leave the hands of the ignorant to fill the coffers of the wealthy and knowledgeable. Those who have will have more—taken from those who do not have. Remember the story of the talent and the servant whose one talent was transferred to the man who already had ten?

There was a time in the 1990s in Ukraine when the criminals in society were getting rich very quickly. But where are those criminal elements now? Some of them are in the grave, and others are in prison. The only exceptions are those who came to Christ and are now serving the Lord. There was no other destiny for such people because they were under the influence and control of money. The law of prosperity says if you make money, you need to keep the balance of it by accumulating information and knowledge about your money. That is why Scripture says, "Wisdom and knowledge will be the stability of your times" (Isa. 33:6). Be prepared and arm yourself with wisdom before you worry about making money. Become rich in knowledge before getting money, because only preparation and opportunity bring lasting success.

If we make money, we need to learn to keep a careful balance by accumulating information and knowledge about it as well. If we do not, we certainly will not retain wealth. Success is a combination of knowledge, wisdom, skills, and hard work. All of these things maximize when the right opportunity arises. We need to dedicate ourselves to developing skills. Above all, we have to be dedicated to working hard without feeling sorry for ourselves. The Lord said, "The harvest truly is plentiful, but the laborers are few" (Matt. 9:37). Any harvest, even a financial harvest, belongs to the one who works hard for it. God takes care of the harvest, but who is prepared to gather it? Only the laborers.

THE YOKE OF FINANCIAL PROSPERITY

Most rich people realized a long time ago that they could not be happy with money unless they were givers. They understand that giving comes back to the giver with a generous return. The United States alone gave nearly $300 billion in 2006 to religious and charitable causes.[1] Most of this money (83.4 percent) came from individual donors.[2] Giving is part of the culture of America and Western Europe.

How must we be givers? First, we need to be givers to God and His kingdom because God determines people's destinies. This involves many things, including giving tithes and offerings and being involved in charity work. This is a principle of many rich people who establish charity funds, endow scholarships, and sponsor hospitals.

I would not be surprised if you find this next statement a bit strange: never lend money to people. You are probably thinking, "Why shouldn't I help someone in need, especially a friend?" Jesus said, if someone asks you, give (Matt. 5:42). This is part of His principle of loving one's enemies. Notice that Jesus did not say *lend*, but *give*. These are two different things. Never lend out what you are not ready to lose or donate. The reason I am saying this is that this practice spoils relationships more than anything else, especially when people fail to give back the money.

If you have decided to lend money, do not be surprised if you do not get it back. In fact, it is better to expect that you will not get it back. Sow the money rather than lend it, and believe that in due time you will reap a plentiful harvest. If someone is asking you to lend a certain amount of money, give as much as you can, and do not expect it back. If someone asks for ten thousand dollars and you can only give one thousand, or one hundred, give the money and explain you can only give that much. Banks were created for the purpose of loaning money. They have a system to regulate the relationship between the borrower and the lender. However, you do not have such a system, so if you lend money to someone and do not get it back, you will not be able to prove anything. Even if you take legal action to force repayment and you win the action by presenting a receipt, your money will be returned to you in such small installments each month that it is doubtful you will ever receive the whole amount back. The act of lending—even to friends and relatives—so often destroys wealth, relationships, and lives.

POVERTY AND RICHES

I want to bring to your attention the testimonies of two members of our church. The first is from Lydia:

> Our family came to church because we had a lot of debts. My husband had a big business and a lot of money, which we used to spend without a second thought, satisfying all of our desires. We bought an expensive car, a cottage, and very nice furniture. We also rented a three-bedroom apartment in Kyiv for our children to use as they attended university there. Besides all that, we had an apartment on the Black Sea in the Crimean Peninsula. My husband was the president of the company, so we had money to do everything on the highest level.
>
> One day my husband made a business deal he thought was going to be very profitable, and he needed to invest a large sum of money that was more than we had. We used to borrow large amounts of money, just as other people in business did. We borrowed and borrowed and then borrowed again. When you do that, you start to think you are rich, but that is far from the truth! Our circumstances made us borrow repeatedly in order to keep the image up. More than that, my husband needed additional money to invest in the business and pay the workers. We used borrowed money for everything.
>
> In the end, we lost everything. We were in significant debt, and people were in significant debt to us. Legal action came from both sides, and court hearings began. People were suing us, and our life was a mess. There was no part of our lives the devil did not attack. The Lord found us three years ago when we were at a very low point in our lives. He began teaching us about finances. Unexpectedly, a partner of my husband gave him his share from a deal they made awhile back. We were excited we got the money, and immediately we went to our seaside apartment for vacation. We thought everything was

going to work out because God is good. It is an old soviet habit; as soon as you have money—spend it!

We had not even applied the four main rules of money that Pastor Sunday had taught us. To make money, multiply it, decrease expenses, and increase profit. We kept spending and spending. When September came, we had to pay rents, send the children to school, buy textbooks, and so on. The problem was, we had no money, though we trusted God. Another problem was a man who lent money to my husband, sued him and had him arrested. After spending three days in jail, they released him without any questions, and the attorney said there was not enough evidence to convict him of anything. We thank God for his time in jail and the chance for His mercy, because this gave my husband time to think about life and our situation. He realized we did not understand the principles of God. My husband came home a new man, thanking God for taking him through this terrible embarrassment of jail to build him up as a Christian.

We went for pastoral counseling and found out that having bad debts is a curse. My husband and I were encouraged to take a very important step. We made a list of people to whom we owed money, and another list of people who owed us money. With the second list, we sincerely forgave our debtors, which was a very difficult thing to do, considering people owed us thousands of dollars. Still, God provided the grace for us to show grace to others. Without Him, we could not and would not have done it. For the first list, we decided we had to pay all our debts back. Because we did not know how to do it, we started attending Joshua Bible Institute, one of the ministries of our church.

In order to study and still support our children, we needed money, and, as if matters were not bad enough, we lost our car. Then I was forced to sell an apartment I owned (before we came to God, I bought an apartment because we were going to get divorced). My husband was trying to convince me to sell it, but I was fighting inside because I was afraid of losing something that belonged to me personally. At that time, we learned of a cost-effective business, where we had to invest money. While I was reading the Bible, God showed me a verse in the Book of Proverbs, and it burned in my spirit: "…gain wisdom and whatever it costs gain understanding" (Prov. 4:7). I realized I did not have this kind of wisdom, but I was wise enough to hand these things over to God. It all belonged to Him anyway, and He knew what to do with it. So we sold my apartment, used the money to get out of some debt, and bought a car. With the remaining money, we invested in the business I mentioned, leaving a small reserve for ourselves.

Very soon thereafter we were without money again. Having invested in business, we trusted people who in six months were gone with our money, and we could not find them. Praise God that in this predicament we learned to trust Him and be thankful for the experience we had. After we had been faithfully serving God in our new ministry of church planting, we forgot we had debtors—and that is exactly when they paid us back all the money they owed us. At this point in our walk with God, we realized that our primary investment should be in the kingdom of God.

During my study at the Joshua Bible Institute, my leader prayed for me and declared that I would only use 10 percent of my income and give the rest to God. Disturbed by this, I wondered who gave her the right to manage my own money. Nevertheless, the seed of the word was planted. Now we see the 90 percent as extra, so it is our desire to use only 10 percent of our income and give the rest for God's kingdom. Our financial situation was getting better when my husband and I decided to become missionaries.

But the devil was mad. The next thing we knew, there was another lawsuit filed against my husband. The man suing us claimed we owed him money that we never borrowed. Even so, my husband insisted we pay the money he was asking for, and we did. We were not concerned because we never took his money, and we left everything in the hands of God. The Lord blessed us so much that we were able to pay him what he demanded, and we even paid extra for his "emotional damages" too. Now this man is our friend, and he listens to our advice and studies the Word of God. Even the judge who heard the case was also willing to listen to the gospel. We now know that the legal situation was a special way to reach those people's hearts. Besides, Jesus said that whoever wants to take your tunic, give him your cloak too (Matt. 5:40), and that is exactly what we did.

God gave us more blessings than we could have ever hoped for. After we paid the money we did not owe, God performed a miracle. Someone who owed us a large amount of money called and repaid us. In the Spirit, we had already forgiven him and never expected the return of the money. It had been two years since we sold my apartment, and by this time, we had already paid close to 90 percent of our debts. After going through all these trials, we became truly rich. A spiritual wealth precedes material wealth, and we are no longer dependent on money anymore.

Praise God for raising and blessing people the way He does. It is a sad thing that when many come to God, they think that prayer alone is going to make everything well. Yet there are things prayer cannot replace, such as knowledge applied. God will give us blessings and opportunities as an answer to prayer, no question about that, but if we are not ready, we will not be able to exploit the opportunity. In order to manipulate money and achieve wealth, we need knowledge and skills.

God knows our level of preparation, and He knows what we will do with money when He entrusts us with it. He knows whether we will invest it or go on a frivolous vacation. When opportunities do not come our way, I think God just pretends not to hear our prayers. We need to study and learn so we can be ready for God to bless us.

This testimony touched in detail some of the truths I have mentioned earlier in this book. It also confirms that it is not wise for us as individuals to lend out money as a practice. Do you see all the trouble that this sister and her family had to go through just because of ignorance in this area?

GIVE, BUT DON'T LEND

Jesus said we should not refuse those who ask of us. In this passage, He was talking about giving to those who ask of us when we are in the position to actually give. If you are not in a position to give because your money is engaged or under obligation, it is better to explain this to the person asking for money. Alternatively, you can give a certain amount rather than lend.

The Bible says we are to lend and not borrow. Yes, even though this injunction is true for us today, still there are mechanisms and structures that are already in place in our societies that enable a legal financial institution to actually lend out money to borrowers. In this case, a believer who wants this scripture to come to fulfillment in his life must also endeavor to do so in the context of the laws of the society. That is to say, if you want to lend out money, you should either own a bank or credit union or some other kind of licensed credit institution. The reason this is necessary, is because there are laws working to protect the interests of lenders when they are licensed as with banks and other financial institutions.

It is not always easy for individuals who lend out money. It is even worse when this money is lent out to your close friends and relatives, because there is no quicker way to start a fight than to lend your money out to friends and relatives.

The second testimony is from Sister Victoria:

> The Lord has been teaching me the principles of money from Scripture for six years now. One of many scriptures that God showed me is Luke 19:13, where it says, "So he called ten of his servants, delivered to them ten minas [$\frac{1}{60}$ of a talent], and said to them, 'Put this money to work till I come." The Bible does not say "spend it." What it says is put it to work, or "invest it." We are supposed to use whatever God entrusts to us according to His perfect will and not our own needs. God gave me this revelation as well as an opportunity to practice it: Money is not for spending but for investing.

It all began on a very sad note when my husband died. He had quite a high position in the society, and he was one of the best directors of the National Bank of Ukraine. My husband managed money very well, and while he was alive, I relied on him entirely. Then he died. When I was alone, with children, God began to teach me to rely only on Him. My children went to the best schools abroad, and it cost a great deal of money. God blessed them, but I was the channel of those blessings, because I trusted the Lord. Even in the worst financial situations, I would only contact people for prayer, not for money.

Once I asked a pastor to pray with me for my financial crisis, which I felt could be solved if the apartment I owned could be leased out. We prayed and nothing happened. I had many brokers come through with potential clients, but there was no deal.

Then I realized that everything I had, including my house, should serve the Lord. My friend and I fasted and prayed in that apartment for forty days, and during that time, I received a revelation that the house was indeed God's home, that He wanted it for His work, and that His glory was going to dwell there. Suffice it to say, we never leased the house.

You might ask where I got the money to educate my children. The Lord had a harvest for me. All my life I was a giver. I used to sow anything I could give away, including money. At first, I did not understand the principle of sowing and reaping, but I had a desire on the inside to give. God was adding to my knowledge and teaching me the principles of money management and the multiplication of finances. I always come to the Lord with my needs. I always prayed, humbled myself, and asked the Lord what to do with money. Only four years after my husband's death, after multiplying the seed and receiving approval from God, I was able to relax and go on vacation.

When God gave me something, He would say, "I trust you with this, but remember it is Mine, and I want you to use it the way I tell you." After I received profit, I would pray and fast to find out how the Lord wanted me to use the profit, how much I should leave for seed money, and how much I could keep for myself. Even during the toughest financial times, I did not dare touch any of the seed money. That is a law. Otherwise, what was I going to sow the next day? I do not just mean by sowing only giving out to bless other people, but more importantly, I mean planting seeds of money in different business opportunities and ventures.

I always prayed when looking for a way out of difficult situations, and God never failed to reach out to me, teach me, and lead me to solutions. Four years ago, I received a vision for creating a Christian bank that would operate with biblical principles. All profit had to go to the kingdom of God. For the last six years, the trial years, I have been learning to listen to God and not to my desires and wishes. Now I am ready to do what the Lord tells me to do.

From these testimonies, it is obvious that the difference between financial success and catastrophe is how much we choose to abide by the laws of money.

PRACTICAL WISDOM
FOR ASPIRING MILLIONAIRES

1. Great men never give up on their dreams, so don't give up on yours!

2. Because success will not come suddenly or immediately, there will be a number of opportunities to give up—but don't give up!

3. Always remember that quitters are never winners, and winners are never quitters.

4. Never quit, even though you may change your tactics, methods, and strategies. Never give up on your dreams.

5.   Dreams make you focus on your future instead of on your present.

6.   Your dreams will give you direction in life instead of going about in circles.

7.   Your dreams will give you life energy; something to work for and live for.

8.   Dreams are important. They make you forget your past and failures, and keep you from wasting your life away.

9.   If you want to be successful, never be afraid of dreaming big dreams.

10.   Divide each dream into small achievable goals, because goals are dreams with deadlines.

KINGDOM PRINCIPLES FROM CHAPTER 6

1.   Success is not an accident; it is subject to laws and principles.

2.   For believers, success is fulfilling what God calls us to do.

3.   You need to stretch yourself to the limit and train your brain to use your abilities and build the muscles of your intellect.

4.   It is possible to have a lot of money and not actually be successful.

5. Worldly accomplishments and success are only necessary as tools to gaining greater influence or platform to declare and establish kingdom influence.

6. When preparation and opportunity meet, you are ready for success and elevation.

7. There is no failure in the world; there are only people who do not know how to succeed.

8. God does not promise that only a diligent Christian would come to wealth, but rather anyone willing to pay the price of diligence.

9. By studying their books and biographies, you can become friends with outstanding businesspeople like Bill Gates, Robert Kiyosaki, Bill Bartmann, Scot Anderson, and Napoleon Hill.

10. Never lend what you are not ready to lose or donate.

Chapter Seven

OVERCOMING FINANCIAL ILLITERACY AND IGNORANCE

BEFORE MOVING ON TO NEW THEMES, LET ME REITERATE SOME things I have already discussed up to this point. Knowledge is the key word when it comes to finances, because money comes to those who have the knowledge of what to do with it. The Lord will not entrust money to those who will only spend it on daily needs and even charity. It is pointless to trust someone like that with money, for this would be the same thing as trusting the foolish and unfaithful servant. Do you remember what the Lord said to the servant who brought ten talents? Since the servant multiplied what he was originally trusted with, Jesus said he would be trusted with even more.

Without the faithfulness to multiply what we have, God cannot trust us with more. The concept is multiplying, not spending. Only money's overflow is for spending. Investing money to produce an overflow is an action God calls wise and faithful. Spending everything to the last cent, even on charity, is what God calls foolishness. We should not spend money before multiplying it. We are free to spend money only after we have invested it and have received a profit. We can spend profit, but never our original capital. That is wisdom in money management.

ASSETS AND LIABILITIES

There are two types of expenses: expenses on capital needs, and expenses on concurrent needs. In financial terms, this refers to assets and liabilities. You buy either liabilities or assets, and you spend money either multiplying assets or multiplying liabilities. Another way to say this is that assets put money into your pocket through your basic investment and do not require you to keep spending to maintain the investment. Liabilities are those things that require you to keep spending. They take money from your pocket after an initial investment. What I want to stress is this: Never invest in liabilities, but only in assets.

On one of my visits to the United States, I met a pastor from Africa who was celebrating a major event in his church. Eight families from the church bought their own houses and no longer had to spend money on rent anymore. They had been saving money to buy a house for fifteen years after having arrived in America. Now they were rejoicing. About 90 percent of us would do the same thing. These people spent fifteen years of saving and celebrated the fact they would not have to rent houses anymore. They spent all their savings buying their first homes.

Rich people, however, would never tell you to spend money like that. They buy houses and cars and other expensive items, but not by using their original capital. They use profit from investments that have produced ten times their original capital amount. They do not spend their last money on liabilities, on expenses that do not produce more money for them, and they never use borrowed money to do so. Borrowed money is only to multiply capital! The rich would rather rent out that house for money flow and live in a more modest apartment until the house generates enough to buy additional assets—another house, or even several other houses.

Yet these families who spent their life savings on homes still live in those homes, which lead to more liabilities. They pay for the maintenance of the house and meet their bank loans every month. But they do not make money on the house. Most people would have handled this like my fellow Africans. They spend their last money buying houses and remain poor for the rest of their lives while paying off debts. In essence, they have become slaves to these houses and banks, sometimes working two or three jobs just to keep up.

In our modern society, people are of the opinion that fulfillment and success mean owning things, such as your own home and car. It is not wrong to own these things, but only after you have multiplied seed or capital. Non-multiplying seed expense does not produce profit, and it is not the way to go. It is merely buying liabilities and spending multiplied liabilities. When we live in the house we have purchased, we are increasing our liabilities because, apart from paying the mortgage (with interest) to the bank, we are adding to the cost of the house through maintenance and upkeep. In the end, this increases the overall cost. It would, therefore, be more beneficial to rent out the house and rent a smaller apartment, so that the tenant in your house ends up paying the expense of the house—mortgage costs, related bills, and so on. It is even possible that the rent the tenant pays for your house is able to further cover the cost of the rented apartment. In this way, your house is in no way a liability but becomes a source of income in addition to being a long-term investment.

The second kind of expense is for capital. When purchasing a house and then renting it out, you keep on receiving money from the house through rentals and savings. This is a capital investment of assets. Some people are very proud that they can get a loan to buy a car, but what happens if that car is involved in a crash the next day? There would be nothing to be proud of then. Buying a car for personal use with a loan or even from your savings and then having to spend money to maintain it is foolish. This is a liability.

It is a different thing when using saved or loaned money to buy a car that is not for personal purposes. For example, the car becomes a capital investment if one uses it as a taxi. If one has money for only one car or one house, then that person is not prepared to live in that house or to drive that car. Rent an apartment for now. Walk or take public transportation—do whatever it takes, but invest your capital. While renting out the house, you could actually take out a loan or mortgage from the bank using the house as surety, and then use the money from the rent to pay off the percentage to the bank. That is why knowledge is the key word when talking about finances.

We think knowledge is found only in universities. Of course, universities teach theory, but unfortunately, they do not teach you how to make money. Most business schools teach students how to manage a business, not own one—how to manage wealth, not create it. Which of the two will be the one with money—the manager or the owner? One cannot always obtain financial education in schools, but people experienced in wealth creation can certainly provide education. Hence, a financial mentor is a major key to financial freedom.

REALIZATION OF PERSONAL WORTH IS A STEP TO PROSPERITY

The 5 percent of people who own 95 percent of the money in the world hold the keys to prosperity—but they hold them in secret. These people only very reluctantly divulge wealth-creation information, and they are often the ones who create the financial system for the rest of the 95 percent of people on Earth. Because of their accumulated wealth, they hold important positions, and society holds them in high regard, making their influence great enough to preserve the status quo. The 95 percent of the population will continue working for the increase of resources for these wealthiest 5 percent.

The truth is that most wealthy people are not interested in giving away their secrets on wealth creation to others. In the kingdom of God, where love reigns, things should be different. I am therefore using this means to appeal to Christian businesspeople and other wealthy individuals reading this book to make it their life goal to liberate others less fortunate than they are from financial slavery and bondage.

There is a story about a president of a large bank who visited one of his millionaire clients, and they got into an argument on the philosophy of money. The millionaire told the banker he did not know what he was talking about. The banker got very defensive, saying, "I have been the most successful graduate of Harvard Business School for the last twenty-five years! I have the largest bank in the country!" In response to this, the millionaire answered, "That's why you are working for me. You are my clerk because you are the best. Despite your degree, you do not know how money works. Harvard is for people like you. They teach you to manage someone else's money. Without me, you do not have a job." The moral of the story is that the person who knows *how* will always control those who only know *what*.

Go anywhere you like to obtain a business degree, but in all likelihood, you will still be knocking on the door of the rich, asking for a job when you graduate. People with money control and determine how much we earn, and as long as we work for a salary, we depend on money. However, there are many ways to make money when we start applying kingdom principles. It is better and more lucrative to know how to create money than how to service it. The person who only knows what to do with money is at the mercy of those who know how to make and how to manage it.

I am sure many of you have been wondering about the strategy or secret that helped me raise two hundred millionaires in two years. One of the secrets is what I will touch on in this part of the book. It is one thing to know the principles, but it is another thing to maximize both the knowledge and the opportunities as they come. In the Club 1000 we created in Kyiv, with chapters established all over the world, we ask successful businesspeople to come and teach their experiences to the young and upcoming. We go beyond this, however. We ask them to share actual business opportunities with the young brothers and sisters.

For example, one of our business leaders in the real estate industry has a successful company posting a profit of over a million U.S. dollars each month. He is a "member of the club," and, as such, has opened doors for younger entrepreneurs by giving them his franchise, the services of his experts, the advice of his lawyers, and other things—almost for free, or for minimum compensation. He does this because he knows we are operating by the kingdom principles of love—do for others as you wish for them to do to you. Even more important is the training we're giving these young people, teaching them not to love money or acquire wealth for status or any other purposes other than expansion of the kingdom of God.

We have several other senior business executives in the church who have helped, mentored, and groomed other Christian millionaires. In fact, if you are a member of Club 1000, you must take responsibility for raising up at least ten other millionaires in the next two to five years.

A particular brother is training over two hundred ordinary Christians with the goal of making them millionaires in the next five years. He himself was just a manager in a shoe shop only three years ago, where he was earning just three hundred dollars a month. Today, his business is running into a hundred million U.S. dollars.

AN EXERCISE IN FUTILITY?

Is this strikingly worldly exercise in wealth creation mere vanity, as Solomon said? I agree that accumulation of wealth for the sake of arrogance is futile. As I have mentioned already in this book, if we are rich toward God and are committed to using our wealth to advance the kingdom agenda of God, then money can be a useful tool to establish righteousness on the earth.

To me, personally, it is an indictment to see so-called prosperity teachers begging for money over the television or in their mailings. It doesn't speak well of our God when even genuine ministers who are doing great work for God have to keep on stretching their hands out as beggars to the ridicule of the whole world. Solomon indeed is right when he said that money answers all things. If all silver and gold belong to God, then we should not be lazy in exploring the secrets of its creation in order to glorify our heavenly Father. It is just good stewardship for Christians to control the resources of the earth if the earth and all its fullness belong to our God.

Galatians 4:1–2 says, "Now I say that the heir, as long as he is the child, does not differ at all from a slave, though he is master of all, but is under guardians and stewards until the time appointed by the father."

As long as we remain financial babies and not sons, we shall continuously be at the mercy of other people, guardians, and stewards who are more matured in financial terms than we are. These people might not be using their knowledge to benefit us, but rather to increase themselves! They use our ignorance to enrich themselves—to dominate and rule over us in financial matters because we remain ignorant and naïve.

To be a part of the world's richest 5 percent, what must we have? Having a college or university degree obviously is helpful and important, but that is not enough to become wealthy. We need to have the greater knowledge and experience that comes from God. We need to become God's representatives in finances and bring back His gold and silver. We need to make money so we can use it for the kingdom of God on Earth and for the deliverance of people the devil holds bound in sin and unbelief. The world cannot teach us how to make money. It can teach us how to work and manage finances, but it does not encourage us to own them. That is why Christians must not be satisfied by just giving out money to churches or lofty Christian ministries. The best stewardship of all is to raise up others to be successful.

We are still only managers, even if our salary is fifty thousand dollars each month. A salary like that may feed the ego, but it does not make anyone financially free. Maybe we can upgrade our Ford to a Mercedes, and maybe we can afford to move out of our apartment into a mansion and send our children to good private schools, but all of that is just constantly creating expenses that lead to bigger and bigger liabilities. After having spent all our money and watching our bills rise, we are back to square one.

The 5 percent keep others—even professionals and educated people—working for them to increase the owner's money and keep on managing it for them. Even if one's salary goes up, so do expenses, which binds us to our jobs even more. Where do we spend our paychecks? Probably in the stores owned by the 5 percent. In this way, the money circles back to them again. We must begin to derive joy from seeing other Christians come out of poverty and begin to enjoy the abundance of the sons of God.

Banks offer enticing conditions for loans and credit cards, but then we are stuck paying fees and exorbitant interest rates, and the money goes right back where it came from. When taking a loan, we need to be smart so that we can use it to our advantages and not end up being enslaved. In short, we need to know the laws of money. Banks offer the most appealing loans, and the rich behind the money are counting on people's ignorance to take the loans. Who created such a system? It was the same 5 percent who control the majority of money all over the world. As children of God, we need to break out of this cycle and become free in our minds through knowing the *whys* and *hows* of money. Because of these teachings in our church, we now send out at least ten full-time missionaries every month, who mostly finance themselves for the missions work they are doing. This is because they have their investments working for them while they work for God.

Rich people do not take loans for liabilities—that is, for expenses they use on themselves that do not earn them more money. Poor people do this, and when they do, the poor get poorer while the rich get richer. The rich only spend their money to buy assets or resources that create more wealth for them, and they only buy liabilities where there are already assets in place to serve the expenses.

THE MIND: AN AREA OF FINANCIAL SLAVERY

Knowledge is a great source of power. Whoever increases knowledge also increases power. People who know the laws of money and how they work—as well as how the financial system of the world works—can make, save, and multiply money more easily than the uninitiated. The world's system of money is designed in such a way that 95 percent of the population struggles and fights for a piece of bread. They kill themselves trying to get some of the rare and scarce resources of the earth. The only force that can break the yoke, however, is taking the time and energy to become knowledgeable about money. I am not talking about taking on the world's system. There is a huge difference between seeking the world's knowledge and taking on the world's character. I am talking about mastering the laws of money so we can begin living our financial lives by these laws, thus crossing over from lack to surplus. We begin to dominate money to gain greater influence for the kingdom of God, and break the stronghold of poverty over individuals and societies. The most exciting advantage of wealth is that it gives us the opportunity to break free from the slavery of "salary work" while we labor for God through our calling and gifting.

"Good understanding gains favor, but the way of the unfaithful is hard. Every prudent man acts with knowledge, but a fool lays open his folly" (Prov. 13:15–16). A good mind is developed and filled with knowledge that comes from God and His truth. We need to understand what makes us slaves and refute it. This world has a lot of money, much more than all of humanity needs. No one will teach you in a university where the money is or how it functions, because professors are also clerks, just as their students will be when they graduate. They do not know how to create wealth. On our own, we need to study the experiences of those who have money on the one hand and knowledge of the laws of God and what Scripture says about money on the other hand. Let us be armed with knowledge and remember that the kingdom of God is taken by force (Matt. 11:12).

Do not think that after you pray for twenty-four hours, angels will bring money to your doorstep. The way of the ignorant is difficult. Yes, we need to pray; that is inherent in the spiritual life. However, we also need to work hard to develop a sound mind and a good understanding— which is the beginning of success. Often when we see and interact with rich people, we merely beg them for money

> THE BEST STEWARDSHIP OF ALL IS TO RAISE UP OTHERS TO BE SUCCESSFUL.

or a job instead of learning from them how they developed wealth. In the end, it is better to learn from people who already understand the laws and principles of money than to continually receive money from them. It is better and wiser to learn how to grow rice than to beg for it all the time.

I teach my pastors that they should never hang around wealthy individuals in the hope those people will bring in tithes. That by itself is slavery. Rather, I tell them to ask the wealthy individuals to come and teach the church the act of making money. The knowledge and secrets of wealth creation are much more important than any amount of monetary handouts from anybody.

Proverbs 13:15 teaches: "Good understanding gains favor, but the way of the unfaithful is hard." The word *unfaithful* refers to the ignorant. The way of the ignorant is hard; they do not study, they do not learn, and they do not have. We need to ask the Lord to help us develop good minds filled with knowledge and understanding. On our own time we can find any information by searching, and this includes financial information. Begin to master information about money and finances, and research for it everywhere. The prudent works with knowledge, and money goes to those who know what it is and how it works. Knowledge is like a magnet for money—attracting wealth, and total dependence on the Holy Spirit leads us so we do not make mistakes with the knowledge we obtain.

On the contrary, in ignorance a fool reveals his foolishness. Ecclesiastes 10:15 says, "A fool's work wearies him; he does not know the way to town" (NIV). We must examine what very successful people have to say about money, even if they are unbelievers. Anybody who has conquered wealth and money must know the *hows* by which money works, and we should study them, balancing their thinking with God's Word. We cannot read only the Bible to know the laws of money. To think that way is to deny that God has already given the knowledge to some. We need to learn from them!

The science of money creation has developed over centuries, and we can possess all that knowledge just by learning. If we only want to read the Bible, we deny the work God has done over the centuries through other great men and women in history.

The labor of a fool makes him tired, and his life is difficult because he lacks knowledge and does not know where he is going. Everything will make us weary if we do not have knowledge. The life of an ignorant person is hard, and so is the life of a financially ignorant person who does not understand financial laws. Anywhere ignorance exists, there is an open door to a difficult life.

One of the great tragedies of the charismatic movement is that it did not empower church members with the financial knowledge to help them create lasting wealth. Most of the teachings of this movement focused on subjective feelings, motivation, inspiration, and faith building. Sadly, knowledge was actually discouraged and considered something worldly. A significant number of churches in the charismatic movement actually require those who are recognized professionals in their chosen fields to set aside their sound, time-tested methods and principles of their field in exchange for their pastors "anointed" but baseless instructions. This is seen in recent financial scandals involving the loss of significant sums of church finances arising out of poor business investment decisions inspired by ignorant church leaders in some megachurches. Even church members were coerced upon instruction and enticement by their church leaders to subscribe and invest in ventures that ended up going belly up. In one particular case, when the business went under, church members were further encouraged to discharge the debts underwritten by certain church leaders in the hope that they would receive a blessing from God.

Consequently, our churches are full of financial illiterates, and this is true even in the so-called prosperity churches. The only prosperity they teach is inspiring people to give. In most of the cases I cited earlier, people in the pews remain poor despite all their giving and all the promises made to them. If a church is to teach on kingdom prosperity, some basic topics must be in focus. The book you now hold is a summarized form of the teachings I did in my church for two solid years, teachings that brought the financial abundance so many of our members are now enjoying.

DOING AWAY WITH FINANCIAL IGNORANCE

Doing away with financial ignorance is the task of local churches. One of the primary obligations of the local church is to set the captives free, free even from financial bondage. We do not learn this freedom only by giving tithes and offerings to the church or pastor. The church should also teach how to create wealth. Unfortunately, most churches and most television preachers teach that giving is the only way to prosperity. This is only half true. Prosperity comes by following financial laws, including giving, but not giving only.

In the beginning, our congregation did not have much money, and we did not know anything about the way to financial prosperity. We had not received any revelations on this, so we started a business center and put one of the pastors in charge of researching finances and opportunities. His mission was to study how to make money and to create an academy of business studies. Many members of our church worked together with the center, increasing in knowledge, finding new ways of raising money, and becoming more qualified in their spheres of business or professional activity. If we do not teach the principles of wealth creation, we do not have the right to ask people to give us what they do not have. Wisdom brings success, so I believe the church must become a knowledge center. "If the ax is dull and its edge unsharpened, more strength is needed but skill will bring success" (Eccles. 10:10, NIV).

I have said this many times already, but it bears repeating. Most people in the world do not know anything about money except that they want it and need it. People do extreme and reprehensible things sometimes because of money, things like committing crimes, engaging in immorality, or working from morning until night because they are enslaved to it. When they come to the Lord, they find it difficult to put God above money. Money controls them because of ignorance.

Extremely wealthy people usually keep their moneymaking secrets to themselves. They might tell stories from time to time, but they do not reveal the most important information. Many will say they got rich because of their education. But if you ask around, people will tell you that their biggest education came from experience on their own. Self-education is the best way to learn the laws of money, and it is the way of success. Formal education does not offer that much, and often it can deplete one's will and initiative.

Self-education is knowledge people find and receive on their own. In ministry…in business…in the professions…in all spheres of life, the most helpful knowledge one can attain is what one personally finds out and learns for himself or herself. Many university programs prepare good servants who will work loyally for the system. Nevertheless, if we take a university graduate and add some self-education in the laws of money, the wisdom of God, and the leading of the Holy Spirit, we develop a true leader full of understanding—not just a servant.

May poverty not become our chronic disease. To avoid that, we must go on a quest for knowledge of the laws of money. Some people have created a myth for themselves and are living in delusion. They think if they migrate to a rich country, they will become rich. The truth is, moving to another country will only change one's circumstances and address. It will not help anyone make money and establish wealth. We cannot change the world system, but we can change *ourselves*. There is no sense being angry with the government or with rich people. Most wealthy people are not bad—what they are is *smart*. We should judge our own ignorance rather than their knowledge of the world system and how it works. Are you angry with those who make dirty money? You should not waste your time and energy, because you cannot change others—you can only change yourself! Work on your character to become the head and not the tail. Change your mentality and fill your head and heart with the right knowledge and understanding. You may not be able to change the country, but you are without excuse if you do not change yourself. God gave you the power for that.

God's blessings are not magic tricks. Some people say they have given their problems to God, but God will not take over your promised land for you. He can only help, but you need to have the corresponding faith and knowledge. Outside of dying for us and paying the price of our sin, God is not going to do for you what you must do for yourself. He would not study for you or take a test for you. He would not brush your teeth for you in the morning. These things you can accomplish on your own.

"My people are destroyed for lack of knowledge" (Hos. 4:6). People perish for lack of knowledge. Ignorance can become a source of problems, suffering, and even death. I have been asking you to consider that perhaps your suffering is a result of information you do not know. If that is true, God is not responsible; you are! We are all responsible for refusing to learn and be teachable. Who needs changing? We all do.

If we are to rise to the next level tomorrow, we need to start doing things we have never done before today. Those things will be the foundation we stand on tomorrow. In order for our financial situation to change, we need to change our attitude toward finances and prepare for the future. A universal principle is that constant change is the key to success, because by changing we receive power and authority over self and circumstances. For example, if you are a nurse and would like to become a physician, you need to buttress your knowledge and skills with additional training, because the difference between a doctor and a nurse is the knowledge they have. Working for a paycheck makes sense only during a transition period, or as preparation for the calling God has for you. In other words, we study and work hard to improve ourselves, not just to make more money. Money is only a result and compensation for our labor.

I want to share the testimony of Viktor, who used to have a high-ranking position in the administration of the president of Ukraine. In a blink of an eye, he lost everything and had to start all over, but this time around, he started over with God. Here is Viktor's account:

> God gave me His grace to realize that poverty is a state of mind that has very little to do with what's in one's wallet. I believe we are what we think of ourselves. The quality of our life determines the quality of our thinking, and so if we think we cannot make a lot of money, then we will not. If we limit ourselves and believe that a small amount is enough, then we will never make more than a small amount. However, God has no limitations. The amount of money God will trust you with depends on the amount of knowledge you have about finances.
>
> The twentieth century was a century of industrialization, but as we can already see, the twenty-first century will be one of knowledge, knowledge that will have spiritual roots. The base of much business today is spiritual principles, and people who do not have a spiritual foundation will find it almost impossible to succeed. Most of them will make profit and then lose it all. I passed this stage myself. I knew how to make a lot of money in the nineties, and I was very proud. I earned five hundred eighty dollars per hour. Yet here is a law: When your income grows and your knowledge stays the same, the amount of money slowly decreases. Nothing happens by itself. As soon as you realize how financial principles work, money begins to work for you.
>
> Before I became a Christian, I used to say, "I can do everything!" I stopped saying that sort of thing after losing everything I owned. When I came to the Lord and, by God's grace, He gave me financial knowledge, I started saying, "I can do all things through Christ who strengthens me" (Phil. 4:13). When we back our knowledge by our actions, and our actions by results, then

we start establishing ourselves financially while being established in God at the same time. This is the most important thing.

In this information age, we can receive some amazing knowledge. This is the information century, where riches are defined by the quantity, quality, and speed it takes to process it all. Yesterday's knowledge is old. The difference between rich people and others is that the rich person is always up to date on societal and financial information. We know many wealthy people have a love of money, and we know the love of money is dangerous—but not money itself. Therefore, with the right goals and the correct ambitions, money will start coming. As Pastor Sunday says, most people do not have money because they do not know what to do with it. They start out buying things like houses and cars and other big-ticket items where they accumulate only expenses and no profits. I have found that hard labor and working three jobs will not earn you money, but thinking, meditating, and birthing new ideas will. These ideas, added to your current knowledge, bring blessings to you and your family.

After reading books with great success stories, some Christians still do nothing. I want to say that a small step or a small deed is often greater than any big dream or promise, and that gaining wealth is a day-to-day job. Today I represent an American firm that is the leading company in growth and development in its field. This company makes a billion dollars a year from one single product. We are working in eighty-three different countries holding training seminars on financial literacy. After nine to ten months, people who have acquired knowledge on the laws of money become great in business, and financial laws are the same everywhere around the world.

I have seen God raise many weak people and make them strong through the financial knowledge they gain. I suggest you do something to realize yourself in the sphere of finances, because the greatest danger is to be satisfied with your present state. If you are completely content with who you are and what you have today, then you have stopped moving forward and have begun moving backward. Someone slower might even be ahead of you tomorrow. I grew up in a country where for centuries we were taught to think first about our country and then about ourselves. This principle is not correct. The better principle is to love one's neighbor as oneself. The rest of the world lives happily because they live by the love-your-neighbor principle. When we have a healthy amount of self-esteem, we immediately rise up and take responsibility. You can only love others to the degree you can love yourself. Prosperity is always striving for excellence. Most people have a low self-esteem and have no desire to improve who they are today. It should not be the same way with God's children. When was the last time you bought new furniture, went out for a nice dinner, or surprised your family with a vacation? You decide how much your life should change or not.

If you have read up to this point of the book, then I'm sure by now you must have begun to consider what you want to do with your financial life. It is even possible that some of you have already started thinking of investments and where to start. However, before you jump in the river, I would like to give you a few practical principles to guide you in the area of investments.

This is a short summary of great truths, and as you meditate on them, I'm sure they will go a long way to help you build a financially secure future.

INVEST IN YOUR MIND

No doubt, a lot of Christians are in the same position that I myself used to be in, having grown up in an African village with no financial education whatsoever. Because of my background, I didn't have an opportunity to learn these principles that I am sharing with you today. Even after my salvation, the Christian and religious books I was reading did not help either. In most cases, some of those writings actually discouraged me from learning more about the laws of money. Ultimately, the impression I was left with is that you should only read the Bible and books by Christian authors if you are a good Christian!

For this reason, millions of people, like I used to be, are locked up in the church prison of financial ignorance while praying for financial breakthrough.

Today, I hope that, like me, you are now convinced that financial prosperity will not come to an empty head—it comes to a developed mind. Furthermore, to possess the kind of wealth the powerful and wealthy people of this world have, we need to know the principles that they know.

I therefore encourage you to invest in your mind by reading the best books on the market about wealth creation, but balance it with the principles of the Bible, and you will never go wrong. Through the principles of the Bible, I have come to realize that it is easy to become a millionaire. Although having said that, I have, through my own experience and the experience of hundreds of millionaires in our church, come to the conclusion that as important as money is in our lives, money will not make you rich! You must make sure you are rich before gaining money, and one of those areas of wealth is being rich in the mind.

PRACTICAL WISDOM
FOR ASPIRING MILLIONAIRES

1. Develop an investment mentality.

2. Never invest in what you do not understand.

3. Investing is the best way to create wealth.

4. Investments demand knowledge.

5. Without the knowledge of money and investments, bankruptcy is inevitable.

6. Get knowledge before acquiring your money.

7. Remember, "The plans of the diligent lead to profit as surely as haste leads to poverty" (Prov. 21:5, NIV).

8. Remember that we don't really own anything in life. All things belong to God.

9. Don't neglect your spouse. Always consider his or her advice.

10. Always give God the glory.

KINGDOM PRINCIPLES
FROM CHAPTER 7

1. Never invest in liabilities, but only in assets.

2. A financial mentor is a major key to financial freedom.

3. The person who knows *how* will always control those who only know *what*.

4. The person who only knows what to do with money is at the mercy of those who know how to make it and how to manage it.

5. It is an indictment to see so-called prosperity teachers begging for money over the television or in their mailings.

6. The best stewardship is to raise up others to be as successful as you are.

7. The life of an ignorant person is hard, especially in the area or sphere of their ignorance. This is especially true of the financially ignorant.

8. Doing away with financial ignorance is the task of local churches.

9.   Money is only a result and compensation for our labor.

10. When your income grows and your knowledge stays the same, the amount of money slowly decreases.

Chapter Eight

FIVE WAYS
TO MAKE MONEY

THERE ARE FIVE MAIN WAYS OF MAKING MONEY. THERE IS A *salary*, where you work and are paid an agreed-upon amount for the work you perform. There is another variation of this when you work on commission, where your pay depends on sales performance or some other measurable standard. Second, there is a *small to medium-sized business*. Third, there is *big business*. *Honorariums/royalties* are the fourth way to make money. Then the fifth way would be through *investments*, such as stocks, bonds, and so on. In this chapter we will look closely at each of these ways of making money.

SALARY—YOU WORK AND YOU ARE PAID

In earlier chapters you learned that no one can get truly rich off only a paycheck, even one from a high-paying job. This is especially true for regular workers at plants, factories, and other large industries. Why do I say this? I say this because you are truly rich only when you can afford not to work yet maintain your standard of living perpetually or indefinitely.

Working for a salary does not make you rich, but it does make your boss and your government richer, because when you have a job, you pay taxes. In Ukraine where I live, many big businesses do not pay taxes at all, and 80 percent of all the money in the country is in the hands of only a few people. Only 20 percent of the money that is left is split among all the average working people, and they are the ones who shoulder most of the burden of taxes. Recently in Ukraine, there was a court trial between an alcoholic beverage company and the government. The company said it had no money to pay taxes, but at the same time, it was sponsoring professional boxing. It claimed that it used all its available money for advertising and production. According to the laws of many countries, money used in this way is capital investment, not profit. To put it mildly, many big businesses are benefiting much more under the new system of capitalism than they did under soviet communism. Of course, it is a vastly different story for the average person. The same is true under any capitalist system of government. The rich people almost never pay taxes; only the middle class and poor do.

Even though in capitalist countries people can own and operate their own businesses, money still enslaves many people in those countries no matter how much they make. Money controls their quality of life and everything else about how they live their lives. A lack of money is a very big problem in these countries, but I suppose the lack of money is a problem with most people on earth. How many people across the world have the opposite problem of having too much money? Actually, there are some, but only a very few. As I've said earlier in this book, they wake up each morning not knowing how to spend all the money they have. This "problem" is certainly better than not having enough money, because not having enough money causes fear and makes people dependent. Those who depend on their salary for income cannot even go on a long mission trip because they have to be back to work to continue benefiting their employers and governments. If they do not go back, their paychecks would stop coming and their bills would drive them crazy. Their salaries are only enough for them to keep on coming back for more work and more salary, a total dependency.

All of this is to say that people who are smart and really rich do not work for money. No, they make their money work for them. They do not have to work, because their money works for them through wise investments. Why, then, do they work? They understand that in the process of work, one accumulates knowledge and learns new skills. As soon as we stop receiving new knowledge about money, it will start moving away from us and going to someone else.

The job of the employer is to control employees and to exercise the law of money. The employer invests money, and as soon as the profit comes, more money is invested again. These people are rich in information about how money works, and the money itself is just a result of this knowledge. Usually this information remains secret, because as soon as it is public, the money from their pockets could flow to others.

Why is it that the average worker does not exercise the law of money? Many people have savings accounts with money just sitting there, but if they invested that money, there would be profit and quite possibly riches. Lack of information on where to invest money is the problem of most people in the world today. Those in the know about money and finances, those who have learned the keys to financial success, should mentor others. I have said earlier that this is where the Christian attitude should be different. Instead of concealing our secrets of wealth, we should share it in the spirit of brotherly love with fellow believers.

Most Christians hardly ever study books on the laws of money. This is why they think that if their paycheck increases they are becoming richer. That is a myth. Without a corresponding increase in financial knowledge, one actually becomes poorer each day—even if the paycheck increases. This is because we don't multiply our money before spending it, thus creating more needs rather than taking care of needs. People who inherit large sums of money often end up with nothing because they do not know the elementary rules about multiplying money. It is too bad there is no requirement for them to know how money works before receiving the inheritance. The knowledge of money is much better and more important than the money itself.

SMALL- AND MEDIUM-SIZED BUSINESS

Small-business owners do not differ that much from the first category of people who earn their salaries. The only difference is that they pay their own salary. But they serve money and are dependent on it in the same way, because they cannot allow themselves not to work. If they do, their business will go bankrupt. Owning a small business can almost never make anyone rich, because all the owner's efforts are spent trying to support himself or herself. Look around. Not everyone who has a small business owns a nice car and a big house. The problem here is the same one as receiving a salary—quite simply, not enough money resources working for him or her. Very rarely do we see people in this category becoming millionaires because most of them are just doing their best to get by. That is not always the case, however. When the small-business owner follows the right business principles, great things can happen.

BIG-BUSINESS OWNERS AND ENTREPRENEURS

Big business is a good way of making money, on the condition one has big capital to fund the business. In other words, much capital is required in the pocket, and many ideas are required in the head. What is the thing most needed in order to survive and be good in big business? Information is worth a lot more than money itself. One will not stay in big business very long without information. Only well-informed people with plenty of ideas will survive.

Big business is fiercely competitive. Even in the United States, the richest country in the world, only 1 percent of the population represents big businesses and those who will become part of the richest 5 percent of people in the world.[1] These people combine big business with big money, and then plow that money back into continuous investment. Another challenge is that only one out of ten businesses started ever survives in the market.[2]

A LOAN IS WORTH TAKING ONLY TO INCREASE YOUR CAPITAL BASE OR TO MAKE MUCH MORE MONEY THAN THE ORIGINAL LOAN.

On a visit to America, a young man around twenty-five years old met me at the airport. It was morning, and I figured he should be at work, but it turned out he was an administrator of the church. Of course, he would not have survived on the salary of a church administrator, so the young man told me his story. When he was nineteen years old he went to the university, but his parents could not afford to pay for his education. He started looking for a job to support himself. One construction company advertised they would help people start their own business, but that first they would have to work for them. The young man worked hard in the field of construction, and then, using the name of the company, he started his own business, hiring his fellow students and teaching them all he knew about construction. Now he employs two hundred people. What does he do with all his money? He invests it by buying homes to rent and, as a result, money works for him while he works for the kingdom of God.

Joseph from the Bible became successful in Egypt, the country known for its wise men. He was famous there due to his biblical wisdom and Egyptian education. He advised Pharaoh of the upcoming seven years of abundance followed by another seven years of famine in Egypt, and devised a plan to store food for the bad times. The Spirit of God revealed to Joseph what the others did not know about saving up for a rainy day. We can be Josephs if we work hard to receive the most knowledge we can, combining it with the principles of the Word of God.

HONORARIUMS/ROYALTIES

Only a very small percent of the world population makes money through honorariums/royalties, and some of the people who do so include writers, speakers, journalists, scientists, and artists. An honorarium is a payment for a particular service, such as speaking, teaching, and advising, on which custom or propriety forbids a set price. Our God is a generous God who gives gifts and talents to everyone, and some earn money by sharing what they know with others. We have to find our gift and work to perfect it, to give everything for our calling.

All workers must be compensated, but not all receive good compensation for their work. Maybe the top 2 percent are really paid well, while others have to struggle for survival. Those who earn money from honorariums are all over the board—they could be in the wealthy top 2 percent, or they could be struggling to survive. This is definitely not the way to become a millionaire for an ordinary Joe, unless you are Bill Clinton, the former president of the United States, who has become very wealthy through speaking honorariums.

INVESTMENTS, SHARES, BONDS, AND SIMILAR OPPORTUNITIES

Now we come to the best and most practical way to make money. Investment is by far the superior way of making money and becoming a millionaire in five to ten years, especially if we know the laws and principles of money. If we begin to study about money and invest it little by little, even if our salary is very small, we will soon see results. Investing is the fastest way to get rich in the world today. This is the way people become millionaires and even billionaires.

I know a man God took to heaven to show how He would entrust Christians with money to advance the kingdom and free people from bondage. After spending fifteen years in poverty, this man decided to look for a way to make money so he could make his own contribution. He moved to Florida and bought a piece of land, knowing that real estate prices were skyrocketing. After that, he borrowed fifteen thousand dollars, and with this borrowed money, he bought three more properties. In a single year, land in Florida tripled in price. He sold his land and paid the borrowed money back. With the leftover profits from the land sale, he invested, and in two years made his first million dollars.

Today this man works full-time studying and searching for opportunities to invest his money. Whereas before he worked hard in construction for someone else, now his current job description is finding ways to make money work for him. This is what power over money means. Only people who understand the laws of money can achieve this kind of result. By investing, we are making money work for us, and this leaves us free to work with our brains and imaginations.

You may think you are poor if you have nothing but a small apartment, however pitying yourself that you are not as successful as others is the wrong tactic to take. Remember, your destiny is in your hands, and your challenge is to find the incalculable number of good opportunities all around you. To do that requires knowledge of what money does. What does the Word of God say about business? In Genesis 2:15 we read, "Then the Lord God took the man and put him in the Garden of Eden to tend and keep it." God gave Adam his personal business, which was to till and keep the earth—not for a salary, but for human fulfillment. It was only in the process of tilling the land that Adam was able to extract wealth from the same earth. This was his reward, to eat from any tree in the garden except the one forbidden tree of the knowledge of good and evil.

Capitalistic idealism convinces us that the only source of money is our paycheck, and everything else is secondary. Many see no viable alternatives. They have become like a herd of animals. Millions work in plants and factories, and when they get old, they are forced to retire. They began their work life with peanuts for a salary. And they end up with peanuts as retired people in a miserable welfare system. Did God create us for a life like this? No, He gave us the gift of life to allow us to serve the Lord and establish His kingdom on Earth. We are not to serve money. We are not to be its slaves. We need to find ways to become masters of money and dedicate our lives to promoting the values of the kingdom of God.

"The poor man and the oppressor have this in common: the Lord gives light to the eyes of both" (Prov. 29:13). God has given everyone eyes to see his or her place or areas of calling. The difference between the poor and the rich is in their eyes. The rich can see opportunities and take advantage of them, while the poor overlook opportunities and complain. "The hearing ear and the seeing eye, the Lord has made them both" (Prov. 20:12). This means God gave ears to the poor as well as to the rich, and He gives sight to the eyes of both. Wealthy people can see because they look around for opportunities, but the poor just lay back and relax. Unfortunately, they will stay poor if they do not open their eyes to wisdom and start practicing it. God did not create people rich or poor; He gave abilities to all. We all have gifts and our lands of promise that we can till and develop for growth and wealth.

WHY ARE SOME PEOPLE RICH AND OTHERS POOR?

Why, then, are some people rich and others poor? I used to think that only a very few were called to serve God in the area of business and money, that only a few were to become millionaires. I thought that because of my call as a pastor and preacher that I did not qualify to be wealthy. Thankfully, I discovered otherwise. God did not choose some to be wealthy and others to be in need. Nor does destiny or luck have anything to do with this.

The reason some are rich is that they work hard and make right choices, and because they see opportunities and maximize them, while the poor do not. My advice is to start seeing. Some mistakenly think wealth or the ability to make money is given to some while others do not have such gifts. Yes, that could be true to some extent, but really, we can all do all things if only we first desire to do them and work hard to accomplish them. The same principles that apply to wealthy people can bring us to wealth if we apply them diligently to our own situations. Geniuses are made, not born. Moreover, if they are born, they are born out of labor.

Proverbs 20:12 says that God gave ears to both the rich and poor. But some ears can hear and some cannot because they are blocked with ignorance. The latter is the common problem among most people. They appear to be listening, but when they walk away, they remember nothing. If the Bible says we can do all things in Christ Jesus (Phil. 4:13), I would rather agree with God than assume I am not good and I am not called to make money.

REASONS WHY SOME PEOPLE ARE RICH AND SOME ARE POOR

1. The difference is that poor people eat their seed, whereas rich people sow or invest their seed.

2. The poor want to live like the rich, so they buy luxuries. The rich, however, never spend; they multiply their money and live off the overflow.

3. The rich know how to identify opportunities, whereas the poor do not see the opportunities.

4. The rich have the "can do" mind-set, but the poor rely on miracles and luck. "Lazy hands make a man poor, but diligent hands bring wealth" (Prov. 10:4, NIV).

5. Poverty is not a state of the purse or pocket, but a state of the mind.

7. For the majority of their time, the poor are not doing enough things in an efficient manner, whereas the rich are experts at what they do and diligent in their work.

8. Poverty is a lack of management, whereas the rich know how to manage resources.

9. Poverty is a lack of savings and investments, whereas the rich understand and practice saving and investing.

10. The poor have not learned how to reduce their expenses, whereas the rich have learned how to overcome their appetite.

11. The rich are masters of their gifts and resources, but the poor have not maximized these.

12. The poor are afraid of failure, whereas the rich take risks.

13. Failure comes by making excuses, but the rich ask, "Why not?"

14. Poverty comes by inability, lack of self-discipline, and unwillingness to confront hardship.

ADDITIONAL STEPS TOWARD PROSPERITY

Step one: acquire knowledge on how money works; godliness is important for true wealth. Step two: work on your character to become righteous and holy. Strive to live by the laws of God, and rid yourselves of all unworthiness, filth, and wickedness. Step three: be free of greed and self-indulgence. Greedy people never escape the nets and traps of the world. Furthermore, a self-indulgent person cannot think straight when it comes to money. Andre, a member of our church, helps us to understand this principle by telling his story:

> When studying the Word of God, we need to allow God to uproot everything that the communists had instilled within us for all those years. I thank God that we can change and step into our calling and receive the inheritances meant for us. Many of us have issues with our self-esteem, and I have noticed this in my own life. When we are in church, we can be very radical Christians, but at home, we live another way—as if we do not know what knowing the Lord is. I believe that if we do not have a break-through at home, we cannot have a breakthrough anywhere else.
>
> God began to break me by His grace. I first had to get free of my money addiction. Because I had no money, I mistakenly thought that an addiction was exactly what I did not have. I thought, "I am not addicted to money because I do not have any!" The Lord taught me how to check whether I am indifferent toward money. You can learn too. Watch yourself to see if you change when you get money in your hands. I remember that when I used to get my paycheck, something would come upon me, and all I would do is go to the store and start buying everything I could see. As money came to our family, so did arguments and disagreements when we ran out of it.
>
> One day when I received my pay, I felt God telling me to put the money in my pocket and not buy anything. In two weeks, I gave up, for I could not hold back any longer. Then the Lord gave me a new deadline of one month. This is how I got my victory. Before, I was tempted every time I passed by a store to go in and buy something. Through exercising the culture of

saving and the ability not to spend money, I was able to control the power of money over me.

Step four: have the courage to take risks. Taking reasonable risks is the way to financial breakthrough, and it ought to be our *modus operandi*. People who lived during the Soviet Union had a much different mentality. For them, having their own house or apartment was a sense of security and something to pass on to their children. When I asked one businessman in our church to conduct a seminar for our pastors on how to reach financial independence, he told them that by having apartments, they were already "sitting on their seed" through which they could become millionaires. Some pastors got offended because to them their home was something untouchable. It gave them a false sense of security, and because of this, they were in no mood to take financial risks. This attitude only leads to a limited and frustrated life. What they did not understand was how to master risk and thrive in it.

Andre's testimony continues:

> What my family really needed was a home, because we were six people living in a thirty-square-meter apartment. We were on a government waiting list for a new apartment, but so were tens of thousands of others. It was a mess! I did not rely on God for our shelter, and so I had to repent and change here as well. While I was praying, an idea came to me to sell the apartment in Kyiv and buy a house in the suburbs. I started researching this idea and was scared to lose my Kyiv registration. I had lived in Kyiv all my life. Thinking about this, I could not sleep at night. "I am from Kyiv! Do I have to give that up?" At the same time other thoughts came. The first one was, "Who is your foundation? Is it Jesus or Kyiv registration? Who saved me, the Lord or the city of Kyiv?"
>
> A false sense of security comes when we put our trust in something other than the promises of the Lord. The change must begin in our mind and values. I made a radical decision to trust the Lord, and I have never regretted it. God was changing me by changing my circumstances, and the changes in my spirit came right before the changes in my situation. Besides

the Lord giving me a nice house for my family, he also set me free from certain strongholds in my mind and in my spirit.

God wants to set us free to have dignity and a great life; but we are holding on to the past in fear of losing something. Yet, the way to lose something is not to hold on to it but rather to miss the opportunity for something better in life. Do not be afraid of risk. Do not be afraid to take a step and do something you have never done before. I took the risk and now my family is in a much better living condition. If we were to sell this house, we would make four times its value due to the renovation and improvements we made. Besides that, God has blessed me with an apartment in Kyiv that is bigger and better than the one I had before.

Step five: listen to the advice of King Solomon: "Do not love sleep or you will grow poor; stay awake and you will have food to spare" (Prov. 20:13, NIV). There is no reason we should not love what we do. Some people who work an eight-hour shift start getting ready to leave half an hour before their shift ends. If you want to be rich, try working overtime. That is what most millionaires do. Successful people usually do not have a set eight-hour working schedule, and if necessary, their day will stretch to a full twenty-four hours. They spend the time required to get the job done. They work hard to become the best in their job. That is a noble practice.

The one who likes to sleep all the time is lazy. That person will never be rich, even if he or she has all the excellent opportunities. Hard work is necessary for attaining true wealth, so let us learn to work hard, even when we are working for others. Because of laziness and complacency (Prov. 6:4–11), most people wait for someone else to give them an idea or to help them become motivated. What about doing this for yourself? Ideas come to those who are always looking for ideas and new information. They come to those who continually work on their character, and they come to the person who is not satisfied with mere bread.

Here is another testimony from a member of the Embassy of God, the church I pastor in Kyiv, Ukraine. Helen received a revelation, gathered information, and worked on herself.

It all began a year and a half ago. I had a small apartment about fourteen square meters, where I lived with my fourteen-year-old child. It was a very difficult situation living in such cramped quarters. I began thinking how I could find a bigger place to live and make things better for us. As I was accumulating information, I realized I had more than one option. I could sell the flat, buy a house in the suburbs, or buy an older apartment on the outskirts of the city. From these options, I chose the safest and most profitable one.

I learned there were three types of apartments—old ones, new ones, and apartments still under construction. The ones not built yet were the cheapest ones. I found a company building an apartment complex, and I decided to invest in the unfinished units as they were being built. That was the deal. Nothing elaborate. I just invested my money from the flat I sold into the new flat under construction, and then I rented another apartment for myself.

Well, I encountered a problem. I only had thirteen thousand dollars from the sale of my old flat, and the new two-bedroom one I wanted was much more expensive at thirty thousand dollars. I was almost twenty thousand dollars short! I researched this problem and came up with additional options. I could invest the money I had and buy a few square meters instead of buying a particular apartment or I could invest thirteen thousand and then make payments on the remaining amount owned. A third way would be to invest thirteen thousand and take a loan to balance things. I chose the last option. The real estate prices were going up, and if I did not buy the whole apartment, the price would have gone up by at least another few thousand dollars. I took a twenty-year loan. In a year and a half, real estate value had gone up dramatically, and when my new apartment was finished, it was valued at between sixty to seventy thousand dollars. I paid back the interest on the loan and continued owing twenty thousand dollars in principal. In a year and a half, my original thirteen thousand dollars turned into forty-five thousand.

Now, I had other options. The easiest one was to move into

my new apartment, which meant "to eat the seed" and then work trying to pay the loan back. I decided, however, to turn the apartment into my capital. If I leased it to someone, it meant I would get about six hundred dollars a month, which I would have to make the loan payments. I decided to sell the apartment and pay back the loan, and then use the rest of the money to reinvest in the building of another apartment complex. But this time I was going to buy two to three apartments and make a down payment of approximately 20 percent, and take a loan for the remaining amount.

This testimony is just part of the long and inspirational story of how Helen became a millionaire in just five years, simply by taking one step and selling her small apartment. She had the courage to take the risk, and she did not fail to seize the opportunity. By ridding herself of the fear of losing her home, she gained much more.

TAKING ADVANTAGE OF THE BANKING SYSTEM

Banks give loans to tie us to themselves for many years. We need to be smarter than the system. Take out a loan for twenty years, but pay it back in a few years. Otherwise, in eighteen years, the interest increases to much more than the amount actually borrowed. You may say, "A Christian should not have debts!" I agree that would be the ideal, and I taught that until I met a man on one of my trips to the United States who was twenty million dollars in debt. At the time I met him, I did not know much about money, but he did. I confronted him and told him it was not good for a Christian to be in debt, especially so much! He said by being in debt for twenty million dollars, he had already made a profit of one hundred twenty million dollars. If being in debt brings such profit, it is worth being in good debt, he thought. He said he simply pays back the interest of four hundred thousand dollars regularly. The bank gave him a loan for thirty years, so in thirty years time, he would have used the twenty million to make four billion dollars. You can have good debts when you use the loan to buy assets that multiply your money instead of buying liabilities that only multiply your debt.

Of course, when one makes so much, it is easy to pay back the twenty million. It is dangerous to take a loan if you do not have your main capital, which should exceed the loan. This man's capital did. He could have paid back the loan at any point, but he decided instead to let the money work for him. A loan is worth taking only to increase your capital base or to make much more money than the original loan. A bad loan is never worth taking. That is when the money you are making from the loan is less than your expenses or when you are using the loaned money to buy liabilities instead of assets. It is also a bad loan when you take a loan for consumption purposes. That is a sure way to bankruptcy.

God is revealing mysteries in these last days to teach us how to make and release money to establish the kingdom of God on Earth and glorify the name of the Father. Never begin a risky deal without doing thorough research and a complete study of all necessary information. Also, never begin any risky deal if your mind is not set on benefiting the kingdom. The only thing that can keep you from success is fear. Remember that fear is the devil's strongest and most persistent weapon. Do not listen to people trying to talk you out of seeking progress, saying nothing will work out and failure is inevitable. Fear will make you a slave. What I have been saying is that the best way to attack fear is to go ahead and do what you are afraid of doing.

TEN HINDRANCES TO BECOMING WEALTHY

1. The greatest hindrance to prosperity is believing that only some people can be wealthy. Remember, we get what we believe. If you are of the opinion that money is the enemy, then it will be. Learn to endure the lack of gratification for a short time while multiplying resources.

2. Lack of financial knowledge is another big hindrance to becoming wealthy. Ignorance is darkness, and Satan rules through darkness. To be wealthy, you must walk in the light of God and the knowledge of what money is and what it can do. To do that, you must develop an

inquisitive spirit. "My people are destroyed for lack of knowledge. Because you have rejected knowledge, I also will reject you from being priest for Me; because you have forgotten the law of your God, I also will forget your children" (Hos. 4:6).

3.   An impossibility mentality is another hindrance to wealth. What must we believe? We must believe we can do it. What Paul said applies to us, too: "I can do all things through Christ who strengthens me" (Phil. 4:13).

4.   Another impediment to wealth is the dictates of mammon or the inability to manage expenditure. That will always lead to poverty.

5.   Lack of a savings and investment culture will not give room to wealth.

6.   Lack of passion and dedication will also rob you of wealth or God-ordained riches.

7.   Lack of an experienced and willing mentor could also limit your possibilities in wealth accumulation.

8.   Lack of right associations can severely limit your possibilities for gaining wealth. Show me your friends, and I will show you who you are.

9.   Not having a never-give-up attitude is a definite impediment to gaining real and growing wealth.

10. An average or mediocre spirit cannot control great wealth. There is no room for average plans here.

Every one of us has a responsibility for what we know. Before you read this book, perhaps you didn't know the information you have now acquired. Now that you are aware of these truths and principles, as individuals and leaders we must be good stewards of what we have learned from this book.

I pray that you will begin to put into practice all that God has taught you in this book. More so, it is my prayer that you will extend these truths to several other people, especially vulnerable people in the developing world that live on less than one U.S. dollar per day.

Let's bring this wisdom to them and make our world a better place!

As part of my contributions to the elimination of endemic poverty in our generation, I have come together with some of my friends in Nigeria, and we have just started a microfinance bank that is meant to alleviate poverty for 40 million people in the next twenty years in Africa and around the globe. Even though this is an ambitious project that demanded the sale of our other investments, GS MicroFinance bank has been successfully launched in Lagos, Nigeria.

I'm therefore appealing to all my readers to think of a way of alleviating and eradicating poverty in our time and age.

PRACTICAL WISDOM
FOR ASPIRING MILLIONAIRES

1. For you to be truly successful, you must build up faith in yourself.

2. Be sure that God has created you for something special and spectacular.

3. You are a chosen generation (1 Pet. 2:9).

4. Fill your life with positive images and thoughts.

5. Fill your life with books. They will help you to generate ideas, creativity, and motivation.

6. Surround yourself with the right people. Show me your friends, and I'll show you who you are.

7. Sometimes old friends and friendships need to be left behind for you to get to a higher height in your calling.

8. Some men are successful because they are destined to be, while most others are successful because they are determined to be.

9. Be determined to be successful by all means.

10. As you move on in life, also be prepared to pay the price that is needed for success.

K I N G D O M P R I N C I P L E S FROM CHAPTER 8

1. Working for a salary does not make you rich, but it does make your boss and your government richer.

2. People who are smart and really rich do not work for money. No, they make their money work for them.

3. The knowledge of money is much stronger and more relevant than the money itself.

4. You can be a Joseph if you work hard to receive the most secular knowledge you can, combining it with the principles of the Word of God.

5. Investing is the fastest way to get rich in the world today. This is the way people become millionaires and even billionaires.

6. The difference between the poor and the rich is in their eyes. The rich can see opportunities and take advantage

of them, while the poor overlook opportunities and complain.

7. Geniuses are made, not born. Moreover, if they are born, they are born out of labor.

8. The poor want to live like the rich, so they buy luxuries. The rich, however, never spend; they multiply their money and live off the overflow.

9. Failure comes by making excuses, but the rich take opportunities.

10. The greatest hindrance to prosperity is believing that only some people can be wealthy.

Chapter Nine

REASONS FOR FINANCIAL FAILURE

IN THE FOLLOWING CHAPTER, WE ARE GOING TO LOOK INTO AND study practical reasons for failure in life and finances. I'd like to start with the heart-wrenching story of one man, Vladimir, who seemed to have all the odds against him.

He was raised on the street and in old soviet-style orphanages, often escaping to sleep in basements and alleyways. He had no family, no hope, and no self-respect. As a result of his unfortunate upbringing, he predictably landed himself in prison, and from the age of seventeen, he strolled in and out of correctional facilities for the next sixteen years.

For the best part of his life, the devil had ruled and reigned. He was involved with gangs and mafia groups and crimes of all types. He had two devastated marriages, and, finally, when he was at the end of his rope, he saw a face of salvation.

About one month after being released from prison, he met a lovely lady who would open the way of reformation in his life. She happened to be a Christian woman who firmly stated that if he was interested in her, he would need to change his ways and come to church. Conforming to her request and hoping to win her heart, he started attending our services.

His heart was won in more ways than one. He dived straight into the living waters, attending all services and seminars and even signed himself up for our two-year Bible-school course.

It was at this time that he also started applying his mind to the financial teachings our church offers, and went further to complete his high school education. He also furthered his studies in business and finance and business communication courses through self-education.

By this time, his life had turned around altogether, and with his new wife, they started applying the principles of wealth creation, making investments and starting businesses and companies.

Today he stands back to look at his life with sincere gratification. In only a little over two years, he and his wife are the owners of several properties, apartments, and houses. They have many companies and projects under their control tallying up to twenty million U.S. dollars.

This was a man who was ruled out by society. Success was not an option for him according to his friends, family, and the society around him. Not even prison could reform this wild card. However, when he came to learn the truth of God's Word for his life and started to understand the principles of life and finances, all that changed. He understood that he was responsible for his life and decisions and that blaming people and circumstances only landed him in trouble and in jail.

Today he is a respected businessman with a passion to help other young businessmen and women. He gives examples out of his rags-to-riches life story of how failure can be turned into success with the right steps.

As *you* step into this chapter, know that no matter how many times you've failed, no matter where you've come from or what you've done, you still stand a chance for success. Just being born makes you a winner already, so apply your mind to knowledge and your heart to understanding, and witness for yourself the impact of truth upon your life.

Only your heavenly Father and you hold the key to your future success. No one else does. Many people try to find excuses for their inability to succeed in life. Some blame their parents; others point to economic hardships in society or a bad government. Some blame God. Is it really so? Would God, who created us in His own image, not want to provide us with everything we need to be successful? I believe He would. Why, then, do people fail? Here are a few reasons people fail on the way to wealth creation.

HAVING THE WRONG ATTITUDE

People fail due to their negative reaction to unpleasant situations or circumstances. It is not the situations themselves that make us unhappy and too discouraged to work hard and achieve our goals. It is a question of attitude. For instance, a young man complains that his bad upbringing and misfortune in life is a result of his fatherless childhood. That is sheer nonsense. I had no father, yet that did not hinder me from becoming who God wants me to be. It is the same for many others too. Another person may claim she failed to succeed because she spent all her life in an unfavorable country. However, if her country was the reason for failure, then no one living in that country should have succeeded. If you know your calling and believe in the Almighty, you have quite enough to realize your dreams. You may argue how impossible that is because of lack of resources and so on. Let me tell you this: God sees your situation. He knows what you do not know. He is teaching you that big achievements begin with small ones.

Small beginnings should not discourage us. In Luke 12:32, Jesus says, "Do not be afraid, little flock, for your Father has been pleased to give you the kingdom." God shows His grace toward us by calling us when we have very little, and later He helps us become great. We should not focus on things we lack today, for we will have them tomorrow. The important thing is remembering that the Lord has called us and is in control of every situation in life. If we give God the little we have today, He will multiply it tomorrow.

Consider the global impact of communism. For all the evil it has brought upon mankind in the name of establishing a new world order, it began as the dream of one man—Karl Marx. In its heyday, communism brought nearly half the world's population under its domination, and its influence still lingers far and wide. Great fires that burn entire cities to the ground and consume untold acres of forests have one thing in common: they all begin with a single spark. So don't despise humble beginnings. Everything that exists began small. It is through the process of growth that God's power comes to bear upon the situation and brings about the desired results.

Our congregation pays tens of thousands of dollars in rent for the large building where we hold services. Vehicle maintenance and postal expenses are backbreakingly expensive as well, but we can afford all this. When I opened the church, I had less than ten dollars in my pocket. For a year and a half, we were up to our proverbial ears in debt. Only God knows how we managed to survive. Yet, He was true to His Word. We began with little, and today we have much. Failure does not depend on the absence of something or on a negative circumstance; it depends on our reaction to our circumstances. Even in my times of lack and ignorance, God still had mercy, although it was so meager that without knowledge it was like eating from the crumbs off the table.

Before I started the church, I had worked at a Ukrainian television station. I made two hundred dollars a month. It was big money at that time, in my eyes at least, and I had a company car to serve my needs. After I entered the ministry, I quit my job, and difficult times began. I had no money to pay the monthly rent for my apartment. I was financially broken. It seemed my only choice was to go to America to earn some money and then come back. I did not do that, however, because I knew God's will was for me to begin a church in Ukraine. That knowledge urged me to search for ways to accomplish those plans. I moved from my three-room apartment to a hostel. Soon I had to move from there to my friend's place because I could not afford the five dollars per month it cost for the one-room hostel. Despite my virtually zero knowledge of the law of money, I had the right attitude.

I kept saying to myself, "There should be some way out of here, and as long as I am alive, I will trust the Lord." One day we will have to make a decision either to succumb to the lies of the devil telling us we will never succeed, or to follow God's purpose for our lives. Whenever we face problems, we must realize there is always a solution. Getting the solutions to our problems requires obedience to God. The first thing we should do is listen to what He commands us to do in our hearts and in His Word. God will provide us with everything needed to accomplish His work, but this first step is required in order to get divine help. Perhaps we have a business that went bankrupt. If our first reaction is to panic, we may fall into a severe depression that might eventually kill us. A negative reaction to a negative situation cannot produce anything constructive. The unfavorable situation will change when we begin thanking God for it, as the apostle James advises us to do: "Consider it pure joy, my brothers, whenever you face trials of many kinds, because you know that the testing of your faith develops perseverance" (James 1:2–3, NIV).

The right attitude about an unfavorable situation will turn our minus into a big plus. The right attitude turns trouble into turnover. This means we need to be in control of our emotions. We do this by trusting the Lord. As our church came under great pressure and accusations by the authorities in Ukraine, some believers left us to join other congregations. They tried to justify their decision by saying, "Maybe the pastor is in error, or maybe he is in sin. Otherwise, the government would not want to close us down."

Others began asking questions like, "Pastor, your church is not the only church in town. So why is so much mud slung at you? There is no smoke without fire. There must be something in all this." Indeed, there was something in it all. Do you know what it was? It was God, for if that were not true, Satan would have had no reason to worry so much about destroying our testimony.

BEING AFRAID TO TAKE A LEAP OF FAITH

We do not realize our plans and dreams when we are afraid to take chances. Most people do not want to take risks, because they like their comfortable lifestyles where everything goes on according to plan and nothing is faulty. People are scared to take a leap of faith. It is very true that faith does involve a certain degree of risk. Faith is a step that conquers the unknown. The risk connected to faith in God's Word is not a risk, however, but rather faith in action.

Sometimes we face situations forcing us to be aggressive, to act in a forceful way without really caring about or thinking about the circumstances. "What will be, will be; if I am to die, so be it." That was the spirit of Saul's son Jonathan in the Old Testament. Whether or not we find ourselves in a similar situation, every man and woman who has been successful took a risk at least once in his or her lifetime. First Samuel 14:1–15 is the story of Jonathan, who, with only his armor bearer, approached the Philistines' garrison and launched an attack against them, killing twenty Philistines single-handedly. Because Jonathan took this dangerous risk, the complete Israeli army and nation stepped out and fought, winning a great victory. We need this spirit to win our own battles.

Only the Lord can give a 100-percent guarantee that you will be successful. Even so, we must be faithful to walk in the Lord in all circumstances. Walking in the presence of the Lord means praying, seeking the face of God, listening to His Word, and living a righteous life as a Christian. It also means working for the Lord and the coming kingdom, and following the leading of the Holy Spirit. The Lord is our most reliable insurance against trouble of any sort. The Bible tells us there are riches that add sorrow to us, but the riches that add no sorrow are the ones God promised (Prov. 10:22).

Hundreds of successful businesspeople win financial wars in the market economy but lose the fight on their home front by losing their families. Thus, it is not about talents but the way we apply the biblical truths of God's Word. We must use them with faith in order to know we will succeed in all areas of life. If we are living according to God's will, should we not have it all? Furthermore, while we are not to gamble, God assures us that we can afford to take reasonable risks. His Word says, "For though a righteous man falls seven times, he rises again, but the wicked are brought down by calamity" (Prov. 24:16, NIV). Don't be afraid of making mistakes. Be willing to take some risks, and remember that faith is a step that conquers the unknown.

In any event, our missteps and failures are temporary, because life does not stand still. An unfavorable situation today can turn into an advantageous situation tomorrow. Things seeming awful today can make us laugh tomorrow. "So we fix our eyes not on what is seen, but on what is unseen. For what is seen is temporary, but what is unseen is eternal" (2 Cor. 4:18, NIV). This scripture encourages us to believe that things we cannot see now will materialize one day. "Now faith is the substance of things hoped for, the evidence of things not seen" (Heb. 11:1). For example, I believe our church will grow to have a membership of hundreds of thousands, although I cannot see it with my physical eyes yet. This assurance encourages me to work harder and take chances as the Holy Spirit guides me.

I believe all the Lord has promised me will someday come true. Heaven and Earth will pass away, but God's Word will endure forever (Matt. 24:35). Do not be discouraged if things turn out in a way you didn't expect. Just remember that everything changes in the final analysis. We know that God Himself is responsible for the things not seen. If God is invisible, which He is, and we believe, then all the unseen things we believe are in His hands. When a doctor diagnoses a certain illness in a person, that means the person is visibly and identifiably ill. As Christians, we know that all visible things are temporal. In the same way, every sickness is a temporal phenomenon, falling under the spiritual law. It will disappear. However, as we trust in God, we must not forget to do what is in our power to do to change the situation. If we are talking about money, you must apply the laws before God can help you.

> WALKING IN THE PRESENCE OF THE LORD MEANS PRAYING, SEEKING THE FACE OF GOD, LISTENING TO HIS WORD, AND LIVING A RIGHTEOUS LIFE AS A CHRISTIAN.

You may currently live on a modest income, but if you strongly believe that some day you will be rich, and you continue to stand on God's promises of provision and abundance, your situation will certainly change. Trust the Lord that what is invisible now will become visible later. We live not by the things we see, but by the things we believe in. Your faith in the invisible will drive away the fear of taking risks, and will give you confidence to discover your calling and start fulfilling it. If you believe God for a multiplication in your ministry, make sure you do all that depends on you, because faith without works is certainly dead.

Maybe you know your calling but do not know how to fulfill it. Write it down. This is important. Try imagining what you want to do. If you are short of funds, start sharing your ideas with others and gathering the necessary information you will need. God has prepared certain people who can help you fulfill your calling, people who have the necessary funds and connections you require. Offer yourself in service to others, because serving is God's way of uplifting (as we saw earlier). There are people in the world who need the gifts and talents God has given to you, so seek those who require your help.

If we have a product or service to offer, we will encounter three categories of people. The first category comprises those who already know about our product or service. For example, in the city of Kyiv, I pastor a church of over twenty thousand people. These are brothers and sisters who already know me. They are a blessing to me, and I believe I am a blessing to them, so they are aware of my products and gifts.

The second category is people who do not know about our product or service but would be interested if we let them know we produce something they need. When they know that this product is available, they will come running to our door to get it. Our church continues to grow because people who did not know about us found out, and now they come running to the church to be a part of it. Others do not know about the product or service we provide, so we need to advertise to reach these people, to let them know there is a product or service we provide that is exactly what they need. They do not come looking for us, so we go to those in need and explain what we have to offer. Therefore, even though I pray and believe God for the church to grow, I certainly need to do what I can in the natural before asking God to do His part.

The third category of people does not know anything about us or our product or service. They would not like to visit our church. Maybe they have the wrong information about the church, or maybe they do not have enough of the right information about me as a pastor. To offer them my "product," I have to convince them I am here to serve them, minister to their needs, and spiritually feed them.

No matter what our product or service, we need to be aware of these three categories of people because they will become a platform of our achievement and greatness. The difference between the second and the third category is that those in the second group are already looking for an answer, while the third group does not even know they need a church or God or whatever products you offer.

NOT PREPARING TO SUCCEED

People fail due to lack of rudimentary knowledge to fulfill their calling. Dr. James Dobson once said: "Enthusiasm is no substitute for preparation." Preparation is often the most overlooked element in the formula for success, but it can be the most critical. Many people fail due to lack of preparation. For instance, you may feel your calling lies in taking care of homeless children. Instead of spending time preparing first, you just go out into the streets to find homeless kids and talk with them. Do you know how your adventure may very well wind up? It is quite possible you will be beaten and robbed. The reason is that you are not yet prepared for this type of ministry.

Before taking to the streets, go to the library and read books about homelessness and homeless children. Go to the Internet to study relevant information, legislation, statistics, and official documents. Also, read about others and organizations already involved in helping homeless children; visit these organizations, and speak to the people involved in the work at the various levels. Learn what the Bible says about your calling. Get all the information available on this subject. The deep knowledge of a subject will keep you from wasting precious time and make it possible to achieve progress, especially in such a complex matter as taking care of homeless children. A popular adage says that knowledge is light. A person who knows little about his or her calling is like someone going around with a bandana tied around the eyes, seeing no light. I know such people, and you probably do too. Seeking quick success, they do not want to spend the "homework" time to prepare themselves thoroughly. Solomon said, "It is not good to have zeal without knowledge, nor to be hasty and miss the way" (Prov. 19:2, NIV).

If we lack knowledge on a particular subject, we will be stumbling around all the time and consistently making mistakes. Consider the life of Jesus Christ. The Lord knew His earthly ministry would span only three and a half years, but He spent thirty years preparing for it. He studied and He earned money at a trade to help His father support the family, and most likely His own future ministry.

The more time we spend in preparing ourselves for a particular task, the more success we will experience at it. Some Christians think otherwise. They enter the ministry not able to tell their right hand from their left. I am not at all saying that if you lack knowledge about a particular subject, the only alternative is to stay at home and not even try. Like the Messiah, we can work hard to prepare ourselves for any task.

NOT TAKING RESPONSIBILITY
FOR ONE'S OWN LIFE

Another cause for poverty lies in unwillingness to take control and responsibility for one's life. What does that mean? Here is an example with which I am very familiar. Communist realities spoiled the mentality of many citizens of the former Soviet Union. During the time of the communist regime, people waited for the state to provide them with housing, medical care, education, and many other things—all free of charge. As a result, these people became inactive. Then the USSR collapsed. Now that the whole system has changed, many of these people do not want to change themselves or their lifestyles along with it. They are used to going with the flow, preferring life to be easy and carefree.

During communism in the USSR, the Communist Party used to make all the decisions for the people, so they had no need to make decisions on their own. The party decided where they had to go, what they were to do, and where they lived. The party even forbade the people from building their own houses. The government made all decisions about personal lives, careers, and futures. It is hard for people in the West to understand, but most of those under soviet control actually preferred that kind of lifestyle. That is why even after communism collapsed and democracy is now in place, many people want to go back to the old system, because they do not like and are not used to taking responsibility for their own lives. They prefer the government to do everything for them.

Such attitudes are unacceptable in modern capitalist countries. People living under capitalism know they have to earn money to buy food and clothing, a place to live, pay medical and educational costs, and so on. They have to take care of themselves because no one else will. Seeking success in life is a normal and natural thing for a westerner. In fact, nothing is more deeply ingrained in the Western way of thinking.

It is time to begin creating your own destiny. Take it in your own hands. If that means you need to work without leisure, go and work as much as you can. You have to do your utmost to gain success. Life is a challenge, and no one ever succeeds without getting rid of hindrances and obstacles. As the people of the former Soviet Union discovered, running away from the realities of life goes nowhere.

I remember the day my second child, Zoe, was born. I went to the maternity home to see my wife and my daughter. This tiny creature, weighing nearly eight pounds and measuring about twenty-one inches, simply enchanted me. I could not take my eyes off her. Eventually my wife asked, "Why are you looking at her so long?" Indeed, as soon as I saw my daughter, I forgot about everything else. I lost track of time and was in deep thought about life, God, His wisdom, and His greatness. Looking at my Zoe, I realized this tiny baby had a part of me in her. That realization radically changed my attitude toward women.

Men and women carry part of each other within them. "God created man in His own image; in the image of God He created him; male and female He created them" (Gen. 1:27). Actually, just one person comprised both male and female until Genesis 2:22, when God fashioned a woman from the rib of man. She became the bone of Adam's bone and the flesh of his flesh. When my daughter was born, I began to look at women not just as persons of the opposite sex, but also as other personalities like me. Now I treat my daughter exactly the way I treat myself. She has always been inside me, even though it was at the maternity home where I saw her for the first time. This was a positive lesson for me that made me reflect in a new way about women.

Although women and men are very different in that we have different sexual functions, we are one. God made us all human beings. I saw in that tiny girl a woman who will give birth to many children, grandchildren, and great-grandchildren. When she was born, she already had her calling through which many will come to Christ. A seed of greatness concealed in this child will yield much fruit in its time.

The same is true for everyone. The Creator puts seeds of greatness in all of us to produce fruit. We should not blame God if things do not go as smoothly as we would like. More often than not, the real cause of our failure is our own unwillingness to follow God's intention for us. Remember, you find out His calling by getting to know Him more, not just by getting to know more about Him. We all have seeds of greatness in us that only need watering with the Word and protection from the weeds.

We have to work hard to change ourselves, to grow and become mature in the Lord. If a child does not eat, move, or develop, eventually he or she will die. The spiritual realm is no different. If we do not fill ourselves with the Word of God or move and grow in Him, we will die spiritually. Do not let this happen. Nothing should stop us from fulfilling our calling. The Old Testament reveals that God's people suffered great hardship and fought against many people to become a strong nation. Some people claim that the Old Testament is a blood-thirsty book, but of course, this is not so. It is full of accounts, events, and characters that teach us countless lessons. Comparing the events of our lives with the events described in the Old Testament, we will soon see that our problems are a good way for the Lord to cleanse us, improve our character, and prepare us to fight for a better life.

> Be strong and courageous, because you will lead these people to inherit the land I swore to their forefathers to give them. Be strong and very courageous. Be careful to obey all the law my servant Moses gave you; do not turn from it to the right or to the left, that you may be successful wherever you go. Do not let this Book of the Law depart from your mouth; meditate on it day and night, so that you may be careful to do everything written in it. Then you will be prosperous and successful.
>
> —Joshua 1:6–8, niv

The Lord gave a great task for Joshua, who had to overcome hardships and strong opposition while fulfilling God's purpose. This is the way it has been and will always be. With each new task to which we are entrusted, God raises us to a higher level of responsibility in Him. This also means we will face stronger and stronger opposition. To help Joshua withstand all the trials, God told him these inspiring words, the same words the Lord speaks to us today, "Be strong and very courageous."

Do not focus on your weaknesses and failures. If you have failed at something, keep trying it repeatedly until you see success. Never stop trying. "Be careful to obey all the law my servant Moses gave you." In other words, fill yourself with God's Word so you can act in wisdom. It has been said that before inventing the light bulb, Thomas Edison tried unsuccessfully as many as 999 times. Only the thousandth try turned out to be a success. When asked what kept him from getting frustrated after so many unsuccessful attempts, Edison answered, "Not one of them was a failure. The Lord was showing me 999 times how I should not have done it." The same is true of financial freedom. Statistics say that only one of every ten new businesses succeed; the other nine end up in failure, which means we need to keep on trying for at least ten times before we can have one guaranteed success. Tenacity is a key to success in life.

REGRETTING THE PAST

Some people cannot overcome their regrets for the past. Perhaps you have attended a school reunion where everyone, especially the athletes, talks about the way things used to be. They all stand around lamenting either their past or the fact that they cannot return to their past. This concerns those who dwell in the past, a serious factor preventing us from being great. Whether we had a good past or a bad past, we should thank the Lord for it. Then we should look ahead. The past is gone, the future looms before us, and God wants to bless our future with many more good things. The prophet Isaiah teaches us that we should not regret our experiences or live in the past: "Forget the former things; do not dwell on the past. See, I am doing a new thing! Now it springs up; do you not perceive it? I am making a way in the desert and streams in the wasteland" (Isa. 43:18–19, NIV). The sooner we start working on the future, the more we will be able to accomplish.

HAVING LOW SELF-ESTEEM

Some people fail in life because they have low self-esteem and cannot seem to rise above their own opinions of themselves. In other words, if we consider ourselves losers, we are losers. With this attitude, it is next to impossible to achieve success unless we reconsider our opinion about our own abilities and worth and begin to look at ourselves the way the Lord does.

Jesus is our prime example. What did He say about Himself? Among other things, He said, "I and My Father are one" (John 10:30). It is possible some of His hearers thought Jesus might be a bit too proud of Himself. The Pharisees harbored feelings even more aggressive. When they heard Jesus make that statement, they were furious and wanted to stone Him to death. Today many people have the same problem. In fact, we all have a bit of the Pharisees' attitude in our hearts and minds.

It is important for you to believe that you are somebody…that you have great value. Otherwise, Jesus would not have said, "You are the salt of the earth.…You are the light of the world" (Matt. 5:13–14). The Lord did not say, "I shall shine, and you will shine through Me." Jesus made us responsible for salting and bringing light to the earth. During His earthly service, the Lord was the light of the world. We have to shine because Jesus said we are now the light of the world and the salt of the earth. We are the ones to assume responsibility for improving the world we live in.

Our opinion of ourselves has to match God's opinion. When the Lord says, "You are my saint," we can't reply, "Oh, no, Lord. I am not what You think. I had a fight with my wife today. I am a sinner." All right, maybe we have sinned against someone. Nonetheless, the Lord is not going to change His opinion about us. God regards us as saints as long as we remain in His presence, clothed in His righteousness, as His daughters or sons. God knows we are imperfect, but He sees the perfection and holiness of Jesus, who lives in us. God also knows that someday we actually will be perfect.

Some people think they can earn God's grace by doing good deeds, but the Lord does not need us to do that. What is important is that we agree with His high opinion about us and live according to His Word. This will reduce our ability to fall. We do not have to become holy before we put our trust in the Lord. If we did, it would be pride and disobedience to God. Rather, we have to acknowledge our own imperfect selves before the Lord.

If the Lord's purpose is for you to become a millionaire, do not think it is impossible because you have no current job and it is hard for you to believe you have such potential. If God sees you as a millionaire, it means you can become one. Throw away false modesty, and agree with the Lord. Do not be ashamed of confessing what the Lord says to you; the confidence in your abilities and qualities will help you fulfill your calling.

LIVING TO PLEASE

Some people cannot excel in life because they try to please everyone. Comedian Bill Cosby once said, "If you want to be a failure in life, just try to make everybody happy." Some people try to show good sense and please everybody at the same time, but they cannot live both ways. People like this usually say things like, "I won't raise my hands in praise and worship or dance before the Lord lest people think I am nuts." Yet, these same people can allow themselves to have an alcoholic drink or two, fearing that otherwise, someone might call them too uptight. As long as we live trying to please people, we will never please the Lord. We have to choose. In Ephesians 2:2, the apostle Paul says that not all people trying to please the world are living according to their will, but according to the will of the prince of the power of the air. Satan controls the lives of those people who live according to human expectations and customs.

That is why when someone decides to give up drinking, drugs, smoking, and committing adultery, that person begins to feel strong pressure. It isn't coming just from other people—it's coming from the prince of the power of the air. If we feel a pressure to do these things and to be people pleasers, we know this leading comes from the devil who wants to subdue us to his will. He wants us to obey him like puppets. We face a choice—either we can be obedient to the Savior of our souls, Jesus the Redeemer, who died for our sins, or we can be lukewarm and serve the enemy of our souls.

When I did not know the Lord, I suppose I lived like most other people. After I repented, everything changed beyond comprehension. It was as if scales fell from my eyes. All of a sudden, I realized whose ways I had been following and the one I had been serving all that time. I call upon you to make your choice and be firm in your decision. Consider the life of the apostle Peter. He was more than merely a believer, for Peter was very close to Jesus. But even Peter succumbed to Satan's temptation. Jesus knew what to do in a similar situation. In Matthew 16:22–23, He refused to accept the views of the world and rebuked Peter for trying to manipulate Him. We have to be as strong as our Lord was, and we can be that strong if we imitate Christ in everything we do to fulfill our Father's will.

Remember that the ways of this world are contrary to God's will and intention. This is not true most of the time; it is true all of the time. You want to live as an honest and righteous person, but the world prevents you from doing so. You want to help the poor and needy, but the world does everything to stop you. You want to lift people up, but the world wants to defeat and humiliate them. I want to suggest that you can enjoy life in this world only on one condition: You must stay in the presence of God, because that is the only thing that makes life meaningful. If you do something wrong before God, repent and keep on walking with the Lord. Repenting means changing your mind and your belief system as often as needed. It is rejecting the old and embracing the new, because the kingdom of heaven is at hand. To walk with the Lord means staying focused on God. If you fall, stand up and ask for forgiveness. Read the Bible. Pray. Do well to others and live according to God's Word. In short, just be a conscientious Christian.

When I say you have to do everything to please the Lord, I do not mean you have to leave your pastor, stop attending your church, and begin serving the Lord on your own terms. That is not the way to go if we are going to be valuable members of the body of Christ. God anoints most pastors. If you believe that, you will recognize that their authority has been established by the Lord Himself. Learning to please

God rather than people will make us strong enough to defend our own position. We will be capable and independent believers able to lead others, rather than living in someone's shadow.

I am sure you have heard the saying that we are all actors and life is really a big stage. Nevertheless, Christians must be aware that the Creator is our one and only audience. We should not wait for others to applaud us, because only Jesus is in the position to approve or denounce our way of living, our work, and our ministry.

DISOBEDIENCE TO GOD

Disobedience to God is another cause of failure. Many people live in sin. Even many Christians live in sin. Did you know that constantly violating God's laws takes His glory away from you? It is true. It began with the story of Adam and Eve, whom God made masters of the earth. He gave them control of everything over the earth. What happened to the original pair? The sin of disobedience caused them to lose their dominion (Gen. 3). The Lord took everything from them that had previously been under their dominion, and they became slaves of these things. Before their sin, Adam and Eve lived under the shadow of the Almighty—but no longer. Their sin made them aware of their nakedness, and so they fashioned some leaves to cover themselves.

The precious blood of our Savior restores us back to the place formerly occupied by Adam and Eve. The Lord has returned to us the right to be masters of the earth. Since living in sin does not agree with God's will, sinners will wind up like our ancestors Adam and Eve. Take smoking, for instance. God created tobacco to fit a certain purpose, but a smoker who indulges in it has turned this innocent plant into an instrument of deadly habit, which now rules the person. Time passes, and one beautiful day, the person realizes that no matter how hard he tries, he cannot quit this filthy, life-threatening habit. The smoker was once a free man or woman but is now a slave.

The same holds true for a person who cannot control his emotions. We have to learn how to convert our hatred into love for people, and with God's help we can, in order to glorify the holy name of the Lord.

Other people sit all day long in front of the television. It has become their god. An ordinary electronic box tragically has turned thinking men and women into senseless robots. Such habits are abominable things, and those living in sin are like caged bears. While in the wilderness, a bear is strong and brave, but as soon as it is caged, the bear becomes helpless and pitiful. By succumbing to sin, we allow it to become our master.

Proverbs teaches us that "He who is slow to anger is better than the mighty, and he who rules his spirit than he who takes a city" (Prov. 16:32). The ability to control emotions is one of our biggest assets, but if we do not use it, our passions may destroy God's plans for our lives. Jesus teaches us to love people because if we don't, we will not be loved and respected in return. Do not allow your emotions and feelings to lead you into sinful desires. In other words, you must not let your body control you and make demands on you to do things you should not do. When sin is committed, confess it to God and ask for forgiveness.

Fasting may be required until you feel you can control your emotions. By fasting in this context, I mean refraining from the things that gratify the flesh. Sometimes fasting could be abstaining from food or abstaining from drinking water for a short period. Sometimes fasting could be abstaining from watching television or playing video games and such things. Declare a war on your problem; do something to solve it. You have to remember that before you decide to conquer the world, you have to learn to first conquer yourself. That is true of all of us. We can conquer the whole world without knowing how to control ourselves, but that will only give the devil a fighting chance to turn us into laughing stocks. Think of the example of Samson in the Bible, who conquered his whole world but became a laughing stock for the enemy due to his inability to control his feelings. Think of television evangelists who operate huge religious empires but who veer off track morally because they are unable to control their emotions and behavior. No one takes them seriously.

Do not even think of trying to fall into the other extreme, saying, "I will become perfect later, after I've succeeded in my career." Acting this way will never make anyone perfect. Conquer the world, and learn to control yourself at the same time. Do them together because learning to conquer yourself and your world is a lifelong process. The apostle

Paul wrote, "But I discipline my body and bring it into subjection, lest, when I have preached to others, I myself should become disqualified" (1 Cor. 9:27).

As long as we are living on the earth, we expose ourselves to temptations. Even the Lord Jesus was tempted. When you are tempted, He will give you the strength to resist your carnal desires. You may fail and fall at times, but you do not have to remain down. Stand up, continue the fight, and win the crown of success at last.

PROCRASTINATION

Another reason some people fail is procrastination. A familiar adage says, "Never put off till tomorrow what you can do today." That, in a nutshell, is what defines procrastination. Some try to put off until tomorrow what they could easily do today. They try to reassure themselves, saying, "It can wait. I will do it later. No problem." If we do this too often, we will fail. Hence, we need to discipline ourselves. We should be more demanding of ourselves. According to Ecclesiastes 3:1, "There is a time for everything, and a season for every activity under heaven" (NIV).

Why are you doing things today that you left unfinished yesterday? You have lost time for it. Other things will arise today that will require your attention, but doing today what was postponed yesterday, or putting off until tomorrow what should be done today, just complicates life and causes you to lose precious time you will never get back.

Many have said that if we added up the hours we spend in idleness, the hours would be equal to as much as ten years of our lives. Learn to treasure every moment. Never leave for tomorrow what you can do today.

I make it a rule to set aside a specific amount of time for every task. Dragging your heels will reduce plans to nothing. Of course, sometimes you need additional time to finish difficult tasks. Great goals take a lot of time, energy, and dedication to accomplish. When planning your time, estimate your abilities, strength, means, and potential honestly. Then set aside enough time for each task. If the time you set aside for a task is not enough to get the job done, never stop moving forward. Move forward without wasting time on a particular task. Work hard—this will help to fine-tune your abilities. The harder you try, the more rewards will come from your labor.

Time is more than just money. It is life. "Whoever watches the wind will not plant; whoever looks at the clouds will not reap" (Eccles. 11:4, niv). One of the members of my church owns a firm where a few Christians work. Recently, he told me he was displeased with their shoddy performance. They are often the most careless and forgetful of employees, and they are always finding excuses for skipping their duties. They never have enough time to finish things when they are supposed to finish. They have a meeting they cannot miss, or they have to be at a church service. Every day, at least one of them has an emergency and asks to leave. My friend said he could not fire them because they are Christians. This is wrong because Christians are supposed to be the most responsible and hardworking people at their jobs. I clearly told him to go ahead and fire all such workers, because they were not good testimonies of the kingdom of God.

I have set high standards for work performance, and I am demanding of those working at my office to meet those standards. If someone proves to be inefficient, I dismiss him or her without regret. I do not discriminate between paid workers or those who volunteer. Jesus said, "But let your 'Yes' be 'Yes,' and your 'No,' 'No.' For whatever is more than these is from the evil one" (Matt. 5:37). It is better not to promise anything at all if you are unsure of being able to keep your promises. The church should be the most efficiently run organization in the world. That is why we have to have high standards and be demanding of ourselves and others, whether they are Christians or not. In fact, I think we should expect Christians to demonstrate a better and higher performance than anybody else.

When God created Adam and Eve, He blessed them and said, "Be fruitful and multiply; fill the earth and subdue it" (Gen. 1:28). In other words, the Creator commanded Adam to work at taking care of the earth and everything on it. Only after that did the Lord allow Adam to enter the Garden of Eden and eat the fruit of the trees. Adam worked and ate, and since the Creation, God's principle remains the same: He who does not want to work will not eat. "Then the Lord God took the man and put him in the Garden of Eden to tend and keep it. And the

Lord God commanded the man, saying, 'Of every tree of the garden you may freely eat'" (Gen. 2:15–16). Adam had reasons not to work: God blessed him. He commanded him to multiply, meaning independent of Adam's desire, the growth would happen. Nevertheless, for Adam to have the right attitude and mind, he had to work.

Many people do not want to work, and this has become a serious social problem. By remaining idle, we consciously rob ourselves of God's blessings. We have to work to receive the blessings the Lord has prepared for us. God has established work as a blessing for humanity and for His kingdom. Work was part of Adam's calling before the Fall. His job was to subdue the earth, tend the garden, and manage the animals. For us, hard work is the key to subduing our own promised lands. Work is the method devised by the Father to help us release our potentials, abilities, and talents from the spiritual world into the physical world. That is why believers must have a strong work ethic and be harder working than nonbelievers are.

INABILITY TO STAY FOCUSED

Another factor preventing many people from having successful careers and happy homes is their inability to stay focused on their primary goals. The devil knows we are trying hard to achieve a vitally important goal, and that is why he tries to distract us from that goal and lead us away from it. To withstand his attacks, we must cleanse our lives from all unnecessary things and reject everything tempting us to sin. This may include anything from empty talk to sexual improprieties. It might include keeping bad company. Do we benefit spiritually from our relationships? Do we influence our friends positively or vice versa? We must access our benefits from every relationship. The basis for relationships is whether we are blessed or are a blessing to others. If neither is true and we simply pass time together, then we might need to let that relationship go.

Of course, we need time to rest, to meet interesting people, and to participate in activities to distract us from everyday chores. Nevertheless, we can plan our free time wisely so it benefits us and helps us to stay focused. For instance, I get the best rest when I spend time with my family, talking to my wife and playing with my children. I advise focusing all effort on your life goals and working hard to accomplish them. Stop the devil from turning your life into a mess, and do not let him disrupt your long-term goals.

KEEPING THE WRONG COMPANY

Keeping bad company can be a hindrance to success. This is true because the people closest to you are most responsible for your success. What the Bible says about this is, "Do not be deceived: Evil company corrupts good habits" (1 Cor. 15:33). Tell me who your friends are, and I will tell you who you are. Because the company we keep can mold us, we must show discretion and wisdom while choosing friends. The people we meet in life fall into one of two categories—either those who learn from us, or those from whom we learn. In the latter category, do you have friends from whom you can gain useful experience, knowledge, and skill? Do they urge you to move forward and encourage you to new heights by expanding your horizons?

No matter how hard we try, good intentions cannot change those who despise wisdom and instruction. This is a spiritual law. You may say to yourself, "Well, my friend likes to drink. I will go to the bar with him and talk about Jesus. I am sure he will receive Jesus as Lord and Savior." This kind of thinking is delusional. You cannot change people, and you should not deceive yourself into thinking you can.

Of course, you may have acquaintances who are not Christians, and you should have friends who are not Christians so you can share the gospel with them. Nevertheless, they cannot be your closest and best friends. For that, be close to others who have received the same values, who have views similar to yours, who are people of real faith, and who lead genuine Christian lives. Remember the wisdom of the Word of God—bad company corrupts good manners.

FALSE CONTENTMENT AND LACK OF DRIVE

The final reason people fail to fulfill their calling is that they think they have done well and there is nothing else for which to strive. Every time we sigh with satisfaction and relief in a completed job, we distance ourselves from our next success, because success is not a one-time event. It is a long and often painful process. It is like a chain reaction—one gain brings about others. We stop developing the moment we think we have done everything we can. Feeling content with today's progress will not allow new successes to come into our lives. In reality, false contentment is a symptom of a much greater problem: small dreams and visions. Christians often limit their visions and dreams through false modesty by not aiming high enough. We must have dreams, visions, and aspirations that are worthy of our great and mighty God. When our dreams and visions are sufficiently big, we will not have the time or inclination to sit around engaging in inordinate celebrations of milestones, but rather we will just keep pressing on. Be bold and audacious in your plans; aim higher than the people of the world who do not have your God advantage!

Instead, having reached one goal, we should set another one and not focus on what we have accomplished already. The only way we can realize the full potential the Creator has put into us is always to expect what is coming next. Make success a constant companion and not a casual visitor. Understand that success will end only when we receive our crown from the Almighty (Rev. 2:10; 3:11).

PRACTICAL WISDOM
FOR ASPIRING MILLIONAIRES

1. Don't compare yourself to others. Compare yourself to your dream and calling!

2. Be ready to admit when you are wrong or when someone has a better idea than you do.

3. Avoid criticizing things that you know little or nothing about.

4. Never be satisfied with present success, status, and achievements.

5. Remember that a successful lifestyle is a constant work of attaining God's goals and purposes for your life.

6. No matter how hard we try, good intentions cannot change those who despise wisdom and instruction.

7. Time is more than just money. It is life.

8. We have to work to receive the blessings the Lord has prepared for us.

9. We should not wait for others to applaud us, because only Jesus is in the position to approve or denounce our way of living, our work, and our ministry.

10. You cannot change people, and you should not deceive yourself into thinking you can.

KINGDOM PRINCIPLES FROM CHAPTER 9

1. Big achievements begin with small ones. Hard work is the key to subduing your promised land.

2. Failure does not depend on the absence of something or on a negative circumstance; it depends on your reaction to your circumstances.

3. The right attitude turns trouble into turnover.

4. You do not realize your plans and dreams when you are afraid to take chances.

5. If you are short of funds, start sharing your ideas with others and gathering the necessary information you will need.

6. The more time you spend in preparing yourself for a particular task, the more success you will experience at it.

7. Some people fail in life because they have low self-esteem and cannot seem to rise above their own opinion of themselves.

8. Some people cannot excel in life because they try to please everyone.

9. Every time you sigh with satisfaction and relief in a job accomplished, you distance yourself from your next success, because success is not a one-time event.

10. Dream and set big, bold, and audacious long-term goals and objectives for yourself and business—levels that will require God's intervention and that will distinguish you from others without God.

Chapter Ten

FOUR PRINCIPLES OF CONTINUOUS SUCCESS

MOTHERS GIVE BIRTH TO CHILDREN. INDEED, EACH OF US IS A fruit containing a seed after its kind. An apple seed planted in the ground will produce an apple tree, which produces apples in harvest. The same was true with the seed God planted into Adam, from whom billions of human offspring have already come. Genesis 1:12 informs us that "the land produced vegetation: plants bearing seed according to their kinds and trees bearing fruit with seed in it according to their kinds. And God saw that it was good" (NIV).

God's seed principle is at work here. The Creator puts a seed in every person that represents our calling, our destiny, and our talents—in short, everything we need to excel and be productive. It is God's seed for the fruitful life, and it has the ability to reproduce itself, multiply, and fill the earth. God gives everyone a chance to become successful. Greatness and fulfillment in life are not just the lot of a select group. The Lord has prepared these gifts for all of His children. In a little boy, we can see an adult man who may father many people. There is a woman in every little girl who, like Eve, may become the mother of many nations. Out of one bird come a flock of birds, and one fish gives birth to a school of fish. "God blessed them and said to them, 'Be fruitful and increase in number; fill the earth and subdue it. Rule over the fish of the sea and the birds of the air and over every living creature that moves on the ground'" (Gen. 1:28, niv).

A great man's gift allows him to sit with the great people of this world. You have the seed of greatness in you as a child of God. You only need to develop it and make sure you put your seed to the ground. That is, you must put your gifts into use for the blessing of God and His creation. Herein is the key to your great and successful life.

Becoming a significant success in life is the destiny of each person. According to Genesis 1:26, God created us in His likeness. This applies to all of us. Do not doubt that He has planted a seed of greatness in you. God did not find and call you into the kingdom in vain. Remember, greatness and fulfillment in life belong to all of us, but blessings come with obedience.

> If you fully obey the Lord your God and carefully follow all his commands I give you today, the Lord your God will set you high above all the nations on earth. All these blessings will come upon you and accompany you if you obey the Lord your God: You will be blessed in the city and blessed in the country. The fruit of your womb will be blessed, and the crops of your land and the young of your livestock—the calves of your herds and the lambs of your flocks.
>
> —Deuteronomy 28:1–4, niv

Heeding God's Word allows blessings to pour into your life. I have seen this truth evidenced in the lives of the pastors in our church. Before their coming to God, they were wretches with no prospects whatsoever for the future. One pastor was previously an alcoholic with a thirty-year drinking record. Another accepted God after three suicide attempts. Still another was on the run from bandits for months. The list can go on. Now these brothers and friends have become leaders in the church and actively lead others to Christ. Each one has said that his life changed the moment he made a decision to follow Jesus. Have no doubt that this will work in your life—and others—as well. However, it is essential to obey God's Word in order to fulfill His plan for your life.

I want to help you learn to maximize God's blessings in your life by introducing you to the four principles of continuous success.

PRINCIPLE #1: NO RESTING PLACE HERE

Never be satisfied with your current state. Admit you have not achieved perfection and that you are still not the person you want—and need—to be. You want to be better, right? If you are satisfied with your current state, then you are complacent. Complacency leads to self-destruction, which is almost like burying yourself alive. We only make progress if we are dissatisfied with our current situation. Dissatisfaction compels us to act, to seek something new.

"I have fought the good fight, I have finished the race, I have kept the faith. Finally, there is laid up for me the crown of righteousness, which the Lord, the righteous Judge, will give to me on that Day, and not to me only but also to all who have loved His appearing" (2 Tim. 4:7–8). Although Paul knew about the reward waiting for him in heaven, the apostle continued his mission, doing the will of God. Like an apple seed growing into an apple tree, your talents will make you famous and successful someday. As long as you believe in yourself, believe in God and His Word, and strive for more accomplishments in your life, success can be a constant companion.

It is those who are displeased with their current positions that make progress. In Philippians 3:12, Paul also wrote: "Not that I have already attained, or am already perfected; but I press on, that I may lay hold of that for which Christ Jesus has also laid hold of me." The scope of your possibilities expands in direct proportion to the number of things you are willing to do for the kingdom. As long as you follow God's leading, no one will ever be able to stop you. Never think, however, that you have attained perfection in anything you do, for there is always room for improvement. The apostle Paul said, "Brethren, I do not count myself to have apprehended; but one thing I do, forgetting those things which are behind and reaching forward to those things which are ahead, I press toward the goal for the prize of the upward call of God in Christ Jesus" (Phil. 3:13–14).

Most people have the mentality of the average person. They say, "I am a normal man or woman. I may not be as successful as someone else, but I am quite satisfied with my life as it is." This attitude is a false assurance to convince others that this person has already done their best and are now resting on their laurels. These people need correction and encouragement to seek new ideas and implement new goals in their lives. Proverbs 3:12 says that "the LORD disciplines those he loves" (NIV).

> ONE THING IS FOR SURE: YOU WILL HAVE NO LEVEL OF SUCCESS IF YOU THINK GOD WILL DO EVERYTHING HIMSELF WHILE YOU JUST SIT AROUND AND MAKE BIG PLANS.

One way God corrects us is through others. Welcome the input from those who encourage you to find new ways to strike blows for the kingdom. There is no limit to your level of success so long as you believe in yourself, in God and the Bible, and work hard to expand your horizons. One thing is for sure: you will have no level of success if you think God will do everything Himself while you just sit around and make big plans. That is not how things work in the divine economy.

NO ROOM FOR COMPARISON

You should compare yourself to no one else except the Lord Jesus. Speaking for myself, I do not want to be like anyone else. According to Deuteronomy 28:13, I have to be the head, not the tail. In other words, since the Creator has prepared something special for me, why should I worry about what people think or say about me? God wants me to succeed, and He wants the same success for you. Be firm in your heart on your identity in Christ, because truly successful people never compare themselves to others.

While some other charismatic leaders in the former Soviet Union were experiencing great success, in our own church, which was young at the time, we were just planning to hold our first conference. I was indeed happy for those successful ministers and did not envy them, because envy and comparison with others impede one's further progress. Now time has passed, and our church has grown into the largest congregation in Ukraine and the former Soviet Union. I believe that if I'd envied those colleagues, I would not be enjoying the level of growth we are now enjoying.

In 2 Corinthians 10:12, the apostle Paul said: "For we dare not class ourselves or compare ourselves with those who commend themselves. But they, measuring themselves by themselves, and comparing themselves among themselves, are not wise." I place a high demand on the church and myself, and I am never at ease with current achievements. The Lord does not see us as we are but as we can—and should—be. Suppose I make a thousand dollars a month, but God has endowed me with a potential for earning ten million dollars. Then naturally, God will wait for me and help me reach my potential. However, while He wants me to be pleased with what I have, He does not want me to become complacent and stop there, because He knows more is planned for me. Therefore, if I do not press on, that means I did not use my God-given abilities fully. In that sense, we could say the Lord is not happy with my current situation. So also it is with comparison and envy of another ministry. God is not happy when we engage ourselves in that.

Envy and comparison with others will definitely impede your progress. As a pastor and church leader, I have never been satisfied with what I have achieved. As a congregation, we are happy our membership is over twenty-five thousand, but it is possible God has even bigger designs for the Embassy of God. Maybe God wanted us to have twenty thousand in the first year alone. Maybe we were supposed to be twice the size we are now, but we stopped short. Sometimes the things we rejoice about makes the Lord sad, so if we stop where we are now, we would have failed to accomplish all God has planned and purposed for us to achieve. The only type of comparison we are allowed to do is with our destinies, the character and works of Jesus Christ, and God's expectations of us. We compare ourselves with our God-given visions and callings.

What does God expect of you? What goals and tasks has He set for you to accomplish? Don't compare yourself with other people; compare only your current status and position with your calling and destiny from God. If you do that, your success will be unlimited. Do you know what the Master calls you to do? Your passion will tell you what your calling is. What are your greatest concerns? What do you long to do? What propels you forward? Knowing the answers is one way to know what God has called you to do. Another way to know your goals and calling is to find out what your talents are—what comes naturally out of you...what instinctual abilities do you have?

Yet another way to know what you were called to accomplish in life is to discover what raises your discontent, what frustrates you. If you are concerned about political practices in your country and have a passion to make politics more honest, or if you get irritated when you see things go wrong, that may be a sign that you are called to make an impact on your world through politics or government.

Here is another example. Some people do not pay the slightest attention to the fact that there are alcoholics in society. Others do little to help them and their families. Still others show anger for the devastation and destruction caused by alcoholism yet have great compassion for the people who use and abuse alcohol. If you are someone who has overwhelming compassion for the person trapped by an addition to alcohol but are angered by the rise of alcoholism in your society, God may well be calling you to address and confront this social ill.

God uses your compassion, talents, and discontentment to help you release hidden abilities and accomplish your calling and purpose in life. As you seek His face, the Lord helps you to discover who you are and what you are to do in life. Don't compare yourself with others or try to copy someone else's lifestyle. To do that degrades your own personality and God's plan for your life.

I once knew a man who made a lot of money and decided to entertain himself with earthly pleasures. He started drinking and became very promiscuous. He tried justifying his bad behavior. After all, he said, most people live this way. The result for him was moral, physical, and financial failure. God's law works, and those opposing it will eventually pay for it in this life.

I know others who recently drove expensive, stylish cars but today are walking on foot. I once asked a drug addict: "Where are your cars?" He replied, "My two Mercedes-Benz 600s are running in my veins."

These people violated God's purpose for their lives by copying the lifestyle of the world, and payment time came. Striving for change in your personal life should be your focus. If you do not oppose evil, you approve it. If you are tolerant of social vices such as pornography, you will not even notice when it creeps into your own life. If you are unwilling to change your wrong manners, beliefs, or behavioral habits, they will crush you. What you tolerate, you allow, and what you allow will eventually rule your life. In the Book of James we are admonished to: "Submit yourselves, then, to God. Resist the devil, and he will flee from you" (James 4:7, NIV).

Live by this golden rule: today's success will become tomorrow's impediment if you stop striving for more achievement.

God often allows problems and crises to enter a believer's life. An example of this is Job in the Old Testament. An unpleasant situation or crisis is not always the enemy. Of course, God does not cause it to happen; He only wants the best for us. Sometimes, however, it comes into our lives because He wants to teach us something, to push us to exert more effort, to raise us to a higher level. He wants to change our status quo. As we continue seeking the face of God and obeying His Word, any situation or crisis can work together for our good (Rom. 8:28).

When our church had a membership of around five hundred, I thought, "The church is only six months old, and already there are as many as five hundred." Soon after, a curious thing happened. The church's growth stopped abruptly. No one joined the church for three months, and this provided me with a good lesson. *Self-satisfaction is a serious obstacle on the road to success.* God helps those seeking to explore new territories in their lives. If a church has a service hall that holds five hundred, and the church leadership and laity are satisfied with that number, it may become an obstacle hindering that church from rising to a new level. It is when we start trying to expand our territories that God will provide His immediate help.

Sometimes problems crop up to serve certain purposes. When our church grew to three thousand members, we began having friction from the local authorities. We prayed hard, stood in the face of trial, and God helped us settle all our problems. Then the church began growing again. Every year brought us two thousand new members. Thanks to those problems, today we experience a special grace, part of which is the awareness that with God's help we have grown into the largest evangelical church in Europe. The Lord has helped us to found over seven hundred churches in forty-five different countries all over the world.

God is mighty, and He is able to turn problems into blessings. Pray about your situation, and do something about it. Above all, pray in times of trial that God would not settle the problem until you learn the lesson He wants to teach you. Never be content with your current state.

PRINCIPLE #2: TURN YOUR TROUBLES INTO STEPPING-STONES

Turn all your troubles into stepping-stones. Some problems prove to be powerful tools that push people into discovering new ideas and open up previously hidden potential and talents from within. Cold weather caused people to invent warm jackets and coats. Large distances made people search for ways to conquer them. As a result, carriages were invented. As the technological revolution progressed, planes, trains, and automobiles came along. To live comfortably, people built electric power plants. These are examples of turning troubles into stepping-stones.

But there are other problems that were just due to foolishness. When you make a foolish mistake, God will show you the way out of that difficult situation and teach you how to avoid making the same mistake in the future. However, repentance is required, along with an honest seeking after God. When you are sincere and truthful, you can always turn all your troubles into your advantages—while learning how to avoid such troubles in the future.

View your problems as tools God uses to promote you and lead you to greatness. Overcoming obstacles in the physical world strengthens your physical muscles. A weightlifter lifts weights to strengthen muscles. A runner runs to build endurance. It works the same way for your soul. In the spiritual world, getting past problems strengthens your spirit. God may allow a problem in your life to teach you to slow down and pursue your relationship with Him. If you have stopped tapping in to divine wisdom and truth in your daily walk, the Lord may use your problems to bring you closer to Him. It is in this way that many people come to Christ—or come back to Him.

The Lord desires to teach us constantly, and the best way to stay on track with His direction is to know Him better. As we strive toward a deeper relationship with Him, we establish ourselves in Him more solidly. Here is a vitally important goal that you must have: "I press toward the mark for the prize of the high calling of God in Christ Jesus" (Phil. 3:14, KJV). This goal of reaching the "high calling of God" is the basic principle of faith. Success without faith leads to total defeat. "Now faith is the substance of things hoped for, the evidence of things not seen" (Heb. 11:1). Progress or growth involves movement toward things not yet visible. Faith is a conviction of things not yet seen by our physical eyes. Therefore, there is no separation between progress and faith. By faith, we look forward to those things we are expecting to have or achieve through prayer. Faith thereby accelerates our prayers and success.

Success without faith is usually short lived, like a bubble bursting the instant it is touched. Success without faith leads to total defeat. This is what happened to the former Soviet Union when they eliminated God, the sole source of faith, from their daily lives. The momentary success lasted only a short seventy years—only a blink of the eye in comparison to eternity.

PRINCIPLE #3: FAITH IS THE VICTORY

Be sure of victory and success. You may say, "At this moment, I see no precondition for my becoming successful in the future." That is only at first glance. It may be true that you lack something important—say, money—to start your business. However, this circumstance is exactly the precondition God will use to carry out His plans for you. If you have everything you need to accomplish your vision, you will have no need for faith. Moreover, without faith, you will never achieve lasting success. So exercise your faith in believing God will bring success to you *while supplying you with the tool (money) you need.* God creates obstacles to teach you to trust Him, to build your faith, making it possible for you to perform your calling and destiny. Your faith is a guarantee of future progress.

Praise the Lord that you lack something, because that lack is the beginning of your faith in things unseen. The apostle James wrote, "Faith by itself, if it is not accompanied by action, is dead" (James 2:17, NIV). If you believe your plans will succeed and that God has planted a seed of greatness in you, don't hesitate to step out and act by faith.

You may be sure that one day you will become a millionaire, although now you make only a thousand dollars a month. Do not lose heart. After all, it is not the amount of money you earn today that counts, but your understanding that each day brings you closer to realizing your dream. Yesterday you earned five dollars; today you have ten; tomorrow you will have fifteen. It is important that you keep moving toward your goal. Your faith will help you achieve this.

PRINCIPLE #4: PROCLAIM THE INEVITABLE

Proclaim by faith things that you expect to have in your life. Speak about your goals and plans as if they are already accomplished. Then promise God you will do your best to attain your goal. Give thanks to God by faith, sincerely, for planting a seed of greatness in you. Above all, work hard to put into practice all the principles and truths you are learning in this book.

PRACTICAL WISDOM
FOR ASPIRING MILLIONAIRES

1. Learn to maintain your momentum.

2. Learn from the best in your vocation, calling, or business.

3. Be humble enough to confess that you don't know everything.

4. Don't allow the fire in you to burn out. Keep the flame alive through prayers and meditating on the Word of God!

5. Turn disadvantages into opportunities.

6. Turn your rejection into resources.

7. Let every disappointment push you forward in your dream.

8. Work harder than anyone else in your profession or surrounding.

9. The fuel and capital of success is hard work.

10. Dedicate yourself to the advancement of the kingdom of God. Seek first His kingdom, and all these things will be added to you!

KINGDOM PRINCIPLES FROM CHAPTER 10

1. The Creator puts a seed in every person, and that seed represents your calling, your destiny, and your talents—in short, everything you need to excel and be productive.

2. A man's gift makes a way for him, allowing him to sit with the great people of this world.

3. You only make progress when you are dissatisfied with your current situation. Dissatisfaction compels you to act, to seek something new.

4. There is no limit to your level of success so long as you believe in yourself, in God and the Bible, and work hard to expand your horizons.

5. Comparing yourself to another will impede your success—don't ever do this.

6. The Lord does not only see you as you are, but also as you can be and should be.

7. God uses your compassion, talents, and discontentment to help you release hidden abilities and to accomplish your calling and purpose.

8. Remember this golden rule: your success today can become an impediment tomorrow if you stop striving for more achievement.

9. Turn all your troubles into stepping-stones.

10. God allows obstacles to teach you to trust Him, to build your faith, and to make it possible to fulfill your calling and destiny.

Chapter Eleven

YOUR CALLING IS THE BASIS FOR YOUR FINANCIAL SUCCESS

GOD CREATED YOU AS A LIVING BEING WITH A SEED OF greatness inside as I've mentioned in previous chapters. How do you recognize that seed? How do you find your place in life or in the body of Christ? How can you know what you were born to do?

For starters, wealth does not measure a truly successful life—success does not depend on our material value. However, at the same time, success is impossible without achieving some measure of material value. God created the material side of our lives. Scripture teaches us how to use and benefit from the material comforts of life.

Some people mistakenly regard themselves as successful. Recently an executive came to my office seeking advice. He said that a few years earlier he had been satisfied with his lifestyle and was sure his successful business was everything he wanted out of life. However, lately he had realized that this was no longer true. He had begun asking questions of himself. One question was, "What do I live for?" His answer was that he lived for money.

I asked him why he thought he was so successful years ago. He said, "Because I was making a lot of money, actually millions of dollars. I thought success lies in making more and more money. But later I came to understand how wrong I was." This man came to understand that stockpiling money has nothing to do with success. During his stock-piling years, he lost his family, his office, and even his son, who became addicted to drugs. As his family was breaking apart, he realized that he was one of the most miserable persons in the world.

I knew that I needed to teach him some things related to the principles of kingdom living. I told my friend that the true foundation of a life had to be based on the Bible, the Word of God. I told him that he needed to receive Jesus Christ as his Lord and Savior, that Jesus died to save him from death and destruction, and that Jesus, the Son of God, came to set him free from his addiction to money. I gave him hope that with prayer and faith his life would become better. Today this man is a living testimony to God's glory. He has his family back, his family life has been strengthened, and the family regularly worships together in church. This man discovered the truth that Jesus is the way, the truth, and the life, as we find the Lord saying in John 14:6.

Life begins and ends with Jesus, because He is the foundation of a successful life. This is what the executive learned, and it is the same lesson we all need to learn. Contrary to what this man once thought, success is a long process and not an isolated event. The measure of success is living your entire life in accordance with the plan of God and in fulfillment of His calling for you. Working hard to accomplish the intentions God has for your life will make you truly happy and successful. When you carry out your calling honestly and diligently, you will find not only spiritual security, but financial protection as well.

Unfortunately, today I am discovering many people in churches who identify their success in life with their material status, or who tend to mistake the American Dream to mean success. There can be no success without first seeking to please God by fulfilling His desires for your life.

TAKING IT TO THE STREETS

One of the hardest lessons I ever learned about ruling my promised land and finding my true calling is that God usually starts at the bottom of society, not the top. Jesus loved to serve "the least of these" (Matt. 25:40)—not the leaders. When Christ was born, the angels went to shepherds to announce His birth—not to Caesar. Jesus ministered to the poor, not the well fed. If we really want to build the kingdom of God, we need to start by serving the people considered the least important and least valuable around us.

This is a lesson I have learned well. I was certainly poor and insignificant when I was born. I was born in poverty. I grew up in Africa and never even wore shoes until I was twelve years old. I had to go to the bush and forest to fetch firewood and then walk many miles from my Nigerian village of Idomila to the next city to sell the wood to richer families. I did this before I went to school to help my family survive. My life was similar to the familiar pictures of children carrying bundles of wood on their heads seen in documentaries and magazines like *National Geographic*. I had to do several menial jobs just to make it through primary and high school. While growing up in this situation, in my mind I thought that some people were chosen by destiny to be wealthy, and others were chosen to be poor. I thank the Lord that I now know better.

I went on to college in Belarus, which, at that time, was a constituent republic of the Union of Soviet Socialist Republics. When I completed my journalistic studies in Belarus, communism was beginning to crumble. Along with some other Christians, I began boldly taking the gospel message to the streets. It was an exciting time, with the growth of new freedoms but the presence still of old powers that had not lost their sting.

Because of my religious activities, the government asked me to leave Belarus. I resisted strongly in prayer, but God said to me clearly and distinctly, "Leave Belarus."

I protested, "No, Lord, this is my promised land. I cannot leave." I had sown my life there for seven years. Now it appeared that God wanted to send me back to Africa. Finally, I gave up the fight. I decided that if the Lord wanted to use me in Africa, the decision was His. I was heartbroken but obedient.

But it turned out that God did not want to send me to Africa after all. Rather, He opened a new door for me to come to Ukraine. I received a call from a television station in Kyiv that needed a journalist who spoke

Russian. My fiancée, Bose, a Nigerian student whom I had met in Russia, agreed to join me there. I started my journalism career in Kyiv, helping to produce and script shows for this pioneering television station. I had much early success, but after only a year in Kyiv, I felt God nudging me to start a church. He told me something that set the foundation for my future life. He said, "Here in Ukraine I want to raise strong, large churches with many thousands of members for the purpose of spreading the gospel throughout the whole world. In the same way the Soviet Union planted communism around the world, so I will use the nations of the former Soviet Union to take the good news everywhere."

I was dumbfounded because the largest church in Ukraine at the time had only seven hundred people. However, the Lord kept impressing on my heart that He wanted me to train reaper warriors to bring in the final harvest, especially in China and the nations of the Arab world. His glory would come to the land of Ukraine as He used the nation to help gather in the final harvest. He said I had not even started my ministry yet. The church I was to start would be my home base for the ministry to which God called and prepared me.

I had arrived in my promised land. I did not quit my journalism job at first, but I knew it was no longer my calling. Journalists always spread the bad news, but I wanted to spread the good news. My mind turned to the strategy I might use to accomplish the goal God had set before me of building a large church in Europe. I was only in my midtwenties, but I made an announcement on television that anyone wanting to study the Bible could come to my house, and I gave the address. I was hoping to attract professors and students from the local university. I envisioned having a church full of rich and powerful people who would come to Christ and do great things for God.

When one of the first people to arrive was Natasha, an alcoholic, I was disappointed. The message of the gospel captivated her, though at first she understood little of it. She simply felt joy at being with us. The others who showed up the first time were also simple people with alcohol and drug problems. They were only a handful, and they looked dejected. This happened again the next week, and the next week after that. Nobody came except a few derelicts. I doubled my efforts and stood on street corners, handing out invitations to normal people. It was strange for a black man to stand on the street corner, inviting people to church. Nobody responded. I became more and more disillusioned. I did not even know what to do with the few down-and-outers who came to the services.

Finally, I went home and prayed, "God, you told me I would build a megachurch for You. Why is nobody coming?" I decided not to sleep that night until I had an answer. At 3:00 a.m., God led me to Mark 12:37, which says, "...the common people heard him gladly" (KJV). That sentence pierced my heart like a burning shaft. I realized that God had sent His friends to me, and I was turning up my nose at them.

God began to minister to me, and through that still, small voice within my soul, said: "Many people think that serving Me means preaching from the pulpit. That is not My understanding of ministry. Preaching and church ministries are just tools and instruments you can use. Ministry is really about touching people. Get rid of your tie and jacket. Go out of your pulpit. Ministry is not about putting on your suit, handing out invitations, advertisements, and expecting people to come hear you at church. Who are you, especially in this society? You are expecting people to go out of their way to come and listen to you. They will never do it. If you were one of them, you would not cross the street to listen to a Nigerian pastor either. How do you expect them to do that? You are not playing basketball or something else they want to see. Moreover, are you to teach them the right way to live? Yes, there is prejudice in this society, but that is not the only problem. You are part of the problem. Your understanding of church ministry is faulty."

I wept when I heard His words to me. God's message to me continued, "Get those ideas of ministry out of your mind. If you want to serve Me, *be like Me.* The ordinary people—the outcasts, the poor, the down-and-outers, the drunkards—all felt welcomed by Me. That is why I said I was naked and nobody clothed me. That is what ministry is to Me. If you can take care of *them,* you will take care of *Me.* If you love them like I love them, you will love Me. If I can trust you with them, then in the years to come I will also be able to trust you with the elite, powerful, strong, and wealthy. But if I can't trust you with the naked and hungry, I won't be able to trust you with anybody else."

My mind was changed that night. All my life I had thought, "If I could only preach well and be eloquent and anointed, I would be a great minister." Yet God's revelation blew apart my conception of ministry. I saw that if I could make ordinary people feel good around me, then I would be like Jesus. I decided then to become trustworthy with the down-and-outers, the outcasts, the unlovable, and the untouchables. This was my breakthrough, and this was when my real ministry began. My breakthrough came when I left the pulpit and went to the streets to look for the outcasts. I had the key. If I could love people with this Jesus kind of love, I could change the world.

If I could sum up kingdom-mindedness in one word, it would be *LOVE*! Love God passionately and demonstrate it by a practical ministry to people.

SATISFACTION, SECURITY, AND PROTECTION

I once received a death threat from a Ukrainian nationalist group. They sent me a threat because I am a black man who pastors the largest church in a nation where less than 1 percent of the total population is black. Not only am I black, but I am also an African black who dares teach the Ukrainian people the things of Christianity. For most people in this nearly all-white culture, my teaching Ukrainians is an insult. After all, Orthodox Christianity had been the official religion in the territory presently occupied by Ukraine for over a thousand years.

Four days after receiving the death threat, I received a funeral wreath as another dire warning. I knew this was serious, so I began to pray as I thought about leaving Ukraine. As I was praying, I heard the voice of God in my heart asking me if it was a man or God who called me? Of course my answer was that God had called me, after which He adjoined me to continue my work until the task is finished—no one can stop me! Moreover, only He who commissioned me to service can terminate my employment.

I answered, "It is Yours, Lord."

Then God asked, "Have you done everything you know to do to fulfill My plan for you?"

Then I began pondering my life, thinking about what else God intended for me to do. After spending much time meditating, I came to understand that my mission in Ukraine was not yet finished.

Soon God revealed Himself to me again, encouraging me and saying that His plan for me remained intact. No one would ever be able to disrupt it. Meanwhile, the nationalist group continued to threaten me that if I continued refusing to leave the country, I would risk losing my life, the lives of my family members, and the lives of many other black people. The nationalists were under orders either to kill me or deport me from the country. This threat lasted for almost five years and to some extent, still continues today.

Some time later, one of the leaders of the nationalist group came to our church in Kyiv out of curiosity. He wondered why their attempts to drive me out did not work. He actually told me later that he just had to go see about this Sunday Adelaja. For him I was a rare bird, and he wanted to know why his plans came to nothing. Why can't we chase this bird away? What was the power behind this black pastor?

I met with this man and took him to my office, showing him a great amount of love and hoping to open his eyes about my mission in Ukraine. I told him I came to Ukraine because God sent me to reach the Ukrainian people with the gospel of the good news of Christ. After that, overcome by the Holy Spirit, he prayed the prayer of salvation with me. He does not attend our church now, because he is a member of the Orthodox church, but we are still good friends. In the interviews and talks that he has given, he spoke very positively about the Embassy of God and about me.

There is no question in my mind that God worked a miracle. I am alive, and my former enemies are now my friends. When you live in accordance with God's will and pursue His directions, no one can destroy or eliminate you—that is, until you have fulfilled God's call on your life. "When a man's ways please the Lord, he makes even his enemies to be at peace with him" (Prov. 16:7). So long as we follow God's will and our calling, we can be confident He will never forsake us. We will find satisfaction, security, and protection in the Lord.

Over the last few years, our church has seen difficult times, including withstanding severe and powerful attacks from government authorities. However, there is no one more powerful against every attack of the enemy than the Lord Jesus Christ. Had I not followed God's perfect will for my life, I would have failed, and no force on Earth could have defended me. Because of God's intervention, our congregation in Kyiv has survived, and the bravery and loyalty of the church members now serve as an encouragement for many newcomers. They say, "If you could withstand that, we can too."

The strong pressure we faced could have broken anyone, yet our congregation did not worry. It remained loyal to God's cause. The secret of a successful personal life and corporate church life lies in finding out and fulfilling God's will. After accepting Jesus as my Lord and Savior, I gave my word I would never allow worries to beat me. It is true that sometimes I do get upset when I cannot understand certain things, but when this happens, I seek God's counsel and direction through prayer and Bible reading. I have since asked God to never allow me to become angry, disillusioned, or fearful regardless of the situation. I know the Lord hears earnest and heartfelt prayers.

With His help, I have barred these negative feelings as much as is humanly possible from entering my heart and mind. When I feel them trying to attack my mind, I now know how to deal with them. In His Word, God says to cast down "arguments and every high thing that exalts itself against the knowledge of God, bringing every thought into captivity to the obedience of Christ" (2 Cor. 10:5). Remember, if you obey God's purpose, fears and anxieties will never harm you. Of course, it is likely that you will have some difficulties and even some dangerous events surface in your life, but if you continually seek God and stay filled with His Word, you will always find a way out.

When trouble or anxiety tries to overcome me, I fight against it by declaring spiritual warfare. The key to victorious spiritual warfare is found in James 4:7: "Therefore submit to God. Resist the devil and he will flee from you." I draw close to God in prayer and stand my ground in faith to resist the enemy. This scripture promises that if we resist the darkness, the darkness will flee from the light. You do not need to accept defeat, worries, fear, or disappointment. You can proclaim the

Word of God upon your life and acknowledge that the Lord has given you a superior mind and the spiritual power to change any situation for the better. *It works!* I know this from my own personal life, and countless thousands of others will affirm the same truth.

To deal with my fears and disappointment, I stand firm in faith. No matter what the problem is in my life, I sleep peacefully and well. I told myself long ago that if God is awake and watching over me (Ps. 121:4), then I would not worry and fret. Another secret to living the successful life is the confidence that God watches over you and fulfills His will in your life. He has done this in my life—and He will do it in yours.

Why am I so confident? That is easy. I'm pursuing God's perfect plan for my life, serving my heavenly Father the best I can, and remaining dedicated to the advancement and expansion of the kingdom.

I am in partnership with God, fulfilling my part of the covenant, with God's help. I know He will fulfill His covenant to me. I recommend that attitude to everyone. If you are still prone to worries and fears, check yourself to see if you have been meditating on the Word and spending time with the Lord in prayer and reflection. If not, your faith is probably not as strong as you may think it is. My suggestion to you is the same I make to every person I meet: commit to daily prayer and Bible reading, and this will make you more brave and daring in the challenges of life.

A DEFINITE SCHEME

This is the story of a young man by the name of Paul. He was born to a large family, living in poverty and desperate circumstances. With few hopes of a decent life, he turned toward an active criminal lifestyle for money and power.

Paul hadn't read the promises of God in Jeremiah 29:11. He didn't know that God had a better plan for his life; plans of prosperity, hope, and blessings! It was only when he came across pamphlets of our church and stumbled into one of our conferences that his life truly began.

By this time, Paul had a growing family of his own and had been forced to continue with his wicked lifestyle just to support his wife and children. Coming to church for the first time, he discovered that God had greater things planned for him than criminal acts and the mafia could ever offer.

More glamorous than the lights of downtown nightlife was the exciting and challenging life that lay ahead for him in the purposes of God.

He immediately gave his life wholeheartedly to the Lord, got set free, and brought restoration to his shattered family. He started attending all services and conferences and enthusiastically learned these principles of life and finances.

Today he is the owner of multimillion-dollar corporations and is also a member of the Christian businessmen's club of our church, overseeing Kingdom of God projects that encourage other up-and-coming businessmen to find their destiny in God.

Paul has also become a member of the local parliament of his state.

"'For I know the plans I have for you,' declares the LORD, 'plans to prosper you and not to harm you, plans to give you hope and a future'" (Jer. 29:11, NIV). Here are six truths I want you to know about God and His plan for you. Knowledge of these six plans will help you to be happy and successful as you walk in the calling and purpose God created for you:

1. God has a plan for your life.

2. Only God knows your calling, and He is eager to reveal it to you.

3. God's plan and purpose for your life is for good.

4. God's purpose for you is not of evil.

5. God is committed to bringing your hopes and expectations to pass.

6. God promises you a secured future.

You are destined to be happy if your lifestyle agrees with God's Word and His plan. So, what is the point of worrying? Scripture says there really is no reason to be anxious about your life (Phil. 4:6). You need to get on the "rails" and rush toward your goals like a locomotive. No man or woman has ever been born by mere chance. Everything takes place in accordance to a divine scheme drawn up by the Lord of life. You can be sure all events follow *His* scheme, including answers to the who, what, when, and where questions. According to Genesis 1:3–7, God created time by creating day and night. After creating time, God created space, which secures physical and material presence on Earth. What and Where? God knew space is indispensable for creating things. After all this, God created the rest of our world and humanity. God is a God of plans and purposes. He has everything under His perfect control.

Some people argue wrongly that the birth of a child is a result of pure chance. God is in control of everything on Planet Earth. I never saw my natural father. Only after finishing school did I learn that the man I believed was my father was actually my uncle. My mother married a man who abused her physically and verbally. When she was pregnant with me, her parents decided to take her from that man. After giving birth to me, my mother got married again, leaving my grandmother to raise me. Therefore, I grew up without either a father or a mother.

Everything surrounding my birth was stacked against me, to the point that some would say I appeared in this world without cause or reason. That is not true. Nothing is accidental. I know why God allowed my birth to take place. He needed me exactly the way I am so He could use me exactly the way He wanted. Only my father and my mother could give birth to me, because other parents would have had a different child. When I was a small boy, children in the street would say I was a bastard. My grandmother always stood up for me, trying to prove to the people living next door that I was a legitimate child. All the while, however, God's plan for me was perfect. Before the creation of the world, the Most High knew that the twenty-first century would be the time of the "great awakening" for me. The Almighty defined the time and the place for it—Ukraine. Although I was born in Africa, the Creator brought me to the place He had chosen for me to fulfill my God-ordained destiny.

I believe there is a great plan for every believer. You may have been unhappy and unfulfilled before accepting the Lord, but now you can forget your misfortunes. They are in God's plans, and His beloved Son,

Jesus Christ, paid a high price for your deliverance. The price for your sin was His sacrificial death. Accepting the Lord and His plan for your life will involve a radical change in your way of thinking. Now you must ask God what *His* plan is for you and where He wants to see you go. Finding answers to these questions will place you in God's will and bring His promises into being. The apostle Paul put it this way: "And we know that all things work together for good to those who love God, to those who are the called according to His purpose" (Rom. 8:28, NIV).

The truth is that God appointed all the events of our lives before we were born. We come to this world to fulfill His definite purpose and drawn-out plans for our participation in kingdom growth. The prophet Jeremiah writes that the Lord said, "Before I formed you in the womb I knew you; before you were born I sanctified you; I ordained you a prophet to the nations" (Jer. 1:5). When? Before. Where? In the womb. Why? To take the message to the nations. We should not pursue success, money, and wealth in isolation or by themselves, but for the singular purpose of pursuing and fulfilling God's desires and purpose for our lives and creation.

God called me to preach when I was nineteen. He revealed to me what He wanted me to become, and to tell you the truth, I strongly opposed God's call at first. Nevertheless, after the Lord showed me this verse in Jeremiah from the Scriptures, I believed Him.

This means not only that the Lord calls us, but also that He has definite plans for us to be great. When I say that God has definite plans for us to be great, I am not just talking about being great in the worldly sense. I do not mean being great in order to have big houses or expensive cars or to be famous all over the world. What I really mean is that we could be great in everything God has appointed us to do. For example, you could be such a wonderful mother or father that your children and neighbors know you are a great mom or dad. You could be a great athlete, famous for physical prowess in one sport or another. We have good cooks all over the world who are famous because they know how to delight the palate. We have great uncles, cousins, and teachers. We might not be the president of the United States, but each person can be great right where God has called him or her to be—in those gifts and abilities He has given them to use for the kingdom expansion. The secret of greatness is going beyond our limit. Greatness is not for fulfilling the American dream but for carrying out God's eternal purposes on the earth.

This is why we need to seek and know Christ better. As you do, He will reveal His plan for your life, and the more you know the Lord and His intention for your life, the easier it will be for you to overcome any difficulty encountered along the way. By knowing the Creator and walking confidently in His paths of righteousness, you can absolve your life challenges through faith in a loving and mighty God. "For whatever is born of God overcomes the world. And this is the victory that has overcome the world—our faith" (1 John 5:4). This verse assures you that your trust in God's purpose will help win the world and overcome your troubles. You can be 100 percent sure that the Lord is in control of your life, that your problems are temporary, that you are above and not beneath, and that He who is in you is greater than he who is in the world. The Word of God endures forever, and your victory depends on how strongly you believe these things.

Many people do not hear the voice of God (in their heart), but this is not because God is silent. The problem is that many people are too busy listening to their fleshly desires to listen to what the voice of God is telling them. The mind of the fleshly man or woman leads to death, but the mind controlled by God's Spirit leads to life and peace (Rom. 8:4–7). Are you walking in the Spirit or in the flesh? Remember, the more you know the Lord and His plan for your life, the easier it will be to overcome any circumstance potentially blocking your way.

God knows your life better than you do, so you need to know God in order to know yourself. The way to get to know the Lord better is by spending more time studying the Word, God's revelation of Himself. God's revelation leads to self-revelation. The revelations one receives are like foundation stones upon which we build our lives, our families, and our calling according to God's plan. By discovering God, we discover ourselves.

If you receive a word of revelation and have an understanding of what God wants you to build and how He will bring it to pass, as you take the steps He expects you to take, then your life and calling become easier. You will find pleasure and delight in them, because it is no longer you who is doing the building—God is! God will accomplish what He has called and appointed you to do.

ADDITIONAL HINTS TO RECOGNIZING YOUR CALLING

Let me give you an additional couple of hints to help you recognize your calling.

The first hint is to look into your inner self and examine your heart; therein is your gift and calling. Watch closely, because your calling is there within you. Genesis 1:12 affirms that everything that God created has seed within itself, as I've stated earlier in this book. Each plant and tree bears seed according to its own kind. Every animal and created being brings forth seed according to its own kind. In other words, the abilities and talents that can make you great already lie within you. This seed often makes itself known early in your childhood.

> THE SECRET OF BEING GREAT IS GOING BEYOND OUR LIMIT. GREATNESS IS NOT FOR FULFILLING THE AMERICAN DREAM BUT FOR CARRYING OUT GOD'S ETERNAL PURPOSES ON THE EARTH.

My grandmother died before I accepted Christ. As a small boy, I used to bombard her with different questions, and she would tell me that when I grew up, I would probably be a lawyer because they too like to ask a lot of questions. I learned that lawyers must be eloquent in their speech if they want people to listen to them. That was not for me, because I had a speech disorder. While in school, I learned that journalists also ask many questions. I decided to be a journalist, and today I hold a master's degree in journalism. It was inside of me all along! Even my grandma saw it, though she was illiterate.

A second hint is to think about the things you especially like, the kinds of activities that give you particular satisfaction. For many people, their job or occupation is actually not their true calling. More often than not, their hobbies could be their calling. Think about it. You may even discover you have several interests or talents. Expand your horizons. Try studying more about something in which you are interested. If you work hard to develop the gifts God has given you, you will be happy and fulfilled in life.

Each person has a divine seed inside that can make him or her great. This seed can never fail. Someday your talent could make you rich and famous. It could bring you before kings, presidents, prime ministers, and other important people who will treat you as an equal. Once Christians know their calling in life, they can succeed at whatever God calls them to do. "Do you see a man who excels in his work? He will stand before kings; he will not stand before unknown men" (Prov. 22:29). The Father will provide everything you need to carry out His divine purpose for your life. He can even put you on the same level as the most influential people, because the design or God's gift is to help you become great for His purposes here on Earth.

How can you achieve greatness through your calling? How can you establish yourself in life? God's gift is the answer, and it is the most efficient solution to your challenges and circumstances, because with these gifts, we meet other people's needs. For example, a tailor makes garments to meet someone's needs. If someone is a manager of a business, he serves the employees and the boss by making efficient decisions. From teachers to preachers, no matter what our occupation, we serve people in some capacity. Service is a major secret to elevation, so use your gifts well in service to others and to the kingdom. It is while you strive to serve that money and wealth follow as you receive material blessings as your compensation.

SERVING OTHERS

What made Jesus of Nazareth the greatest person the world has ever known? Unlike the hypocrites of that time, Jesus was not ashamed to declare that the main purpose of His coming into this world was to serve people. He said, "I am the resurrection and the life. He who believes in Me, though he may die, he shall live" (John 11:25). He also said, "I am the way, the truth, and the life" (John 14:6). He never said about Himself, "I am Jesus." When He spoke of Himself, the Messiah always referred to the calling the Father ordained for Him. Great men and women become great by discovering other people's problems and providing answers to them.

Our problem as imperfect people lies in being too constrained. Our earthly expectations cause us to suppress our natural feelings. Often we are even reluctant to mention our true calling for fear of ridicule. We should not hesitate to reveal our true calling, however, because each of us represents the solution to someone's problem. The reason the health-related and legal professions are so popular is that they can address people's needs. Those who work in these areas usually receive handsome rewards because they offer solutions.

The surest way to become great is to serve other people. It is important to build a life on the principle of loving your neighbor. If you do this by serving other people, success and greatness will follow. Serving people means ministering to them. Your services are the products you offer other people. The more people you serve, the better you are known. If you serve ten people, only ten people know you. If you produce ten cars, only ten people will know about you and your car. However, if you want to serve motorists by building hundreds of thousands of new cars and improving their technical characteristics, hundreds of thousands in the car-buying public will know you. This really is the difference between successful people and great people. The person producing ten cars is successful, but the one producing hundreds of thousands is more than merely successful. That person is great because he or she influences and impacts more people. That is greatness. That is true success.

There are limitless ways in which you can attend to other people's needs and problems. By serving others without expecting anything in return, you will receive the love and respect of those you serve. In this way you will succeed, even if you work for free, yet your reward will be greater than the physical salary you could get.

Do you want to offer your knowledge and experience in solving problems? First find out what people need. Is it repentance, Christian growth, discipleship, healing, or financial success? Once the Lord has revealed to you what people need, you will know what kind of service you can offer, perhaps in the form of a profession such as a pastor, teacher, dentist, or financial advisor.

A successful man or woman is constantly searching for people with whom they can share their own wisdom, life experiences, and skills. Everything we need has already been entrusted into other hands. When you put your gift at the service of other people, or when other people put their gifts at your service, blessings flow from God and together we help fulfill the great commandment of love: "Love the LORD your God with all your heart, with all your soul, with all your strength, and with all your mind, and your neighbor as yourself" (Luke 10:27).

We often think of a commandment as something limiting our freedom to act. That is not so. God's commandments are a gift and blessing to us. They are designed to help the person who, in keeping them, is on the way to becoming a distinguished individual. We received the commandment of love so we can achieve a spiritual and physical satisfaction. We should follow the example set by Jesus. If our love is sincere, we will be willing to reach as many needy people as possible with our gifts.

Even when asked to stay, Jesus never remained long in the same place. He answered that He had to visit other towns, and He sent His disciples in pairs where He could not go Himself. Ministry and any kind of work are not for earning money but for performing our call. It is never wise to work only for a paycheck. If you work to fulfill your call, economic blessings will come to you anyway. The basic aim of work should be ministering to people. Like Jesus, your desire to serve people rather than your salary has to be the major motive of your work every day. Your job is not just *a job*. It is a platform God gives you to enable you to change your world.

Jesus lost His life in doing this, but He gained the whole world.

As you freely offer yourself to the service of others, money will follow (Matt. 6:33). When you seek to fulfill God's kingdom purposes, all other things like money come automatically as a spiritual law.

WHAT DO YOU HAVE TO OFFER?

I hope it is clearer now why ministry and even secular work of any kind are not primarily for earning money. Rather, our work is to fulfill our unique callings, both in life and within the church. In fulfilling our calling, we will be fulfilling ourselves. Jesus had important things to offer to the world, including peace, truth, and eternal life. What do you have to offer? The answer is that you have a lot to offer your world, no doubt more than you realize.

First, you have your own experiences that God has allowed you to accumulate in the course of your life. Maybe you think it was a tragic mistake that an alcoholic mother or a drug addict father raised you. On the other hand, perhaps you grew up in some other negative circumstance. You felt disregarded, unloved, and lonely. Your childhood may have been difficult, but because of the hardships you endured, you gained priceless knowledge that may be of great help to those living through the same harsh situations. This is knowledge no one else has, for no one else has lived your life.

Do you know the story of Joyce Meyer, well-known Christian author and evangelist? Her father abused her from the time she was a young child until she came of age. Yet today she is one of the best preachers in the world because, as she tells the story of her life, she offers a remedy to people who have found themselves in a similar situation.

Second, you can offer the world the priceless experience of your mistakes. Perhaps your marriage failed and you remarried for the second or third time. What you have learned could be helpful to others who are unhappy in their marriages. Sharing the lessons you have drawn from your own mistakes, tragedies, and missteps may be of real help to others. Your lessons learned will be an invaluable object lesson for many others. This is true with many life-debilitating or destructive issues, including alcoholism, abortion, or prostitution. You have great authority to be able to say, "Listen, I used to be like you. I've been through and overcome what you are experiencing now. I can help you because I made the same mistakes and was in the same troubles you are in now. I can give you the wealth of my experience."

The experiences we share can help others to see things from a different perspective and help them to solve and recover from their own difficulties. Sharing the experience of our mistakes is a valuable commodity that we can offer in service to others, because it blesses them while bringing gratification to us.

Third, you can share your life experiences in overcoming almost anything imaginable, including financial difficulties, marital infidelity, joblessness, and so on. You could even set up a program for people suffering from these problems who do not know how to deal with them. In the final analysis, each of us has something to offer others as a remedy for insecurity and pain. Fulfilling your calling is the surest way to win the world to Jesus Christ. Your victories or failures are your successes to salvage the world. Don't hesitate to share these life experiences.

Fourth, the most important gift you can offer anyone in the world is salvation. You and I are spiritually safe, but millions of other people are not. You know Christ, but what about your next-door neighbor or the man you see every day at work? Does that person know Christ? You can launch a ministry to bring the lost to God. You have priceless gifts and ministries to share with others. Don't allow your gifts to remain unknown and useless to the kingdom of God.

Don't bury the wealth God has entrusted to you. Happiness, peace, and fulfillment are yours if you love people and serve them with what God has given to you. That brings glory to God, and it could even eventually bring you fame and success, because nothing is impossible with God. So tell the world about yourself as Jesus did, and always be ready and willing to go out to the hurting and the needy and declare to them that you know the solution to their problems. You can help many people rise up and start anew.

God has engineered you to be alive at this very moment in time. Who is to say this is not because someone needs you, your wealth, your life experience and insights into your mistakes, and your unique service?

You must live up to God's expectation. If you do not exercise your gifts to serve others, you will live an empty, useless life—no matter how successful you may be according to the world's standards. What a day it will be to hear these words from the Lord after fulfilling your calling: "Well done, good and faithful servant! You have been faithful with a few things; I will put you in charge of many things. Come and share your master's happiness!" (Matt. 25:21, NIV).

The purpose of wealth should be for service to God and man. It becomes your gift and platform from which you reach out to those in need of your abilities. Financial freedom is intimately tied to gifts and abilities, how much you devote to its discovery, the discipline you exercise in developing and pursuing that purpose, and the tenacity with which you overcome the challenges on your way to pleasing God.

The reason I've endeavored to devote two whole chapters to the topic of your calling and gifts is because finance is given in exchange for something. This is the best way to financial fulfillment: when you know what you can offer the world in exchange for their money. Your best product to sell to the world is your gift and ability. Hence, it is crucial that we all know what we do best, and as we offer it out even for free, not looking for money, we will discover that, nevertheless, money will find us out.

PRACTICAL WISDOM
FOR ASPIRING MILLIONAIRES

1. Life begins and ends with Jesus because He is the foundation of a successful life.

2. Love God passionately and demonstrate it by a practical ministry to people.

3. So long as we follow God's will and our calling, we can be confident He will never forsake us.

4. Remember, if you obey God's purpose, fears and anxieties will never harm you.

5. Commit to daily prayer and Bible reading, and this will make you more brave and daring in the challenges of life.

6. You may have been unhappy and unfulfilled before accepting the Lord, but now you can forget your misfortunes.

7. Remember, the more you know the Lord and His plan for your life, the easier it will be to overcome any circumstance potentially blocking your way.

8. Look into your inner self and examine your heart.

9. For many people, their job or occupation is actually not their true calling.

10. We should not hesitate to reveal our true calling, however, because each of us represents the solution to someone's problem.

KINGDOM PRINCIPLES FROM CHAPTER 11

1. Working hard to accomplish the intentions God has for your life is what makes you truly happy and successful.

2. If you really want to build the kingdom of God, you need to start by serving the people considered the least important and least valuable around you.

3. Preaching and church ministries are just tools and instruments you can use. Ministry is really about touching and serving people.

4. If you can love people with a Jesus kind of love, you can change the world. Summed up in one word, kingdom-mindedness is *love*.

5. When you live in accordance with God's will and pursue His directions, nobody can destroy or eliminate you— that is, until you have fulfilled God's call on your life.

6. God is awake and watching over you (Ps. 121:4); don't worry or fret.

7. You are destined to be happy if your lifestyle agrees with God's Word and His plan.

8. You have come to this world to fulfill His definite purpose and drawn-out plans for your participation in kingdom growth.

9. For many people, their occupation is actually not their true calling—their hobby is.

10. Great men and women become great by discovering other people's problems and providing answers to them.

Chapter Twelve

MAKING MONEY
WORK FOR YOU

PUT ASIDE ALL IDOLS FROM YOUR LIFE. IN PAUL'S LETTER TO THE
Philippians, there is a wonderful passage of Scripture:

> I am not saying this because I am in need, for I have learned
> to be content whatever the circumstances. I know what it is to
> be in need, and I know what it is to have plenty. I have learned
> the secret of being content in any and every situation, whether
> well fed or hungry, whether living in plenty or in want. I can
> do everything through him who gives me strength.
> —PHILIPPIANS 4:11–13, NIV

Church offerings are not meant to enrich the church or the pastor in
any way. I do not preach economic well-being to gain a profit from church
offerings. The purpose of the gospel of prosperity is not to enrich the man
of God, not at all. It is to enrich the people, to open their eyes on how to
make money and prosper in order to be a blessing to God's work.

The apostle Paul said he could live in need as well as abundance
because the purpose of life is Christ, not money. (See Philippians
4:10–13.) If you could choose to live in either poverty or abundance,
which would you choose? Which one is better? Most of us would say
that living in abundance is better than living in need. As long as we

live on this earth, we will have needs, and it is impossible to meet them without money. That is why the Bible says that money answers all things (Eccles. 10:19). We must learn to live above money, thus having power over it. Many people have almost no money, but they are still slaves to it. It is our job to change this situation and destroy the financial lack in our life and ministry.

According to the Word of God, we are not to be slaves to money; on the contrary, it should serve us. We will not be able to serve God fully and satisfactorily if we do not have abundance in our lives. Paul said, "I can do all things through Christ who strengthens me" (Phil. 4:13). Being able to do everything means we can earn money through Christ who strengthens us. We can become millionaires, live in abundance, and become a blessing to others! As believers, we can actually do all things with faith in Christ and His mighty power working in us.

Unfortunately, the United Nations Development Report 2007/2008 shows that half of the world—nearly three billion people—live on less than two dollars per day.[1] They lack not only money, but also even the most basic of necessities. Many millions of people cannot afford a single square meal a day. According to UNICEF, out of 2.2 billion children in the world, 25,000 to 30,000 of them die each day due to poverty. The report says they "die quietly in some of the poorest villages on earth, far removed from the scrutiny and the conscience of the world. Being meek and weak in life makes these dying multitudes even more invisible in death."[2] This is beyond scandalous because there is so much money in our world and yet there is such horrible suffering and poverty.

> THE FIRST THING TO DO IS TO MULTIPLY YOUR RESOURCES SO THAT YOU BUILD ONLY FROM YOUR ABUNDANCE AND NOT FROM YOUR SEED.

The situation must change. Something is desperately wrong. We need to teach people across the globe the knowledge of how money works.

As believers and Christians, we need to labor so the world around us becomes better and more fulfilling. As children of the Almighty God, we can do everything in Christ who strengthens us.

In previous chapters, we discussed how to create a financial base or capital. Every person needs a financial platform on which to build a future. As one lays a spiritual foundation through Christian fellowship, Bible study, worship, prayer, and so on, one lays a financial foundation in the same way. We need to know certain things about money, because money goes to those who know how it works.

I want to give you an additional three financial laws that will help you to realize your potential in Christ and your ability to preserve your money. I have already made some of these statements in this book, but I want to emphasize these truths again.

Learn to decrease expenses and control your desires.

"Now godliness with contentment is great gain" (1 Tim. 6:6). Some will never be prosperous or financially independent because they do not know how to be content. A person who is never content or happy is poor, even if that person has millions of dollars. Greed is a sickness that prevents prosperity and financial happiness from entering our lives. A person under the control of his buying desires eventually becomes bankrupt. When the Soviet Union fell apart, people who made illegitimate money were prospering. One told me about his life. "First, I got a BMW, and then I got a Mercedes, then a Mercedes 600. Then I got another and another. I had all the women I could have, gambled in as many casinos as I wanted, and built a mansion with a sauna..." How did he end up? This person's lavish lifestyle brought him to our church's drug rehabilitation center. He sold all his cars for drugs. He said he had to try everything in life, and this was possible for him because he had so much money. When he tried drugs, he could not stop.

Why did things turn out that way? Greed, self-indulgence, and discontentment are the answers to this question. The man from our story used to have houses in Spain and in the Bahamas, but everything he once had was now gone. He was never content with what he had. The lesson for us is that if we do not learn to be content and happy, we cannot become financially prosperous. Money will destroy us before we will be able to retain it. Our desires want to rule our lives, and we need to learn to control those desires and rise above them. We cannot just spend our money impulsively. We need to learn to make capital investments that will produce lasting wealth.

Make every dollar count.

Do not give money away until you know it has worked for you. Banks operate by taking your money and making a profit from it. When you withdraw your money with a little percentage of interest, you are only taking a small portion of the profit the bankers made off your money. You need to invest your money to make a profit for you, not for someone else, and you need to do it before spending it all. Let every dollar make ten dollars before releasing or spending it.

Teach yourself to live and work by a budget.

Every family should operate on a budget. This is an estimated and documented list of expected income and expenses for a given period in the future. Think of it as an itemized allotment of funds and resources. Budgets help you keep your expenses in check, and they remove unexpected expenditures from your life. They bring order, a plan, and a focus on our finances. In addition, you need to keep a budget in order to increase your profits, because a budget helps to separate needs from desires. It draws a strict line between what you merely want and what you truly need.

Budgets help protect us from our own greed and curb our inclination to go on spending sprees. For example, you may have a budget of one hundred dollars per month allotted for money you can spend on your children. That amount has been earmarked for your children—you cannot spend it on anything else, yourself included. The same principle applies for budgets on food, clothing, shelter, and other things. If you deviate from the plan through lack of discipline, then the purpose of the budget (to help you keep expenses in check and remove unexpected expenditures) is nullified. It would be a waste of time and effort.

Do not be in a hurry to begin a large building project for your church, because it will require a lot of money. You could probably find the money to do it, but your ministry would suffer because you cannot neglect the people while putting up a building. You cannot ignore the drug addicts who need salvation, or the homeless and alcoholics who need to be clothed and fed. And you cannot forget the street children who need serious care and a soft human touch. There may be others in your community or church who desperately need your ministry. The first thing to do is to multiply your resources so that you build only from your abundance and not from your seed. Your seed must first bring in the harvest.

Our church is now in her fifteenth year, yet we have yet to build our church building. First of all, my priority must be right, which is people first, the changing of the culture, and a holistic and undeniable impact on the nation! These must come before a church building.

We can now begin thinking about having our own building since we've recently recorded over two million salvations in our Kyiv church alone! Secondly, I don't want to venture into a building project until we have at least ten million U.S. dollars in our building fund. This means we have done enough multiplication on our seed before commencing on a building project so as not to put a burden on our church members.

It is the same reason I didn't rush to build myself a house or drive expensive cars, because even if I've made my first million, I must obey the same laws if I don't want to put excess burden on myself or on the church.

People have said to me, "Pastor Sunday, you are the leader of a megachurch, and you don't even have a house. You live in a small apartment with your wife and three children. Why?" This bothered them much more than it did me. Although things have changed now, I knew that everything had its divine timing. I needed to multiply my resources first, especially if I do not wish to use any of the church's money for personal gain. This law must first work in my life.

Keep a record of your money to help you stay away from overspending. Learn to endure the lack of gratification for a short time while multiplying resources so that your joy and blessing do not affect your other needs and areas of life.

BEWARE OF GREED

1. Greed is the deep desire driving you to the point you are willing to do anything to get what you want. Proverbs 1:19 says, "So are the ways of everyone who is greedy for gain; it takes away the life of its owners."

2. Greed makes you want something so badly that you are willing to violate the rights of others to get it.

3. Greed is not just about money. It is about being driven by whatever you want so badly.

4. Greed is the desire to get something quickly—whether money, sex, power, recognition, leisure, or other things.

5. Greed can be both subtle in nature and aggressive.

6. Greed steals your joy of life because you are never content.

7. Greed can destroy your financial security. "A stingy man is eager to get rich and is unaware that poverty awaits him" (Prov. 28:22, NIV).

8. Greed will bring trouble into your family. "He who is greedy for gain troubles his own house, but he who hates bribes will live" (Prov. 15:27).

9. Greed brings spiritual bankruptcy. "There is one who makes himself rich, yet has nothing; and one who makes himself poor, yet has great riches" (Prov. 13:7).

10. Greed will destroy your integrity. "A faithful man will abound with blessings, but he who hastens to be rich will not go unpunished" (Prov. 28:20).

11. Greed creates a false sense of security. "He who trusts in his riches will fall, but the righteous will flourish like foliage" (Prov. 11:28).

12. The root of greed is *coveting*, which is the desire for more and more and the desire to be hasty for gains.

The danger of greed has been well displayed to the whole world from this recent Wall Street financial crisis that has consequences the world over. Banks are collapsing, businesses are closing, even nations are declaring bankruptcy. Our whole world is in danger just because of the greed of some Wall Street executives. Let's be truly aware of greed.

DO NOTHING; BECOME NOTHING

The fact that greed is bad does not mean we should not do anything to move forward to the things we want. To do nothing is the way to be nothing. Greed or willingness to avoid the love of money is not an excuse for laziness. It only means you must watch after your heart.

1. Idleness brings more trouble than hard work.

2. Action subdues fear. Master your fear by being proactive.

3. People judge you by your actions, not your intentions. "If you know these things, blessed are you if you do them" (John 13:17).

4. If you do not do it, you do not really believe it.

5. One deed is better than ten thousand words.

6. Prayers do not mean lack of actions. When you pray, you do so to commune with God.

7.   Nothing is more exhausting than searching for easy ways to make a living.

8.   Laziness leads to poverty. "Lazy hands make a man poor, but diligent hands bring wealth" (Prov. 10:4, niv).

9.   Do not try to get something for nothing.

10.   Most people only dream of what they will be, while some stay up late at night to make their dreams happen in reality.

It is my deep belief that every Christian can become a millionaire. You do not need a calling to be a millionaire. You only need to know the laws and principles of money.

Many would argue that they don't need "a million" to be happy. Yes, but that is when you're only thinking of yourself. Egoism makes us only think about ourselves, and think that we don't need more money. Well, you may not need more millions, but your access to more millions will produce a greater impact for the kingdom of God. The orphans of your city need more millions, the senior citizens who are in a desperate state in your society need more millions! And the list goes on...

So let's all get out of our comfort zones to conquer money and become deliverers of our world and for the expansion of the kingdom of God.

FREE TO SERVE THE KING

What I've discovered is that money *does* make a difference in the life of a believer. In fact, money has the ability to set you free to do the work of the ministry. There is a well-known saying that says, "Money makes the world go round," and to some aspect this rings true for Christians who want to spend the majority of their time serving God. That is to say, if you are spending most of your life in a time-consuming job, when will you afford the time to fulfill your calling or explore your God-given talents? However, if you are making money work for you, then you have the time and opportunity to work for God.

We have many such examples in our church, and every week more and more people come to the front to tell their "liberation stories."

One example is of a gentleman who for many years worked as a security guard for a certain company. He worked many hours every day and hardly had any time off. For the hours of his life, he earned minimal wage and therefore found himself in frustrating circumstances. However, when we started teaching practical lessons about investments and how to maximize your income, he decided to make a move.

He opened his eyes to the financial opportunities around him and sold his apartment. With this money he made several investments and in a short time started doubling his money. He later quit his job and gave his time to serve in the security ministry of the church.

Moreover, he was again able to take up his favorite pastime of art. He started painting again and even posted these on a private Web site for sale.

So, from working too many hours for too little money, he went to working only a few hours each day—making considerably more money—and is now able to serve God and enjoy his everyday life!

Money really turned his world around!

PRACTICAL WISDOM
FOR ASPIRING MILLIONAIRES

1. Poor attitude and reactions are the number one reason for the failure of our dreams.

2. Blaming others, self-pity, and disillusionment will paralyze your dreams.

3. Remember that faith demands risk, but when we trust in God's Word, our risk becomes secured by God Himself.

4. The fear of risk-taking will steal success from any person.

5. A successful man is an ordinary person who dares to risk.

6. When you risk and act out in faith, you are not secured from mistakes and failures, but this should only challenge you to launch forward for more.

7. Always find enough time and effort to prepare for your tomorrow.

8. A man who sows today will reap tomorrow.

9. Most people fail because they refuse to work on their moral weaknesses. Make sure to work on yourself.

10. Treat people well. Be positive with people, and make sure that you leave a positive impression with people in your dealings with them.

KINGDOM PRINCIPLES FROM CHAPTER 12

1. Church offerings are not to enrich the church or the pastor in any way.

2. Some will never be prosperous or financially independent because they do not know how to be content.

3. You need to keep a budget in order to increase your profits because a budget helps to separate your needs from your desires.

4. Budgets help to protect you from your own greed and curb your inclination to go on spending sprees.

5.   Greed is the deep desire driving you to the point that you are willing to do anything to get what you want.

6.   Greed can be both subtle in nature and aggressive.

7.   Idleness brings more trouble than hard work.

8.   Action subdues fear. Master your fear by being proactive.

9.   Nothing is more exhausting than searching for easy ways to make a living.

10.   Learn to endure the lack of gratification for a short time while multiplying resources.

Chapter Thirteen

PROTECTING YOUR GAIN

I N THIS CHAPTER, YOU WILL LEARN HOW TO BE TRULY RICH—AND maintain it. Many people in the world can get rich, but not very many know how to protect that wealth and stay on that mountaintop. We need help from falling when we become rich and wealthy.

> People who want to get rich fall into temptation and a trap and into many foolish and harmful desires that plunge men into ruin and destruction. For the love of money is a root of all kinds of evil. Some people, eager for money, have wandered from the faith and pierced themselves with many griefs. But you, man of God, flee from all this, and pursue righteousness, godliness, faith, love, endurance and gentleness.
> —1 TIMOTHY 6:9–11, NIV

TEN PRINCIPLES FOR PROTECTING WEALTH

These principles will protect both you and your wealth from the dangers mentioned in the scripture above:

1. *Do not love money.* Search your heart because this temptation is always out there. The devil will push you, but you need to guard your heart so you do not get attached to wealth. Always make God your love and your passion.

2. *Prosper in righteousness and holiness, always striving for high godly standards in everything you do.* Put God first. Do not deceive or cheat people, and do not try getting your gain through unrighteous ways, because the seed you sow in another person's life, good or bad, will come back to you multiplied. Knowing and following this advice prevents you from forfeiting your future through craftiness and deceitfulness. Instead, pursue the true wealth. The only way to stay pure in this evil world is to fill yourself with God and His Word.

3. *Practice godliness.* Godliness is being in God's will, being like God, having the character of Jesus, and living in righteousness. Never let riches—or the lack thereof—change you. Success, money, and fame usually affect people in a bad way. Often it fills them with pride, but Christians must always be humble and modest. Wealth will allow you to be around powerful and rich people, and often this changes those who have no spiritual foundation. If your allegiance is with God, you have nothing to be afraid of. "Command those who are rich in this present age not to be haughty, nor to trust in uncertain riches but in the living God, who gives us richly all things to enjoy" (1 Tim. 6:17).

4. *The righteous live by faith, so work on strengthening your faith by trusting God more.* Do not let disappointment, failure, betrayal, deception, and infidelity break you. Your faith in God should be invincible. You can overcome all obstacles with that kind of faith.

5. *Walk in love, even with your enemies.* Loving your enemies is one of God's commandments. As you get closer to God, your relationship with Him becomes stronger, and when that happens, you are simply unable to hate people. For example, I may not agree with everyone I meet or approve of all they do, but I love them and bless them nevertheless. Do not let hurt, pain, and offense capture and dominate your heart, because God is love, and God created us for love. When you act in love, you strengthen the mind and renew the system. When you act outside of love, there is a constant fight inside, an imbalance, and as a result, untold sicknesses—and even death—can befall you. We were created to love, so all actions counter to love cause internal conflict. No matter what someone does to you, love and forgive.

6. *Develop patience.* No one can attain or maintain lasting success

without it. Work on being patient in love. The Bible says that we need patience, so that having done the will of God we can receive the promises made to us. God's promises are real, but only those who have patience inherit them.

7. *Be humble.* Some people cannot maintain wealth because pride stands in their way. Despise arrogance and pride. The Bible says God opposes the proud and gives grace to the humble. If you do not want God to oppose you, be humble, for the proud shall not succeed. "Therefore humble yourselves under the mighty hand of God, that He may exalt you in due time" (1 Pet. 5:6). Jesus said it would be easier for a camel to go through the eye of a needle than for a rich person to enter the kingdom of God (Matt. 19:24). If you make riches your idol, it can only lead to death. If you would be refused entrance to the kingdom of God because of money, it would be infinitely better not to have any. A person errs by putting trust in anything other than God. When you have money, even millions, act as if you do not have anything. Walk as if God has taken your millions and they are no longer yours. God delivers those who trust in Him, and money has not saved anyone yet, eternally speaking.

8. *Beware of haughtiness.* This problem comes from money as well. A haughty person wants to dress nicer than others, have a nicer car—a problem that has destroyed many people. Haughtiness will cause you to spend money that you are supposed to invest to become better than others. Another way to say this is that sin needs to be financed. You can still cultivate a good image, but avoid haughtiness at all costs. Paul wrote that he was comfortable with living in both abundance and lack (Phil. 4:12). We should be the kind of people who are content living with little as well as plenty.

9. *God alone is the source of all riches.* He gives the power and strength to receive wealth. Remember this because after accumulating wealth, the devil might come to you saying that you have achieved all this success on your own. Nothing is further from the truth. Having knowledge is one thing, but having the grace for building up wealth is quite a different thing.

10. *When you decide to do something—do it!* Three qualities make a

difference in your ability to realize your dreams and meet your goals. They are determination, ability to mobilize, and momentum. The most fundamental of these is determination. When listening to an exciting speech or reading a challenging book, almost everyone is filled with an immediate inspiration, making a decision to do something or to change some part of his or her life. However, over time, the fire goes out for many people, and the decision is swept under the rug. A few may have a more sensitive conscience and keep feeding the fire of inspiration with promises of "tomorrow I will start." But a majority of people are indecisive and do not have adequate perseverance and endurance to accomplish their goals. On the other hand, people who achieve success in life never postpone and procrastinate with their vision. Those who can minimize the distance between decision and real action are those who become great.

Some people spend their whole lives doing something they could have accomplished in a year or ten years. Most people in the world stay on the bottom, not because they do not have valuable gifts, great ideas, or worthwhile skills, but because they are indecisive and complacent. There is no inner engine driving them through life. It is easy enough to calculate the quotient of our decisiveness. The perfect decision quotient is 1:1, meaning that each time we decide to do something, we do it, but no one can achieve that. Companies specializing in thought leadership and process innovation say the most effective people in the world have a decision quotient of 3:4 or 2:4, meaning that for every four decisions they make, they act on two or three of them. People who simply talk about doing but seldom follow through have a decision quotient of 2:10 or 2:20—for every ten or even every twenty decisions they make, they act only twice. This is what Jesus was talking about when He said, "Let your 'Yes' be 'Yes,' and your 'No,' 'No'" (Matt. 5:37).

In addition to determination, the qualities of mobilization and momentum make a difference in your ability to realize your dreams and meet your goals. There are people who have this great quality called the ability to mobilize. Mobilization is when one is able to concentrate strength and effort on achieving a set goal. This also includes the ability to mobilize others. Another great quality is momentum, which is a drive or an inner force that enables you to build on your success continuously. These two qualities allow you to renew strength and effort so that your dreams and visions never cool down. When you are rooted in God, this staying power never burns out. You need to be on fire and burn for God, and mobilization and momentum are important qualities of people who realize their dreams and reach their goals.

TURNING DECISIONS INTO MANIFESTATIONS

My wife says I have an amazing drive and staying power. If I decide to do something, I do absolutely everything in my power to make it happen. I often even call myself a fanatic. I think there is a positive side to fanaticism. Jesus said that our "yes" should be "yes" and our "no" should be "no." I take this to mean that a deed must follow a word, and an action must follow a decision. When a person deceives himself or herself on not following through on a word or decision, it is the same as if they were deceiving a neighbor. Many people always try to do what they say, but often, because it is something they promised to themselves, they take it lightly. However, everything having to do with success and prosperity starts with self-discipline. If you are not sincere with yourself, then you are not sincere at all. Integrity is measured by how much you are able to hold on to the promises you make daily to yourself, the ones no one else knows about.

> WHEN YOU HAVE MONEY, EVEN MILLIONS, ACT AS IF YOU DO NOT HAVE ANYTHING.

Measure your level of integrity by how often you keep the promises you make to yourself. The ratio of promises and faithfulness to those promises will tell you how well you have developed your character. I now want to share with you ideas on how you can preserve your staying power to fulfill and accomplish what you have.

TEN IDEAS TO HELP PRESERVE STAYING POWER

I believe the following ten pointers will help us all in our change process, acting upon our decisions, and preserving our staying power to turn decisions into realities.

TIP 1: *When you decide to do something, make sure something else reminds you about your decision on a day-by-day basis.* Write it down in your diary or on your calendar or leave a note for yourself on the refrigerator. Put a picture in a frame if your decision has to do with a specific person. If you decide to become a millionaire, put this book on your desk or carry it with you so it reminds you of your decision. If you hear a sermon and make a decision to follow Christ or come closer to God, buy the tape and play it in your car and at home. Let it be your reminder.

TIP 2: *On a daily and systematic basis, it is important to find time to be alone in order to pray, read, study, and listen to God.* This quiet time will equip and guide you to accomplish your plans. The quiet time is usually the time in your day when new and fresh ideas will come to mind. When they do, write them down. It is important to keep track of things. You will remember things better when you write them down, and since you will always be able to go back to what you have written, it is another way to get closer to your dreams. Meditate on your decisions and ideas, and organize them to help you produce a program or a plan. Your plan is perfected as your knowledge grows.

TIP 3: *Do something about your decision every day so you will not forget it.* Pray about it every day. Ask the Lord for wisdom to accomplish your goal, and do not doubt you will receive what you are asking for. In the Book of Joshua we learn that by meditating and thinking, we not only remind ourselves about our decision, but we also enrich it and ourselves. "This Book of the Law shall not depart from your mouth, but you shall meditate on it day and night, that you may observe to do according to all that is written in it. For then you will make your way prosperous, and then you will have good success" (Josh. 1:8). Reminding yourself about important truths through reading, meditation, and note taking leads to living successful and righteous lives, and there is not a successful individual who does not work in his or her mind the same way.

TIP 4: *In order to maintain the fire and desire to reach your goal, discipline yourself to take steps toward that goal every day.* Read the Bible every day, pray every day, and seek God every day—all these practices bring you closer to your dreams, even if you cannot see the difference immediately. If you combine all the small investments of time, it turns out to be a big deal. Remember, no one can become a millionaire in one day. No one can become anything in a single day. Singers need to work on their voices and rehearse repeatedly. Athletes must work out on a daily basis to develop skills. One of my own goals in life is to be healthy and in top physical shape, and I want this to last at least until I am seventy years of age. I used to think that physical health and shape depended entirely on one's genes, but today I understand that being healthy in older years depends on a person's eating and exercise habits in younger years. Look after yourself! My wife helped me in this area by teaching me to eat healthy foods and live a healthy lifestyle. I would prefer living to age ninety before going home to be with Jesus. However, what is the point in living to ninety if I cannot walk at seventy or eighty? Disciplining yourself is a systematic and day-by-day process in moving toward your goals.

TIP 5: *Giving your decision or idea staying power and seeing your plan come true requires doing something new each day.* Living a long and healthy life means studying and always collecting new information about what it takes to stay in shape and live a healthy lifestyle. To be a millionaire, the same thing applies. Study, obtain new information, and gather facts each day to encourage forward movement. Doing something new each day increases your knowledge and renews your determination. Where do you get inspiration to do something new each day? First, agree that you do not know it all. No one knows everything, even about a given subject—not even if you hold a PhD. If you think you know as much as you should know, you are deceived. A PhD holder in mathematics cannot know everything about the field of mathematics. A pediatrician cannot know everything about his area of medicine. Hence, we all need daily improvements.

When some Christians come to God, they read only the Bible and refuse to touch any other books. Don't limit yourself in this way, because you still need other sources of information. Even if you are the smartest person on your block, you still do not know everything there is to know. There are truths that took centuries to discover and took many cycles of knowledge, experience, and meditation. Your life will not be enough to repeat the author's path, so read their books. Uncover truth wherever it may be found, even in books that are not necessarily Christian. John Calvin said:

> We cannot read them without great admiration. We marvel at them because we are compelled to recognize how pre-eminent they are.... Those men whom Scripture calls "natural men" were indeed sharp and penetrating in their investigations of interior things. Let us accordingly learn from their example how many gifts the Lord left to human nature.... If the Lord has willed that we be helped...let us use this assistance.[1]

There is abundance of gold and penetrating knowledge in books, even secular books, so use them, and do not take them for granted.

Maintain an attitude and willingness to learn from everyone you come across. In this way, you will always maintain a teachable spirit. It often happens that we end up getting information we could never have thought they possess. Tune in to learn from every situation and person.

TIP 6: *Learn to specialize in your area of interest and study rather than just casually browsing general information of all sorts.* If you want to be a physician, you have to prepare to master the medical field of your choice. You cannot do that with generic study. The same is true if you want to be a scholar in the field of history. It is true with every field and every calling. Exhaust all sources of information on your subject of interest. Do not be casual in your search, because the more thoroughly and deeply you dig, the more treasures you will find. God will honor your hard work and effort, and you will attain your goal. We become specialists in our area of interest by studying hard and reflecting long, accumulating knowledge so that we know what to teach others.

TIP 7: *Find inspiration in your obstacles.* Obstacles will come your way as soon as you determine your goals. Learn to see impediments to progress as stages of success. Everything you overcome will bring you closer and closer to your dream. It is like a ladder in that the higher you climb, the more effort it takes. Every step seems like a test or trial, but it brings you closer to your endgame. Teach yourself to have this kind of positive attitude toward obstacles. If you have a problem at work with a colleague or boss, do not panic. Treat the problem as a step higher up your ladder toward your goal. Be courageous and do not be afraid to accept the challenges of life. These challenges come to us for a purpose. God allows difficult situations in our lives to make us stronger, to build our character, and to make us into the men and women He wants us to be. Without trials and hardships, you will not develop character and spiritual muscles.

The Book of Psalms says, "As they pass through the Valley of Baca, they make it a place of springs; the autumn rains also cover it with pools. They go from strength to strength, till each appears before God in Zion" (Ps. 84:6–7, NIV). This is a great revelation. The valley of tears, which is the meaning of the Valley of Baca, is full of difficulties and trials, which of course we would rather not have to go through. How often does it ever enter our minds that passing through this valley can help us become stronger? Often, it is the only way we become stronger. In the midst of a tragedy, we discover a hidden source of blessings and support, receive strength and become stronger. The valley of weeping is the passage to salvation and eternal life for many people. Perhaps it was for you. When facing problems and trials, do not be discouraged, do not be depressed, because these problems offer another chance for revelation of God. When we let obstacles stop us, we cannot overcome them and will be unable to see them as another source of blessings.

Only when you rise up over your trials can your eyes see new horizons, allowing you to see what you could not see before—new blessings, new prospects, new people, and a new life, of which you could not have dreamed. Remember, no one rises to the top without making a concerted effort. Accepting life's challenges and overcoming obstacles in your way will move you from strength to strength, and you will find yourself walking in the purposes of God for your life.

TIP 8: *Learn to enjoy your work, and do not procrastinate with it.* The person who makes a decision and follows through with it is a disciplined man or woman. We are not born with this discipline; we need to learn it. In addition, we need to work hard. I have not met a single successful person in business, the professions, ministry, or politics who is not a hard worker. I thought I was a hard worker until I visited Sweden and saw how hardworking Swedish people are. Hard work made them wealthy and helps them stay that way. Sweden is one of the richest countries in the world, because long ago the Swedish people disciplined themselves to work hard. In Germany also people work very hard, and they are not a people who do anything lightly. (See Proverbs 10:4.) The Protestant value and ethic has always emphasized hard work as a noble Christian characteristic.

TIP 9: *You can preserve your staying power and accomplish what you have decided only when you make a decision to do everything as unto God.* Be responsible toward God for all you do—on the job and off. "Seek first the kingdom of God and His righteousness, and all these things shall be added to you" (Matt. 6:33). Remember that God sees all your deeds—it will give you extra incentive to work hard to attain results to benefit the kingdom.

TIP 10: *Always be ready to help people with the knowledge, finances, or whatever else you have.* Help them without expecting a return. When arbitrarily doing something for another person just to help that person out, God will compensate your efforts and bless you. Compassion and kindness are the best qualities you have, and when you show these traits to others, God often unexpectedly does something for you in return.

IDEAS FOR PROTECTING YOUR GAINS

1.   Begin to make money consistently. Guard yourself against get-rich-quick investments. Schemes to make instant and large sums of money are deceptive, so never jump at them.

2. Protect your money and gains by putting security measures in place, such as life insurance, family businesses, and assets.

3. Always work with experts who know more than you do in business, investments, and the legal field.

4. Never take what you have for granted. You will not save what you do not treat with care.

5. Do not be interested only in results. Be meticulous in the process of running your affairs. Do not just focus on accumulation, but also take the time to monitor wealth.

6. Watch out for economic changes, and learn how to adjust to them.

7. Make sure you have multiple streams of income. Spread risk. Do not put all your eggs in one basket.

8. Don't let greed and emotional blindness make your decisions for you.

9. Never change your core values—even though ideas and insight might change.

10. Protect secrets and weaknesses.

11. Stay informed.

12. Live a life of giving, being generous with God and others.

BE A FAITHFUL STEWARD

The Bible tells us in 1 John 5:19 that the whole world lies in evil. As much as we would like to think it is not like that, that is the reality of our world today—the whole world lies in evil.

As we have learned in this book, there are a lot of evil schemes being devised by millions of people working day and night to steal and take away your wealth. There are organizations that are formed especially to rob naïve and ignorant people of their hard-earned money. Hence, it is important for you and I to be watchful and extremely careful about whom we entrust our money and precious financial information to.

As I've stated earlier, it is even more difficult to retain money than to gain it. The servant with one talent was condemned by Jesus for not retaining the value of the money he was entrusted with. It was easier for him to get the money than to retain it.

This happens over and over again today. Many people are entrusted with money by God and others, only to end up losing it because they don't have the discipline to retain and increase the value of what they have been given. That is why this last chapter is essential for you to pay special attention to.

As you work hard to make your money, be careful to protect your gain as well. No doubt these principles will go a long way to helping you do just that!

THE REASON FOR IT ALL

As I'm about to conclude this book, I again want to stress to all of you, my dear readers, that the reason for all this is to expand the kingdom of God in all the spheres of life we have been called to, and to bring good to our neighbors. In the Gospels, Jesus says that if anyone will make the sacrifice of giving up anything in His name, namely, house, land, properties, money, family members, that that person would receive one hundred times more in this world and in the world to come. It is my firm belief that if we will go the extra mile to give up anything small or large to support and meet the needs of the world's poorest of the poor, we will not become poor for it, but God will surely give us a hundredfold more in return. I would like you to keep in mind information and statistics of world poverty that you read in the first chapter of this book. It is the motivation behind my willingness to make known to you the secrets of financial well-being so that you can go out and help the rest of the world conquer poverty. We are all called by God, not just to be blessed, but more so to be a blessing (Gen 12:2).

As we go all over the world to tackle the problem of poverty, the citizens of the poorest nations will definitely respond by believing the good news faster than when we just talk to them without meeting their needs. Jesus not only preached the gospel but also demonstrated it practically by meeting the needs of His audience (Luke 8:1).

From my experience, I have discovered that when you don't just preach to people but you also meet their needs, their response is better than when you only preach without meeting their needs. I believe that this is a vital key to carrying out the Great Commission. More money means more opportunities, but these opportunities must be used to expand and establish the kingdom of God on the earth.

Out of my major joy and excitement is the GS MicroFinance bank project, it is unbelievable to see what a little amount like ten dollars could do in the life of a whole family. So much joy, happiness, even death prevention through ten dollars.

However, more than the money, what we do at GS MicroFinance bank is to give all our clients financial education—the same as in this book. After this we provide them with a starting capital without any collateral, only their identity card. We then give them a mentor who will help them start a business, monitoring them until they return their loan.

It is amazing that the default level with the poor of the world is less that 2 percent, that is 98 percent actually pay their debt on time and with interest too, which is later used to help others also.

I, therefore, want to encourage all of you, my readers, to think of a way of improving the lives of the needy around you.

Your joy, satisfaction, and fulfillment will be beyond words!

PRACTICAL WISDOM
FOR ASPIRING MILLIONAIRES

1. If you think you are beaten, you are.

2. If you dare not, you do not.

3. If you would like to win but think you cannot, it is almost certain you will not.

4. If you think you will lose, you are lost.

5. Success begins with the will; it is all in the state of mind.

6. If you think you are outclassed, you are.

7. You have to think high to rise.

8. You have to be sure of yourself before you can ever win.

9. Life's battles do not always go to the smarter or wiser.

10. The man or woman who wins is the man or woman who thinks he or she can.

KINGDOM PRINCIPLES FROM CHAPTER 13

1. We were created to love, so all actions counter to love cause internal conflict. No matter what someone does to you, love and forgive.

2. God's promises are real, but only those who have patience inherit them.

3. When you have money, even millions, act as if you do not.

4. Be the kind of person who is content living with little as well as with plenty.

5. If you can minimize the distance between decision and real action, you will no doubt become great.

6. If you are not sincere with yourself, then you are not sincere at all.

7. Do something about your decision every day so you will not forget it.

8. Tune in to learn from every situation and person.

9. Only when you rise up over your trials can your eyes see new horizons, allowing you to see what you could not see before—new blessings, new prospects, new people, and a new life of which you could have never dreamed.

10. Guard yourself against get-rich-quick investments.

FOUR TRUTHS TO REMEMBER ON YOUR WAY TO A GREAT AND SUCCESSFUL LIFE

THIS BOOK IS FILLED WITH IMPORTANT INFORMATION TO HELP you discover the truth that *money won't make you rich—but knowledge and hard work can.* Now that you know something about the laws and philosophy of money, financial freedom, the meaning of true success and the hindrances that prevent success, the meaning of prosperity, the reasons for financial failure, and the ways of money, you are on your way toward delivering the gift God wants you to offer to the world. What do you do next? Let me wrap up this book by reminding you of four important truths for you to bear in mind and follow.

WRITE IT DOWN

Get a notebook to write down all God reveals to you. Write down His plans and intentions for your life and the ways He wants you to achieve your targets. Then write down all your observations about people and life around you. "Then the Lord replied: 'Write down the revelation and make it plain on tablets so that a herald may run with it'" (Hab. 2:2,

NIV). There is a difference between looking and seeing. You can look at yourself—as a divorcee, a poor fatherless child, or a successful professional—but it is another thing to see yourself as God does. This scripture speaks about the kind of godly vision that helps you to see what you will be like in the future, and what God has in store for your life.

The first part of this verse teaches us to write down everything pertaining to God's purpose for our lives. We may see ourselves as artists, evangelists, entrepreneurs, architects, or as anything else. Draw up a clear and detailed plan of your future actions that will take you to whatever you know to be God's purpose for you. If you are unclear about God's purpose for you, seek His face, and ask what direction you should go.

This is what I have done in my own life. I know God wants me to reach five million Ukrainians for the Lord. There is no doubt in my mind. I have written down this vision, and now I am working to accomplish it. How will I do it? I will preach and build churches. I will bring people to repentance, raise and train disciples, and send out missionaries to all corners of the earth. That is not all. God has other tasks for me, and I have written them down too. God has an interesting agenda for me, and He has an equally interesting one for you. However, if you do not write His plans down, there is very little chance you will be able to fulfill them in the best way possible. Why? Because writing down God's visions will discipline you.

Writing down God's visions for you will make you more responsible and precise in everything you do. Even if you think you know the purpose of your life, consider it unknown until you have written it down. When a purpose is not fixed, it will be vague and unclear in your mind. Committing things in writing helps your actions become more organized and purposeful.

There was a time in my life when the media in Ukraine accused me of all possible sins. I could have left everything, escaped the pressure, and gone to America or Africa. If I had, I might have become a successful preacher in those places. Here is the difficulty, however: I know what I am to do, and I know where God wants me to be. Dedication to God's guidance makes me strong enough to endure any hardship. When we are certain of God's direction and agenda, it is easier to dedicate ourselves to its fulfillment.

I know my calling, and that is why it is vital for me to be dedicated to fulfilling it. Dedication to your purpose gives the strength to overcome problems and difficulties. When you have concrete work and plans set before you, then you can better dedicate yourself to them. Moreover, when you look through your notes, you will be able to reflect deeply on God's purpose for your life, and pray it through in the Holy Spirit.

How do you pray through all God reveals of His plans and intentions for your life? Here is what I suggest: When you pray quietly in the morning, meditate on the things you feel God is putting in your heart to do and about the things He calls you to do. If you are a Spirit-filled believer, you could let your spirit loose and begin to speak in other tongues. The point is, pray your needs through in the Spirit. During your time of prayer and meditation, the Holy Spirit will reveal some ideas and give you a picture of how exactly you can fulfill the things God calls you to do. Be open and prepared for God to suggest new ideas and strategies to help you fulfill His purpose as efficiently as possible. I advise you to pray about your calling at least one hour a day. Fervent prayer in the Spirit is important, because you do not know what obstacle or difficulty you may encounter on the way. The Spirit of God mediates for us when we do not know in our mind what to pray about. Romans 8:26 says: "Likewise the Spirit also helps in our weaknesses. For we do not know what we should pray for as we ought, but the Spirit Himself makes intercession for us with groanings which cannot be uttered."

Prayer says, "Lord, please act on my behalf." God will begin ministering to you by sending the people and the resources you need. He will ordain His angels to open doors for you. While you pray, try picturing in your mind God's plans already fulfilled. Visualize your goal, and be armed with a plan and a picture. Doing that helps to achieve goals regardless of your current circumstances. This advice is in line with the apostle Paul's letter to the Ephesians: "Now to Him who is able to do exceedingly abundantly above all that we ask or think, according to the power that works in us" (Eph. 3:20).

As you can see, we pray for our own benefit. When you pray, you are not doing a service to God. You are not helping Him. When you pray, you become a co-worker with God, and you absorb His presence, His glory, and His strength. While you are praying for a request or a need in your life, you are saying that you are open to the Lord to fulfill His desires. Your prayers facilitate your life here in the visible world. Normally in most churches, few people show up for prayer meetings even though wisdom tells us that when we pray, even in small groups, we are united in God's strengths and possibilities. Through prayers, we prevail. This is an advantage and a good thing when we spend time with God in prayer, because He is already willing to do much more for us than we dare to ask or think.

Perhaps you cannot boast today of having much to your name. If that is true, do not be discouraged. Learn to be happy even with modest achievements. Every step that brings you closer to the realization of your dream is important. For instance, I am not at all upset that I am still far from realizing my dream of bringing five million Ukrainians to Christ. The salvation of one person makes me happy and confident that I am moving in the right direction. I know that He who is in me can do much more, and I continue praying for God to work great things through me. I believe this, and I know, according to His Word, that it certainly will happen some day. The time will come when I realize my dream of five million souls. I firmly believe that he who does not take time to plan his future is planning his failure. So, apart from praying, I must plan and do all that depends on me, as I have said earlier in this book.

I am sure your dreams will come true someday too. If you are willing to take time to write down your goals and plans, pray and follow the principles, you can be sure that great results will not be long in coming. Careful planning always results in success, but if you fail to plan, you are planning to fail.

PUT FIRST THINGS FIRST

Philippians 3:13–14 hides the second tip: "Brothers, I do not consider myself yet to have taken hold of it. But one thing I do: Forgetting what is behind and straining toward what is ahead, I press on toward the goal to win the prize for which God has called me heavenward in Christ Jesus" (NIV). To achieve a particular goal, draw up a daily agenda where prayer comes first.

While planning your day, arrange assignments, problems, considerations, or courses of action in the order of their importance. Be sure you have covered them all. Following such an agenda will enable you to see what needs are first, and it will allow you to work on a priority basis. I can tell you that I begin my workday by reading my notes from the previous day. Sometimes I find entries that have nothing to do with my goals for today. Often we allow the devil and worldly problems to interfere with our plans. This should not happen, because we are God's servants, and our lives are precious to Him. We need to get to work and take our destiny seriously.

I advise you to begin by making a list of all you have to do in the course of the day, and then write these things down according to their importance. This will help you do the most important things before the less important ones. Apart from this, make a list of your life's priorities and arrange them in their order of importance. Keep in mind that your relationship with the Lord comes first. My most important priority is spending time with God. I spend a certain amount of time each morning talking with the Lord, and I never leave home unprepared from lack of prayer. Meetings, sermon preparation, the church's daily duties, and chatting with colleagues and visitors—these all come after my personal communication with God, never before. The time of day and the amount of time you spend praying may differ from mine, but the point is to do it. My second priority is my family, my wife and children. No matter how urgent other things may be, I attend to them only after spending enough time with my family. My ministry and calling are my third priority.

Every month I dedicate one week entirely to the Lord. It is not a strictly fixed date, say, the first or the second week of each month. Therefore, this time with God may vary from month to month, depending on circumstances. I fill that week up with Bible reading and study, prayer, fasting, and serious meditating over the Word of God. Naturally, during this week I cancel all the routine church matters and dedicate myself to being with the Lord.

I want to stress the absolute importance of efficient time planning. Determine your priorities, arrange them in a proper order, and then strictly follow it. I will always list my first priority as the Lord, my second priority as my family, and my third priority as my ministry. That is how I manage my life and time.

If you have a young family, make it a rule to come home early enough in the evening to play with your kids and have some time for your spouse. In my own case, I schedule three days in a week to be at home no later than seven o'clock in the evening. Four days a week, I come home later in the evening to allow me to care for pressing things happening in the church. Such planning makes everyone in the family happy. As far as my ministry is concerned, I set priorities there as well. Although I receive many invitations to preach outside Ukraine, I always give special importance to the church I pastor in Kyiv. Church matters also need careful planning, and so my work with the pastors comes first in the day, and then comes meetings with my assistants and the agenda for the rest of the day. Then I schedule time to meet with various ministry leaders of the church-run programs and other members too. Unless I arrange my priorities correctly, I find it difficult, if not impossible, to carry out any job as an efficient pastor, let alone to attain financial independence.

What you make your first priority is up to you. However, the question is: Does it agree with God's purpose for your life? Keep a reasonable balance in all you do. Here is a good example of being out of balance. I know pastors of big churches who have children who are drug addicts or unbelievers. Such things often happen because the priorities are wrong. These pastors regard their calling as their first priority, and some of them may not even be aware they have made wrong choices. They may be traveling around the world, preaching in other countries, enjoying respect and popularity, while their family and possibly even their church is on the verge of falling apart. Make sure that your priorities are in the right place. This becomes a major challenge, especially as your businesses and wealth grow. So make sure you set your priorities right now.

Give place to five things in order to facilitate the development of good habits—praying, reading the Word of God, reading good books, listening to teachings and talks, and attending church services on a regular basis. Your work has to be carefully planned. You must study and reflect constantly to enrich yourself with new understanding. In return, blessings will come to you abundantly.

I have developed for myself a self-education program. I read a book and listen to tapes or CDs with messages every week. Devise your own program. Maybe you want to read a book in a week or in a month, or two books in a month, or whatever. Maybe you want to listen to one message in a week or two messages in a month. The point is to keep at it. By studying constantly, you will be able to keep abreast of the latest developments, receive new information to update your knowledge and skills in the area of your choice, and promote your self-development.

If you choose the right priorities and manage your time correctly, your life will be filled with special meaning and peace, and your ministry will flourish. The efficiently arranged priorities prevent you from turning your life and falling into a mess. I know this is true because I have seen it happen many times.

I once paid a visit to an extremely rich man who was quite influential in political circles. He told me his story. His business earned him millions of dollars, but it took up all the free time he could share with his wife and children. As a result, his marriage was on the verge of breaking up, and he was in despair. A man who was in control of thousands of employees was crying before me like a little child. I explained to him the cause of his misfortunes. I told him that his inability to put first things first had reduced his business successes to nothing and turned his personal life into a failure. Thank God for this man, for he gave his life to Christ and became a child of God. His family is doing well now, but this became possible only after he learned how to arrange his priorities efficiently.

To tell you the truth, I am amazed at how many people readily sacrifice their personal lives and family for riches and popularity. Some succeed in doing one thing while neglecting another. Life without God is a sad and futile adventure. When we reject God's principles, first we lose peace of heart, then righteousness, and eventually we will discover we have lost everything. That is why God must be your first priority. You cannot live a successful life independently of your source, and your source is God.

FOR EVERYTHING THERE IS A SEASON

Under no circumstances should you overburden yourself with too many obligations and promises. "Be still, and know that I am God; I will be exalted among the nations, I will be exalted in the earth!" (Ps. 46:10). Having too many obligations will leave you without enough time and strength to cope with them. If you are in the situation where too many things are expected of you, begin with the goals, plans, or problems that are most urgent. Learn how to distinguish between urgent tasks and those that can wait. In other words, learn to distribute your time in the most efficient way because "there is a time for everything, and a season for every activity under heaven" (Eccles. 3:1, NIV).

While drafting a daily agenda, concentrate on the tasks you have enough time and strength to attend to, and do not plan more than you can deal with.

"Whatever your hand finds to do, do it with your might" (Eccles. 9:10). It is much better to delegate to another person a task you cannot do well or on time. If you persist in doing it yourself, there is a good chance you will mess up the whole thing and end up frustrated. Once you have drawn up your agenda, share your plans with family, friends, and co-workers. They are God's tools for making you great. Choose people who have something valuable to contribute to you and to whom you can be helpful as well. The Lord will provide you with people who have exactly what you need (finances, connections, knowledge, friendships, and so on) to carry out His ideas and goals for your life. In turn, you will find many others who need the gifts God has given you. Show love and concern for your neighbors, and be on a constant search for people you can serve. This is especially true in the place you work because so often there are wonderful opportunities out there.

This advice goes along with what we just learned in the third tip: Learn to arrange objectives and work within a particular time, because there is time for everything under heaven (Eccles. 3:1). According to your plan, there are some things you should have done yesterday, and if you wait to tackle them today, you might not be able to do what you have planned for today. If the time to do certain things has passed, it is better to leave them and face today's challenges until you find some free time to do what remains to be done.

REMAIN BLESSED IN HIM

May your life and your family be blessed both spiritually and financially. I have tried to outline for you in this book the biblical principles to help make your life flourish. I pray you will consider them seriously and put them into practice: Declare war on poverty. Get to work and take your destiny seriously. Arrange your priorities and objectives. Never be content with your current state; always pursue your life goals. Remember to consider God's purpose for your life to be unknown until you have written it down. Make your relationship with God your utmost priority, and make prayer a way of life. Ask Him for wisdom, and do not be afraid of failure. Failure is one of the main ways God teaches you and guides you. He uses challenges as platforms to lift us. The way to become great is to serve others. Take chances, but do not take on too many obligations, and do not make too many promises. Concentrate on what you have the time and strength to do. Do not keep bad company.

For financial health and welfare, do not love money! It is only paper, and it will not make anyone happy. Be free of the power of money over you. Money serves you—not the other way around. Work is not primarily for making money, and righteousness is true wealth. Prosperity comes with inner changes. True millionaires invest not only money but also time in getting more knowledge and wisdom. Continuous education is the minimum requirement for achieving success. Study constantly, and follow the world economic trends. Know the laws of money, including the fact that wealth accumulation begins with saving. Understand the principles of wealth creation and turn everything into investments. The reason some are rich while others are poor has to do with hard work and right choices. Speak about your goals and plans as if they already happened. Never sow good seed into bad soil. Keep a budget—and live by it. Pay yourself second, and make sure God is always first. Beware of lending out money, and never give money away until you know it has worked for you.

May the lessons inside this book touch, bless, and transform your life and many other lives, and may those lives play a dynamic role in the advancement of Christ's church and the kingdom of God. If you go for the best in God, your life will be an example of the success and prosperity that is possible for all believers. May the Lord use these financial principles to help ignite and revolutionize your potential in Christ. May He bless and empower you, so you will be a blessing to countless others around you and in our world.

NOTES

PREFACE
A WORD FROM THE AUTHOR

1. Statistics may be accessed at www.globalissues.org/povertyfacts andstatistics.

CHAPTER ONE
THE REALITY OF POVERTY IN OUR WORLD

1. For more information on the definitions of poverty, see "Global Poverty: What Is Poverty?" *Net Aid*, http://www.netaid.org/global_poverty/global-poverty/ (accessed July 29, 2008).

2. Fight Poverty, "Recent Facts," http://www.fightpoverty.mmbrico.com/poverty/facts.html (accessed July 29, 2008).

3. The World Bank, "News and Broadcast," http://web.worldbank.org/wbsite/external/news/0,,contentmdk:20034434~menupk:34463~pagepk:64003012~thesitepk:4607,00.html (accessed November 5, 2008).

4. Country Studies, "South Africa," http://countrystudies.us/south-africa/66.htm (accessed November 5, 2008).

5. WorldOil.com, "Industry at a Glance," http://www.worldoil.com/infocenter/statistics_detail.asp?statfile=_worldoilproduction (accessed November 5, 2008).

6. *New York Times*, "Full Text: Bush's National Security Strategy," September 20, 2002, http://www.nytimes.com/2002/09/20/politics/20STEXT_FULL.html?ex=1218686400&en=41d8f69ca4bb5aa1&ei=5070 (accessed July 29, 2008).

7. United Nations Children's Fund, *The State of the World's Children, 1999,* cited in John C. Holveck et al., "Prevention, Control, and Elimination of Neglected Diseases in the Americas: Pathways to Integrated, Inter-programmatic, Inter-sectoral Action for Health and Development," *BMC Public Health 2007,* January 17, 2007, http://www.biomedcentral.com/content/pdf/1471-2458-7-6.pdf (accessed July 29, 2008).

8. World Health Organization, "Facts and Figures from *The World Health Report, 2005,*" http://www.who.int/whr/2005/media_centre/facts_en.pdf (accessed July 29, 2008).

9. "Global Poverty: What Is Poverty?" *Net Aid*, http://www.netaid.org/global_poverty/global-poverty/ (accessed July 29, 2008).

10. Fight Poverty, "Recent Facts," http://www.fightpoverty.mmbrico.com/poverty/facts.html, (accessed July 29, 2008).

11. BioMed Central, "BMC Public Health," http://www.biomedcentral
.com/content/pdf/1471-2458-7-6.pdf (accessed September 9, 2008).

CHAPTER TWO
WHY EVERY CHRISTIAN CAN BE A MILLIONAIRE

1. Curriculum available via La Red Business Network, http://www.lared
.org/Home/.

2. Famous Quotes and Quotations, "Thomas J. Watson, Founder of IBM,"
http://www.famous-quotes-and-quotations.com/thomas_j_watson_founder_
of_ibm_1.html (accessed July 30, 2008).

3. *Apollo 13*, directed by Ron Howard (Universal City, CA: Universal,
1995).

4. MSNBC.com, "U.S. Savings Rate Hits Lowest Level Since 1933,"
January 30, 2006, http://www.msnbc.msn.com/id/11098797/ (accessed
September 9, 2008).

5. "Our Hidden Savings," *BusinessWeek*, January 17, 2005, http://www
.businessweek.com/magazine/content/05_03/b3916043_mz011.htm (accessed
September 9, 2008).

6. Ibid.

CHAPTER FOUR
MAXIMIZING OPPORTUNITIES FOR FINANCIAL PROSPERITY

1. Library of Congress, "NLS Other Writings," http://www.loc.gov/nls/
other/acbnfb2001.html (accessed November 5, 2008).

2. U.S. Census Bureau, "Americans Spend More Than 100 Hours
Commuting to Work Each Year, Census Bureau Reports," March 30, 2005,
http://www.census.gov/Press-Release/www/releases/archives/american_
community_survey_acs/004489.html (accessed September 9, 2008).

3. Purdue University, "Office for Continuing Education and Conferences,"
https://www.cec.purdue.edu/docs/Presidents%20Forum%20Presentation%20
Handouts.pdf (accessed November 5, 2008).

4. U.S. Department of State, "The Real Axis of Evil: Removing the
World's Remaining Dictators Through Diplomacy," November 5, 2003,
http://www.state.gov/s/p/of/proc/26789.htm (accessed September 9, 2008).

CHAPTER FIVE
FINANCIAL FREEDOM AND THE BASIC LAWS OF MONEY

1. Chris Joyner, "Bank Robberies Up Around USA," *USA Today*, accessed
at http://www.usatoday.com/news/nation/2008-06-15-bankrobberies_N.htm
(July 31, 2008).

CHAPTER SIX
AVOIDING THE DECEPTIONS OF MONEY
1. "Americans Set Charitable Giving Record in 2006," *MSNBC*, June 25, 2007, accessed at http://www.msnbc.msn.com/id/19409188/ (July 31, 2008).
2. Ibid.

CHAPTER EIGHT
FIVE WAYS TO MAKE MONEY
1. UExpress.com, "Figuratively Speaking," http://www.uexpress.com/figurativelyspeaking/index.html?uc_full_date=20080323 (accessed November 5, 2008).
2. Articlesbase.com, "Why Most New Small Businesses Fail?" http://www.articlesbase.com/business-ideas-articles/why-most-new-small-businesses-fail-361035.html (accessed November 5, 2008).

CHAPTER TWELVE
MAKING MONEY WORK FOR YOU
1. Human Development Report 2007/2008, *United Nations*, page 2, accessed August 5, 2008. A full downloadable copy of this report may be accessed at http://hdr.undp.org/en/media/hdr_20072008_en_complete.pdf.
2. "A Spotty Scorecard," *UNICEF, Progress of Nations 2000*, http://www.unicef.org/pon00/immu1.htm (accessed August 5, 2008).

CHAPTER THIRTEEN
PROTECTING YOUR GAIN
1. Covenant Presbyterian Church, "John Calvin on Two Kingdoms," http://www.covopc.org/Two_Kingdoms/Calvin_on_Two-Kingdoms_Natural-Law.html (accessed November 5, 2008).

It's time to transform
YOUR WORLD!

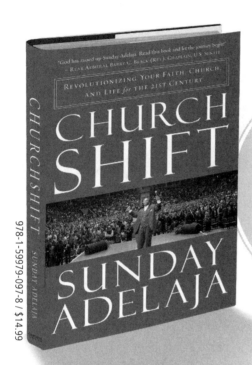

ChurchShift, based on the true story of Sunday Adelaja, gives you the keys to revolutionizing your life, faith, church, and community.

Let this book inspire you to get busy with God's assignment for you!

Visit your local bookstore.